Diasporic Feminist Theology

Diasporic Feminist Theology

Asia and Theopolitical Imagination

Namsoon Kang

Fortress Press
Minneapolis

DIASPORIC FEMINIST THEOLOGY

Asia and Theopolitical Imagination

Bible quotations, unless otherwise noted, are from the New Revised Standard Version Bible, copyright 1989, Division of Christian Education of the National Council of the Churches of Christ in the United States of America. Used by permission. All rights reserved.

Quotations marked Inclusive are from The Inclusive Bible: The First Egalitarian Translation, copyright 2007, by Priests for Equality. Published by Rowman & Littlefield Publishers, Inc. Used by permission. All rights reserved.

Cover image: © Anthony Armstrong

Cover design: Laurie Ingram

Library of Congress Cataloging-in-Publication Data

Print ISBN: 978-1-4514-7298-1

eBook ISBN: 978-1-4514-8972-9

The paper used in this publication meets the minimum requirements of American National Standard for Information Sciences — Permanence of Paper for Printed Library Materials, ANSI Z329.48-1984.

Manufactured in the U.S.A.

This book was produced using PressBooks.com, and PDF rendering was done by PrinceXML.

In celebration and gratitude for the diasporic lives of these thinkers,

their double mode of seeing and worlding the world

with their passion for ethics of singularity and justice-to-come,

each in one's own unique way

Hannah Arendt

(October 14, 1906-December 4, 1975)

Jacque Derrida

(July 15, 1930-October 9, 2004)

Edward Said

(November 1, 1935-September 25, 2003)

Gayatry Chakravorty Spivak

(February 24, 1942-   )

We are all mediators, translators.

–Jacques Derrida

Contents

Preface

This book is a collection of essays, the pieces of which have been in the making over a contextually different period of time. Although each chapter has its own mode of approach and primary entry point, feminist theological discourse resonates consistently as a theme that runs through the entire book. In this sense, the chapters not only interlink but depend on one another to weave interconnected claims about power differential, identities, multiple subjecthood, alterity, or *différance*. I believe that different contexts of readers govern the reading and reception of a work. One's act of reading is like exploring a city because "a book is like a city, and not every reader is native to its complexities."[1] In this sense, what a reader may encounter in this book will depend on her or his context and mode of reading, seeing, and longing.

There seem to be two ways of writing a book. On the one hand, one can write a conventional book *about* a theme, period, or figure within the logic of a representational voice, as I did in my *Cosmopolitan Theology*. On the other hand, one can also write a book as a collectivization of multiple points of entries and arrivals. This book is an instance of the latter approach. Each of the essays

1. Donald Marshall, "Foreword," in Stephen W. Melville, *Philosophy Beside Itself: On Deconstruction and Modernism*, Theory and History of Literature 27 (Minneapolis: University of Minnesota Press, 1986), xiii.

here has both its own particular context and, at the same time, is a part of a process of engagement, transformation, reconstitution, and mediations. It is hard to find a book title for this kind of collection, which has multiple contexts and intersections. However, one must begin somewhere. I find the point of entry in the word *diaspora*, in the complex intersections and locations, negotiations and passions of my world that I am still processing. The diasporic longing embodies deterritorialized and transterritorialized utopian daydreams for enhancing an *ethics of singularity*, building connections and solidarities across territorial and epistemological boundaries, and refashioning homes at multiple crossroads, intersectional points, and heterotopic spaces. Throughout my arguments on Asia, I have no exceptionalist or representational claim to make for Asia simply because I am only one of countless mediators or translators, as Jacques Derrida says.

I have been writing from an in-between space as a *border thinker*—a philosopher-theologian/theologian-philosopher, teacher-scholar/scholar-teacher. My identity as a border thinker remains and will remain both in my personal and professional journey with different emphases, engagements, and longings for the world to come.

Acknowledgments

A book is always a product of multilateral interactions with and stimulations from others. In this sense, proper and full acknowledgments to all individuals, groups, and institutions that made this volume possible would involve a complete cartography of my overlapping professional and personal landscapes, an autobiographical excursion that I am unable to make at this time and in this space.

I must, however, thank Michael Gibson at Fortress Press for embracing this book project with enthusiasm and also the rest of the Fortress editorial staff for their dedication. I thank Kyle Warren, my research assistant at Brite Divinity School at Texas Christian University, for his astute assistance in the research and the preparation of the index. I am grateful to Steven Sherwood at TCU for reading the manuscript and providing expert comments that were extraordinarily helpful.

I thank my students—former and current, distant and near—whom I have encountered at Methodist Theological University in South Korea; at Faculty of Divinity, University of Cambridge; and at Brite Divinity School, Texas Christian University, for their empowerments, affirmations, and inspirations that have made my life journey as a teacher-scholar enriching, meaningful, and joyous.

This book wouldn't exist without my ongoing encounters with those students who constantly have reminded me of the significance of diasporic border traversing.

Permissions

I am grateful to the respective publishers for permission to reprint in full or in revised form the following journal articles and book chapters: "Asia as Theopolitical Imagination" appeared first in a different form in *Postcolonial Theologies. Divinity, Hybridity, and Empire*, edited by Catherine Keller, Michael Nausner, Mayra Rivera (St. Louis, MO: Chalice Press, 2004). "Radical Border-Traversing" appeared first in *Concillium* (2013/2). "From Epistemology to Hermeneutics" is a revised version of my work in *Journal of Asian and Asian Theology* (2013). "Out of Places" appeared first in *Out of Place: Theologizing at Crosscultural Brink,* edited by Clive Pearson and Jione Havea (London: Equinox Publishing, 2011). "*Glocal* Feminist Theology in an Era of Neo-Empires" is also in *Christian Theology in Asia,* edited by Sebastian Kim (Cambridge, UK: University of Cambridge Press, 2008). "*Transethnic* Feminist Theology in an Era of Globalization" is also in *Oxford Handbook of Feminist Theology*, edited by Sheila Briggs & Mary Fulkerson (Oxford, UK: Oxford University Press. 2011). "Negotiating the Alternative" appeared first in *Journal of World Christianity* (vol. 3, no. 1, 2010). "Resurgence of Asian Values" appeared first in a different form in *Asia Journal of Theology* (vol. 18.1. April 2004).

1

Diasporic Feminist Theology

Politics of Diaspora and the Critic on the Fringes

"Theory" is a product of displacement, comparison, a certain distance. To theorize, one leaves home.
—James Clifford[1]

Dwelling, in the proper sense, is now impossible. . . . The house is past.
—Theodore Adorno[2]

The peace of "living together" . . . exceeds the juridical, even the political.
—Jacques Derrida[3]

Existence *is with*: otherwise nothing exists.
—Jean-Luc Nancy[4]

---

1. James Clifford, "Notes on Theory and Travel," *Inscriptions* 5 (1989): 177.
2. Theodore Adorno, "Refuge for the Homeless," in *Minima Moralia: Reflections from a Damaged Life*, trans. E. F. N. Jephcott (London: Verso, 1974), 38, 39.
3. Jacques Derrida, "Avowing—The Impossible: 'Returns,' Repentance, and Reconciliation," in *Living Together: Jacques Derrida's Communities of Violence and Peace*, ed. Elisabeth Weber (New York: Fordham University Press, 2013), 26.
4. Jean-Luc Nancy, *Being Singular Plural* (Stanford: Stanford University Press, 2000), 4.

Diaspora: Reality, Theory, Metaphor

One must begin somewhere. In order to write or express, one must find one's point of entry. I find my point of entry in the adjective *diasporic* because the diasporic has been a way of seeing and experiencing where I am and what I am: an academic in the United States, who could not find an academic home in her own place of birth. Here the binary approach to the issue of diaspora in terms of voluntariness or involuntariness does not work because the two poles inextricably intertwine. In diasporic life, the both sides are somehow always an aspect of each. James Clifford illustrates how theorizing requires one's experience of displacement: "'Theory' is a product of displacement, comparison, a certain distance. To theorize, one leaves home. But like any act of travel, theory begins and ends somewhere. In the case of the Greek theorists, the beginning and ending were one, the home polis. This is not so simply true of traveling theorists in the late twentieth century." [5] As Clifford points out, the point of departure and the point of arrival hardly remain the same in theorizing one's diasporic life in a contemporary world.

When one is away from home, whether empirically or metaphorically, whether voluntarily or involuntarily, the very idea of living together, of the *we* that living together implies, becomes daunting. The issues of home and identity recur in every sector of our reality. Theodor Adorno, who lived a life in exile, a life of away from home, starts his book *Minima Moralia* with a quotation by Ferninand Kürnberger: "Life does not live."[6] What it means to live one's life becomes so difficult to answer due to the entangled nature of the world we inhabit. Needless to say, to live is not merely to survive and sustain one's biological life. In a world of inhumanity, alienation,

5. Clifford, "Notes on Theory and Travel," 177.
6. Adorno, *Minima Moralia*, 19.

and indifference, Adorno's statement, through Kürnberger's voice, is telling. A significant task that theologians, philosophers, religious practitioners, and intellectuals face today is to address the issue of living together, especially when many feel and experience that life does not live. My adoption of diaspora as a guiding concept for this book is an attempt to address one of the most urgent predicaments of our time—displacement. The issue of displacement, of home and identity, has inextricable links to the issue of living together.

My use of the diasporic is not just about one's geographical and historical location but more about epistemological, theopolitical, or metaphorical position and location. Wherever one resides, in this context, doing feminist theology that contests the existing world and envisions a new one means always already living a life of diaspora. I adopt the term *diaspora* neither as a mark of pure victimhood or of privilege, nor as a universalizing or totalizing representative human condition in general. Generally speaking, scholars use the term *diaspora* in two ways, empirical-historical and metaphorical, and the two often get entangled and interrelated in the construction of diasporic consciousness and subjectivity. Although one can interrelate the two, my primary focus is on the metaphorical function of the diasporic mode of existence that creates a special agenthood for theopolitical and epistemological change, along the lines of Paul Gilroy, James Clifford, Stuart Hall, R. Radhakrishnan, or Rey Chow, whose postcolonial diasporic discourses understand diaspora as metaphorical, not merely as an empirical, historical reality of geographical dislocation. Although one's geographical dislocation may contribute to the construction of one's diasporic consciousness, one's diasporic consciousness is not simply an automatic consequence of geographical dislocation. One's geographical dislocation often constructs a new mode of being, thinking, knowing, and seeing the world. Hall, for instance, articulates his understanding of diaspora as follows:

> Diaspora does not refer us to those scattered tribes whose identity can only be secured in relation to some sacred homeland to which they must at all costs return, even if it means pushing other people into the sea. This is the old, the imperializing, the hegemonising, form of 'ethnicity.' We have seen the fate of the people of Palestine at the hands of this backward-looking conception of diaspora—and the complicity of the West with it. The diaspora experience . . . is defined, not by essence or purity, but by the recognition of a necessary heterogeneity and diversity; by a conception of identity which lives with and through, not despite, difference; by hybridity.[7]

In a vein similar to Hall's articulation of diaspora, I choose diaspora as a guiding concept of this book because of its possibility as a mobilizing and effective concept that denaturalizes, disrupts, intervenes in, and interrupts existing institutional structures, discursive strategies, and current configurations of the world that territorialize and naturalize to maintain the status quo. Furthermore, diasporic consciousness calls for an alternative configuration of discourses and practices to existing institutional, theopolitical, and epistemological constraints and confinements in order to eventually enlarge the circle of radical inclusion in religion and the world. By using the term *diaspora* more metaphorically than empirically, however, I intend neither to romanticize the diasporic life nor to distract our sociopolitical and economic attention away from the harsh reality of historical, geopolitical diaspora. Whether forcefully exiled or voluntarily migrated from a homeland to a host country, a diaspora lives a life in between home and away, here and there, and lives in "dwelling-in-displacement."[8] Diaspora studies have recently

---

7. Stuart Hall, "Cultural Identity and Diaspora," in *Identity: Community, Culture, Difference*, ed. Jonathan Rutherford (London: Lawrence and Wishart, 1990), 235.

8. James Clifford, "Diasporas," *Cultural Anthropology* 9, no. 3 (August 1994): 310.

emerged and challenged people's perception of culture and various boundaries of nation-state. These diaspora studies give attention not only to the diasporic experience of the people in their materialized lives throughout the world in an age of globalization but to its theoretical, metaphorical, epistemological implications as well. The notion of diaspora is significant in dealing with issues of minorities and majorities and of nationalism and transnationalism, although diaspora studies emerged only recently.

Etymologically, the term *diaspora* first appeared in the Septuagint and midrashic rabbinical writings to denote the Jewish diaspora, or their expulsion from the "homeland."[9] The word *diaspora* comes from the Greek διασπορά, meaning "sowing," "scattering," or "dispersion," and appears in the Greek translation of the biblical book of Deuteronomy: "Thou shalt be a diaspora in all kingdoms of the earth" (Deut. 28:25). It is interesting, but not surprising, to see that the "scattering" or "sowing of seeds" which the word *diaspora* implies gets closely related to male sperm in Judeo-Christian and Islamic cosmology. In the traditional sense, therefore, the word *diaspora* refers to "a system of kinship reckoned through men," in which addressing "the questions of legitimacy in paternity that patriarchy generates"[10] becomes a recurring task. In this Greek version of the text, one can hardly see any negative connotation in the word *diaspora*. However, the original Hebrew text indicates a clear negative attitude toward the Jews, presenting them as an "object of horror," which does not necessarily mean a geographical and physical dispersion: "You shall become an object of horror to all the kingdoms of the earth" (Deut. 28:25). The Jewish destiny in the original Hebrew text sounds more threatening and horrifying than being simply diaspora in its Greek

9. Jana Evans Braziel, *Diaspora: An Introduction* (Oxford: Blackwell, 2008), 11.
10. Stefan Helmreich, "Kinship, Nation, and Paul Gilroy's Concept of Diaspora," *Diaspora: A Journal of Transnational Studies* 2, no. 2 (Fall 1992): 245.

translation.[11] In this biblical context, diaspora can symbolize a "diminished spiritual and eschatological condition, connected to the negative idea of exile, homelessness, and a yearning for a return to Zion under the guidance of Messiah."[12]

Due to the mystified notion of return to the eternal home, the Zion "under the guidance of Messiah" who has not yet come, some religious Jews such as the ultra-Orthodox groups declare, "Jews who lived in the Holy Land were just as much in exile as those who lived in the diaspora,"[13] regardless of whether they lived in Israel as a sovereign state. Jews' perception of diaspora, of home and exile, has made up, historically speaking, their daily practice and subjectivity, regardless where one resides and lives. Those strictly religious Jews of Eastern Europe, for instance, would regard even the idea of physical return to the Holy Land "before the advent of the Messiah" anathema.[14] In this sense, their idea of "return" is, theologically speaking, neither literal nor physical but eschatological.

Nowadays, one cannot apply the fate of diasporic life only to the Jewish people. Although scholars once used the term *diaspora* to portray primarily "Jewish, Greek, and Armenian dispersion," numerous scholars today use it to indicate "immigrant, expatriate, refugee, guest worker, exile community, overseas community, ethnic community,"[15] based on a general definition of diaspora as "segment of a people living outside the homeland."[16] William Safran further

---

11. For the comparison between the Greek and Hebrew version of this verse, see Caryn Aviv and David Shneer, *New Jew: The End of the Jewish Diaspora* (New York: New York University Press, 2005), 3.

12. Ibid.

13. Aviv and Shneer, *New Jew*, 4.

14. William Safran, "Diasporas in Modern Societies: Myths of Homeland and Return," *Diaspora* 1, no.1 (Spring 1991): 91.

15. Khachig Tölölyan, "The Nation-State and Its Others: In Lieu of a Preface," *Diaspora* 1, no.1 (Spring 1991): 4.

16. Walker Connor, "The Impact of Homelands Upon Diasporas," in *Modern Diasporas in International Politics*, ed. Gabriel Sheffer (New York: Harcourt, 1986), 16.

extends the definition of diaspora by applying it to those who belong to "expatriate minority communities" that share parts of the following features: (1) being dispersed from their original homeland; (2) retaining a collective memory about their homeland; (3) not having a full sense of belonging to the host society; (4) regarding their place of origin as their true, ideal home for a final return; (5) believing in the collective commitment to restoration of their homeland; and (6) having a continuing, ongoing relationship to the homeland in various ways.[17] Most diasporas, with the exception of the Gypsies, tend to internalize the *myth of return* to the *true* home. Interestingly, Safran categorizes the Gypsies as *metadiaspora*. Due to the lack of the myth of return and to the economic rootlessness, the Gypsies neither retain the myth of return and nor form a "Gypsy problem," while other groups' diaspora tends to construct a "Jewish problem," "Polish problem," or "Palestinian problem," for instance.[18] These scholarly analyses introduce major empirical characteristics of diaspora in their specific historical and sociocultural contexts. Here, the "triangular relationship"[19]—the diaspora, the homeland, and the host society—is always the operative aspect in dealing with diaspora discourses and practices.

In his book *Global Diasporas*, Robin Cohen categorizes various diaspora into five types: *victim* diasporas, *imperial* diasporas, *labor* diasporas, *trading* diasporas, and *cultural* diasporas.[20] These various types of diaspora display, Cohen points out, some of following nine features: (1) a dispersion from one's homeland, often forcefully; (2) a

---

17. Safran, "Diasporas in Modern Societies," 83–84.
18. Safran, "Diasporas in Modern Societies": 87. Since people often regard "Gypsy" as a racial slur, it would be better to say "Romanis" instead of "Gypsy." I use however "Gypsy" here due to the general use of it in most works on the diaspora discourse.
19. Cf. Gabriel Sheffer, ed., *Modern Diasporas in International Politics* (New York: Harcourt, 1986), 1–15.
20. Robin Cohen, *Global Diasporas: An Introduction* (Seattle: University of Washington Press, 1997), x.

relocation from one's homeland to other countries to seek work, to pursue commercial developments, or to exercise colonial desires and ambitions; (3) retaining shared memories and fantasies about their homeland; (4) a romanticization of their original homelands; (5) a commitment to a movement for an eventual return; (6) sustaining a steady and long-standing group identity; (7) a distressed relation with the host countries; (8) a sense of alliances with fellow ethnic groups in other places; and (9) a possible life of prosperity in receptive or affirming host societies.[21] One should note that not all diasporas retain the desire for ideal return to the homeland. The Indian diaspora, for example, does not share cultural institutions such as language and religion with India and does not show any strong desire for return to their homeland.[22] Cohen relates his treatment of diaspora primarily to the empirical, historical experience of people physically dislocated from their homeland. Such diasporas always carry the image of their homeland from which they get separated. The image of homeland they always keep in their hearts can be a physical place, an existing country, or an imagined space, a country-of-not-yet, like Zion for some religious Jews. In this context, the relationship between diaspora and the homeland becomes crucial in the process of constructing both an individual identity as a diaspora and a collective identity as diasporic community.

In an era of cyber-communication, one's physical ties to and residence within the homeland that were once inevitable to maintain a close relationship with the homeland become much less significant. The diasporas can instantly involve themselves in the politics of the homeland, for instance, via cyberspace, and can form a kind of political peoplehood. In this context, diasporas can be "outside the state but inside the people."[23] Here one can see two types of diaspora

---

21. Ibid., 180.
22. Amitav Ghosh, "The Diaspora in Indian Culture," *Public Culture* 2, no. 1 (Fall 1989): 76.

paradigms: one that takes geographical borderlands between home and away as the most central issue, and the other one that has more interest in multilocale diaspora cultures than rigidly fixed specific geographical places. It becomes more complex than ever to identify the range and scope of diasporic phenomena and experiences in the twenty-first century, in which one's geographical distance becomes reduced and in a way pointless due to technological developments for means of travel, cyberspaces for audio and video communications, and various social-networking services. Moreover, defining diaspora exclusively in a context of one specific racial and ethnic group also has its limits to capture the complex scope and aspects of diasporic experience in multiple contexts of border-traversing, hybridity, migration, exile, deterritorialization, transnationality, or transculturality. Diasporic discourse invites, I argue, one to acknowledge two profound aspects of one's longing for the homeland: a historically real homeland and a symbolic or metaphoric one.

Politics of Diaspora:
Diasporic Dis/Location and Intersubjectivity

One can perceive the notion of diaspora through two paradigms. The old paradigm, or the classic model of interpretation, portrays diaspora as associated with a "unified, solidary community and a thematic of territory and memory."[24] In this classic model, diaspora is a unified entity whose cultural, ethnic, racial, or religious identity people define as oneness, stable, unchanging, or fixed. The diasporic

---

23. Yossi Shain, *Kinship and Diasporas in International Affairs* (Ann Arbor: University of Michigan Press, 2007), 124.
24. Christine Chivallon, "Beyond Gilroy's Black Atlantic: The Experience of the African Diaspora," *Diaspora* 11, no. 3 (Winter 2002): 359.

identity is, according to the classic model, inescapably essentialist in its construction of identity, which suppresses the differences and heterogeneity among and within the same diasporic group. The explicit operative metaphor for this model is *roots*.[25] The diasporic community of this model maintains its life centered on the stories and practices of memories, foods, culture of the place of origin, and the idea of the final return to true home. In this sense, the classic interpretation of diaspora tends to fix the diasporic community into the past time and space and lacks a sense of mobility, alterity, hybridity, or liminality.

Scholars like Hall, Gilroy, Homi Bhabha, and Clifford offer a different interpretation of diaspora: the model of hybridity, which portrays diaspora not as a fixed, essentialist, unitary entity but as a moving, becoming, interconnecting, negotiating, and hybridizing one. However, the model of hybridity does not exclude in its discursive construction the diasporic experience from the classic model. Instead, it takes the notion of *roots* that is most crucial in the classic interpretation but turns it to *routes* as a guiding metaphor and reference. James Clifford articulates this metaphor of *routes*[26] as being antiessentialist and one that celebrates hybridity and difference in its construction of diasporic identity. However, *roots* and *routes* are not in contradiction or in a binary position but in a constant spiral movement back and forth.

Diaspora discourses evolve around the issues of deterritorialization, dislocation, detachment, uprooting, or dispersion. Scholars of diasporic discourse, such as Gilroy, Hall, and Clifford, transvalue the diasporic state from a negative to a positive condition and a subjectivity of alterity, hybridity, counterterritorialization, or

25. Ibid.
26. Cf. James Clifford, *Routes: Travel and Translation in the Late Twentieth Century* (Cambridge: Harvard University Press, 1997).

multiple locationalities. The diasporic location can be a site of creative engagement with the world. Diaspora is a "signifier, not simply of transnationality and movement but of political struggles to define the local, as a distinctive community, in historical contexts of displacement."[27]

Here it is important to note that diasporic consciousness can be both negative and positive. It can be negative in terms of its internalization of discrimination, alienation, and exclusion. When this diasporic consciousness operates in one's life in a negative way, it is hard for a diaspora to make an inventive, passionate engagement with a given context. Occupied with a negated, negative self-image of the "inevitable self-questioning, self-disparagement, and lowering of ideals which ever accompany repression and breed in an atmosphere of contempt and hate,"[28] dispersed people tend to feel a sense of victimhood, rather than an agenthood, which can overshadow the diasporic life. Here, diasporas can fall into the danger of ethnic absolutism when they lock themselves in a compound box of exclusion from the host countries. Paul Gilroy contends that both blacks and whites can produce the "continuing lure of ethnic absolutism"[29] in the black diasporic world. Diasporas could live, in this context, with a paradoxical consciousness of despair and hope, of painful suffering and persistent spirit of survival. He contends that the racism against the black Atlantic cultivates the "need to project a coherent and stable racial culture as a means to establish the political legitimacy of black nationalism and the notions of ethnic particularity on which it has come to rely" and makes the black Atlantic unable to see the "displacements and transformations" as

---

27. James Clifford, "Diasporas," *Cultural Anthropology* 9, no. 3 (August, 1994): 308.
28. W. E. B. Du Bois, "Of Our Spiritual Strivings," in *The Souls of Black Folk* (1903; Rockville: Arc Manor, 2008), 16.
29. Gilroy, *Black Atlantic*, 3.

"enriching or strengthening" but regard them as "cultural contamination."[30]

W. E. B. Du Bois introduces the notion of double consciousness—paradoxical features of black Atlantic's diasporic consciousness: "It is a peculiar sensation, this double-consciousness, this sense of always looking at one's self through the eyes of others, of measuring one's soul by the tape of a world that looks on in amused contempt and pity. One ever feels his [*sic*] twoness,—an American, a Negro; two souls, two thoughts, two reconciled strivings; two warring ideals in one dark body whose dogged strength alone keeps it from being torn asunder."[31] This double consciousness arises from the "unhappy symbiosis between three modes of thinking, being, and seeing," as Gilroy points out: "The first is racially particularistic, the second nationalistic in that it derives from the nation state in which the ex-slaves but not-yet-citizens find themselves, rather than from their aspiration towards a nation state of their own. The third is diasporic or hemispheric, sometimes global and occasionally universalist."[32] In the early 1960s, various groups, such as the "separatist" Nation of Islam and the "integrationist" NAACP, SCLC, CORE, and the like adopted Du Bois's notion of double consciousness in their discussion of paradoxical, ambiguous aspects of African American life.[33] The geopolitical meaning of Du Boisian double consciousness, as a form of sociopolitical alienation, can also imply both negative and positive meanings and effects.

It is necessary to shift diasporic consciousness from a narrow, negative concern of alienation, ambiguities, or ethnic absolutism to

---

30. Paul Gilroy, *The Black Atlantic: Modernity and Double Consciousness* (Cambridge, MA: Harvard University Press, 1993), 97.

31. Du Bois, "Of Our Spiritual Strivings," 9.

32. Gilroy, *Black Atlantic*, 127.

33. Ernest Allen Jr., "Ever Feeling One's Twoness: 'Double Ideals' and 'Double Consciousness' in the Souls of Black Folk," *Contributions in Black Studies: A Journal of African and Afro-American Studies* (Special Double Issue: African American Double Consciousness) 9/10 (1990–1992): 55.

a more positive, planetary commitment to transracial, transethnic, transnational, transreligious, transgender, transsexual, alternative visions for the world of freedom and justice that require a different sense of temporal spatiality. Here, the diasporic double consciousness can be enormously positive. The person with a positive diasporic consciousness can expand his or her sense of belonging to *everywhere*, in the sense of ever embracing multiple contexts, and, at the same time, *nowhere*, in the sense of making a decision not to claim any sense of ownership and territorialized fixation. In this sense, the diasporic person can inventively engage with multiple contexts, each time anew. Here, everywhere and nowhere are not in contradiction. Instead, they reveal the entangled nature of belonging and nonbelonging, or home and away, while never claiming an absolute ownership of any fixed space, discourse, or movement. A person with a positive diasporic double consciousness can always already remain open to engage inventively with each specific context, taking each context as a unique one every time. Edward Said characterizes a positive mode of a life of exile in his quotations from Hugo of St. Victor: "The man [sic] who finds his homeland sweet is still a tender beginner; he to whom every soil is as his native one is already strong; but he is perfect to whom the entire world is as a foreign land."[34] Such a person, for Said, exemplifies the positive figure as an exile:

> Seeing "the entire world as a foreign land" makes possible originality of vision. Most people are principally aware of one culture, one setting, one home; exiles are aware of at least two, and this plurality of vision gives rise to an awareness of simultaneous dimensions, an awareness of simultaneous dimensions, an awareness that—to borrow a phrase from music—is *contrapuntal*. For an exile, habits of life, expression, or activity in the new environment inevitably occur against the memory of these things in another environment.[35]

34. Edward Said, *Reflections on Exile and Other Essays* (Cambridge: Harvard University Press, 2000), 185.

When diasporas are fully aware of and constantly negotiate the entanglement of rootedness and routedness, of local and global, of microdimensional and macrodimensional, of here and there, of dwelling and traveling, of continuity and discontinuity, of memory and countermemory, belonging and nonbelonging, or of history and counterhistory, they can construct positive, innovative, empowering diasporic consciousness and discourses.

One cannot guarantee, however, that diasporic experiences automatically contribute to the construction of geopolitical, critical, and subversive discourses and actions. People can commodify diasporas in a wide range of practices and discourses under the banner of multiculturalism and respect for cultural diversity, for instance. Multiculturalists can celebrate the culture of the diaspora's homeland, often homogenized, nativized, and exoticized, but dehistoricize and depoliticize the lives of diaspora in a concrete reality by not taking the "low-wage sweatshops," for instance, to the sites where multicultural diversity is being celebrated.[36] The act of multiculturalization of the diasporic minorities, under the banner of multiculturalism and in the name of cultural diversity, can then function to mislead and distort diasporic experiences and consciousness. Homi Bhabha offers insightful critique on the discourse and practice of liberal multiculturalism's endorsement of cultural diversity. Bhabha distinguishes between cultural diversity and cultural difference and points out two problems with the liberal endorsement of cultural diversity.[37] First, the host society or dominant culture formulates and administers a "transparent norm," a

35. Ibid., 186.
36. Cf. Getty Center, *New Geographies of Performance: Cultural Representation and Intercultural Exchange on the Edge of the 21st Century: Summary Report* (Los Angeles: Getty Center for the History of Art and the Humanities, 1991), 124–28; quoted in Clifford, "Diasporas," 313.
37. Homi K. Bhabha, "The Commitment to Theory," in *The Location of Culture* (New York: Routledge, 2006 [1994]), 55–51.

"containment of cultural difference," which implies "these other cultures are fine, but we must be able to locate them within our own grid."[38] Second, the universalism of liberal multiculturalism ironically encourages diversity while disguising "ethnocentric norms, values and interests."[39] In this sense, liberal multiculturalism can function to represent "an attempt both to respond to and to control the dynamic process of the articulation of cultural difference, administering a *consensus* based on a norm that propagates cultural diversity."[40] As a result, the manipulated false consensus of liberal multiculturalists on the host society suppresses the hybridity, alterity, and heterogeneity of cultural difference between different cultures. The host culture can often hide its "pathos of hegemony" under the depoliticized "celebration of differences, but only of differences in the aestheticized form of recreations," relegating the minority cultures to space of the "mere repetition of ethnic or feminine exotica."[41] One should note that discourses, practices, and the sociopolitical implications of multiculturalism vary to an extreme and can be categorized into five types: conservative, liberal, pluralist, left-essentialist, and critical multiculturalism.[42]

Diasporic consciousness can be "an intellectualization of an existential condition"[43] and implies "the reality of being intellectual"[44] today on the part of those who would embody the transnational, border-crossing reality—not only empirically and historically but also

---

38. Homi K. Bhabha, "The Third Space: Interview with Homi Bhabha," in Rutherford, ed., *Identity*, 208.
39. Ibid.
40. Ibid., 208–209.
41. Abdul R. JanMohamed and David Lloyd, "Introduction: Toward a Theory of Minority Discourse: What Is To Be Done?" in *The Nature and Context of Minority Discourse*, ed. Abdul R. JanMohamed and David Lloyd (New York: Oxford University Press, 1990), 5, 6.
42. Cf. Joe L. Kincheloe and Shirley R. Steinberg, *Changing Multiculturalism: New Times, New Curriculum* (Berkshire, UK: Open University Press, 2011 [1997]), 3–26.
43. Safran, "Diasporas in Modern Societies," 87.
44. Rey Chow, *Writing Diaspora: Tactics of Intervention in Contemporary Cultural Studies* (Bloomington: Indiana University Press, 1993), 15.

metaphorically and existentially. Diasporic intellectuals embody and contest the question of borders of various kinds: borders of language, race, ethnicity, gender, class, sexuality, citizenship, nationality, religion, and so forth. The diasporic location is a space of liminality, a space of in between here and there. One's diasporic location deterritorializes a fixed notion of borders and negotiates one's naturalized, essentialized identity that people socioculturally formulate based on one's place of origin and its relation to one's present home—whether it be geographical, epistemological, ontological, or political. How many hyphens or what kind of hyphens one carries around in one's work, life, and relationships with others reveals the layers of diasporic conditions, locations, and positions.

Although the diasporic location is twofold—geopolitical and metaphorical—these two locations are not completely dissociable. Instead, both often intertwine and have one thing in common: both evolve around the issue of power—linguistic, discursive, sociocultural, geopolitical, economic, symbolic, and the like. A geopolitical diasporic location reveals how power in various forms interplays in every sector of one's life and in the formation of one's consciousness through languages, systems, institutions, daily practices, and so forth.

For those who dwell in the hyphen and live a hyphenated life such as Asian-American, African-American, or Hispanic-American, which part of the components that the hyphen joins best represents the person is an extremely complex question. In a similar vein, I would not need to label my theological discourse as "feminist" if my theological position did not fundamentally contest traditionally normative parameters of theological discourses. Furthermore, I would not need to indicate my work by using or being labeled as "Asian feminist" if my ethnicity or race belonged to the mainstream feminist theologians whose works automatically become universal and normative without any process of translation or mediation, or any particular racial, ethnic marker. People often locate sexual-minority persons in contexts that require a particular marker such as homosexual, queer, gay, lesbian, transgendered, and so forth, whereas heterosexuals do not need to use such sexuality-specific markers simply because they belong to the mainstream, the universalized, and normativized group. In this context, a society where heterosexuality constitutes the sexual normativity, this default sexuality puts a sexually minority person in a diasporic location.

The question of how one's diasporic location would then function in one's personal and institutional life becomes extremely significant because more people than ever live their lives in diasporic locations, both empirically and metaphorically. In this context, diaspora, Gilroy contends, "offers a ready alternative to the stern discipline of primordial kinship and rooted belonging . . ."[45] A woman is not born a feminist simply due to her biology. Instead, she *becomes* a feminist. In the same vein, one does not automatically come to have a diasporic mode of seeing, sensing, thinking, acting, and a deterritorial pluralism, openness, or passion for justice simply due to one's geographical dislocation. Regardless of one's geographical and physical dislocation, one needs to cultivate, practice, and constantly radicalize a diasporic mode of existence and consciousness in the way it contributes to promoting a community of justice and living together.

In his seminal work *Minima Moralia*, Theodore Adorno declares: "Dwelling, in the proper sense, is now impossible."[46] The impossibility of dwelling in one's life also implies the impossibility of homecoming in its proper sense. Homecoming, whether physical

---

45. Gilroy, *Black Atlantic*, 123.
46. Adorno, "Refuge for the Homeless," 38.

or metaphorical, requires a sense of certainty of returning, arriving, or completing one's itinerary. For the diasporic subject, however, embracing the uncertainty of the point of departure and of arrival is a part of the conditions for his/her life. Here, being unable to have a life of homecoming can bring both despair and promise. Living a diasporic life always already signifies a life in transit, a life on the move, a life of wandering in an epistemological, cultural, linguistic, racial-ethnic, or physical dislocation and relocation, in which one never claims a sense of territorial ownership. Diasporic scholars such as Edward Said point out that those who have resided in countries other than their own place of birth see themselves as the other: "Identity—who we are, where we come from, what we are—is difficult to maintain in exile. . . . We are the 'other,' an opposite, a flaw in the geometry of resettlement and exodus."[47] Here deterritorializing becomes a condition for a diasporic life. A diasporic life, in which dwelling, an absolute belonging, is impossible, creates a different mode of being, thinking, seeing, judging, or acting. Being unable to dwell in one's heart language, in one's sociocultural history, or in one's static identity makes one always see double and see something that dwellers do not see. In this sense, diasporic identities are "constantly producing and reproducing themselves anew, through transformation and difference."[48] In this context, one constructs a diasporic identity only in a provisional way across differences and alterity.

When one becomes a feminist, one cannot live a life as it used to be. One sees, smells, touches, feels, or experiences patriarchy wherever one goes, from private sectors to public ones. A feminist gradually finds her or his mode of existence by becoming diasporic,

47. Edward Said, *After the Last Sky: Palestinian Lives,* photographs by Jean Mohr (New York: Pantheon, 1986), 16–17.
48. Lawrence Grossberg, "Cultural Studies and/in New Worlds," *Critical Studies in Mass Communication* 10, no. 1 (March, 1993): 11.

especially one's home: the space of familiarity turns into a space of unfamiliarity, a space of unfreedom, and a space of contestation and resistance. In this case, one is in exile, living a diasporic life, in more than a political, geographical sense. Rather, living a diasporic life is a state of being, a mode of existence in the world—to be skeptical, rigorously critical of what-it-is, to intentionally distance oneself from the mainstream way of thinking and practicing, to long for the world to come. Being diasporic is, therefore, a sensitive, multiple mode of seeing the world and the people living in it. Diasporas experience their sense of "belonging only through the experience of nonbelonging: separations, rejections, ruptures, exclusions."[49]

Here, it is important to note that Rey Chow, a diaspora intellectual herself, warns against the danger of "sanctification of victimization"[50] in those Third-World diaspora intellectuals in the West:

> The space of "third world" intellectuals in diaspora is a space that is removed from the "ground" of earlier struggles that were still tied to the "native land." Physical alienation, however, can mean precisely the intensification and aestheticization of the values of "minority" positions that had developed in the earlier struggles and that have now, in "third world" intellectuals' actual circumstances in the West, become defunct. The unself-reflexive sponsorship of "third world" culture, including "third world" women's culture, becomes a mask that conceals the hegemony of these intellectuals over those who are stuck at home. For "third world" intellectuals, the lures of diaspora consist in this masked hegemony.[51]

Some third-world intellectuals often use the sanctification of victimization in their pursuit of power in the Western academy, while the First-World scholars enjoy the unconscious ethnocentrism that remains intact in this rhetoric of exaggeration and sanctification

49. Derrida, "Avowing—The Impossible," 27.
50. Chow, *Writing Diaspora*, 19.
51. Ibid., 118.

of victimization, as long as the third-world intellectuals or minority diasporas remain within that boundary of exotica of victims.

One of the significant roles that a diaspora could play is to produce, create, write, and disseminate multivalent narratives to complexify and diversify the monolithic narratives. A diasporic mode of existence helps one invent counternarratives to resist master narratives of all forms of imperialization, colonialization, dominations, exclusive nationalisms, or subjugations. In this process of resisting, one in a diasporic mode of existence comes to realize the intercontextuality between seemingly different contexts and realities that make people affirm the worldliness of our existence as *Mitsein* ("being-with"). In this sense, Theodore Adorno makes a thought-provoking statement: "it is part of morality not to be at home in one's home."[52]

Diasporic Homelessness: A Condition of Critical Understanding of the World

Diasporas are not a unitary entity; therefore, "diasporas-in-general" are impossible. Hannah Arendt's distinction between "pariahs" and "conscious pariahs" is helpful for seeing the complex degree of diasporas. Arendt's notion of conscious diaspora offers insights into how one can turn one's marginality by imposition not just into an absolute outsidership but into critical marginality, where one can develop a diasporic consciousness, the transformative mode of seeing, reading, and writing that one cannot do otherwise. Arendt makes a distinction between four types of diaspora in her "The Jewish as Pariah." In her articulation of diaspora, Arendt uses the terms *pariah*, *parvenu*, and *conscious pariah*, which she adopts from Bernard Lazare,[53] an exemplary figure for Arendt of a conscious pariah. The

---

52. Adorno, "Refuge for the Homeless," 39.

four types of pariah follow: first, the *schlemihl* by Heinrich Heine; second, Bernard Lazare, the *conscious pariah*; third, the *suspect* by Charlie Chaplin; and fourth, *K* in Franz Kafka's novel *The Castle*.[54] Interestingly, Lazare is the only real person, whereas the other three are fictional. Each type has its unique features, with some coinciding similarity to another type of pariah in terms of its political attitude: *antipolitical*, *apolitical*, and *political*.

The first type of pariah, the *schlemihl*, from Heine's poem *Princess Sabbath*, is a figure of innocence. The *schlemihls* with "the noblest hearts" have the "attitude of denying the reality of the social order and of confronting it."[55] This type of pariah becomes apolitical or antipolitical by escaping into the "higher reality"—into such universal things as "the sun, music, trees, and children,"[56] and is "always remote and unreal." This pariah stands "outside the real world and attacks it from without."[57] This first type of pariah does not give up a deep-seated desire to assimilate happily to the mainstream and remains completely apolitical as "the pariah who aspires to become a *parvenu*,"[58] with his or her utopian land of dreams.

By contrast to the *schlemihl* type, the second type of pariah, exemplified in an actual historical figure Leonard Lazare, is what Arendt calls a "conscious pariah,"[59] who does not unconsciously accept his condition of marginality but turns it into a politically significant condition. Lazare turns his experience of marginality by imposition into a critical marginality by choice. Both the *schlemihl*

---

53. Cf. Bernard Lazare, *Job's Dungheap: Essays on Jewish Nationalism and Social Revolution*, trans. Harry L. Binsse (New York: Schocken, 1948).
54. Hannah Arendt, "The Jew as Pariah: A Hidden Tradition," *Jewish Social Studies* 6, no. 2 (April 1944): 99–122.
55. Ibid., 102, 104.
56. Ibid., 103.
57. Ibid., 105.
58. Ibid., 110.
59. Ibid., 107.

and Lazare do not feel at home; they are homeless, diaspora in the world. They take this homelessness, nonbelonging in completely different ways: the *schlemihl* being apolitical and Lazare being critically political. Lazare does not pursue a happy assimilation into the mainstream like the *schlemihls* do. Instead, he becomes resistant to the mainstream for the oppressed people.

The third type of pariah, exemplified in "the Suspect" from Charlie Chaplin's film of the same name, shares a similar condition with the other types in terms of their stateless condition and remains thereby outside the world. Thus, Chaplin's pariah is the stereotype of the pariah as suspect: "always and everywhere he is under suspicion. . . . in the guise of the 'stateless,' the living symbol of the pariah."[60] Both the first and the third types of pariah are powerless by attempting either to escape or circumvent the laws and contexts of the corrupt world rather than to resist and transform them.

Arendt takes an example of the fourth type of pariah, *K*, from Franz Kafka's novel *The Castle*, the only novel from Kafka that deals with the "Jewish problem." K, a typical figure of diaspora, is a stranger and a nobody, who "belongs neither to the common people nor its rulers."[61] The harsh reality that diasporas face is manifest in the painful illustration that "[s]ociety . . . is composed of 'nobodies'—'I did wrong to nobody, nobody did wrong to me; but nobody will help me, nothing but nobodies'—and has therefore no real existence."[62] K can be an example case for diasporas who try to assimilate themselves to the world of the universal humanity, but without success. All pariahs, of whatever type, experience exclusion and marginality against their will. However, the way in which they adopt their experience of marginality and outsidership becomes utterly different from one

60. Ibid., 111.
61. Ibid., 115.
62. Ibid., 113.

another in terms of their politicization of marginality and commitment that they will to make. Their attempts to get recognized as universal humans with their particular features as Jews or as diasporas illustrates the recurring problem of taking a binary approach to the issue of human particularity and universality.

The issue of particularity and universality is a long-standing and recurring issue in nearly all the disciplines. One's identity as such pertains to the question of particularity and universality, especially when one's gender, race, ethnicity, or sexuality does not belong to a site of normativity in the mainstream world. For an Asian, a woman, or a Jew, for instance, one's admission to the ranks of the universal humanity, but without having to negate who one is, is in a way the goal of every liberation movement for a social change. The concept of the universal here is not a superficial, deductive notion that the modern project has invented but a lived, inductive reconfiguration that affirms every individual human as being as equal as anyone else, regardless of who one is. I use the notion of universality, as Judith Butler articulates, not as an "exclusive negative and exclusionary term," but as "a non-substantial and open-ended category" and as "a future-oriented labor of cultural translation."[63]

Humankind's first exile, a diasporic experience, begins in Genesis. God expelled the first humankind, Adam and Eve, from the Garden of Eden (Gen. 3:23), their homeland, and condemned them to live a diasporic life, a life with the impossibility of homecoming. Abram, whose name and tradition are significant in so-called Abrahamic religions—Judaism, Christianity, and Islam—turns into Abraham through his life as a diaspora after he follows the divine command to leave his own homeland (Gen. 12:1). The narrative of human exile in Genesis fascinated me during my seminary period. Why

---

63. Judith Butler, "Preface (1999)," in *Gender Trouble: Feminism and the Subversion of Identity* (New York: Routledge, 2008 [1990]), xviii.

does Eve's encounter with the tree of knowledge, which supposedly gives such a great power to discern the good from the evil, become the very ground of human exile from the ideal Home, the Garden of Eden? I wondered, when I was about to leave Korea, my place of birth, for Germany in search of knowledge and self-fulfillment, whether my journey to quench my intellectual and existential thirst for knowledge of life would also become the ground of being exiled from my community and home where I used to belong and feel homely.

In retrospect, it seems true that my ongoing exposure to new knowledge of life, of good and evil, of right and wrong has become the ground of living in exile in my own homeland. I came to experience that my exile experience, my diasporic experience, not just as a geopolitical condition but more as an epistemological and intellectual one, began with my exposure to the tree of new knowledge such as the discourses of feminism, deconstruction, postmodernism, or postcolonialism, which fundamentally challenge and shake the existing reality and the structure of knowledge with which most people feel comfortable. Since then, it has been difficult for me to feel at home wherever I am. I have always felt in exile, even in my own homeland. After years of intense struggles with patriarchal institutions, I decided to leave my physical homeland to find, rebuild, and reshape my intellectual, epistemological, ontological home, which is however always evolving and in the making.

What, then, would be the functionality of assuming the status of one who leaves the familiar place that people call home/land and being a diaspora? God commanded Abraham, whose name was then Abram, a seventy-five-year-old man, to leave his home without offering any substantial explanation for why he should leave his familiar space, the home, to receive the blessing from God: "Go from your country and your kindred and your father's house to the land that I will show you. I will make of you a great nation, and I will bless you, and make your name great, so that you will be a blessing" (Gen. 12:1-2). Although Genesis does not offer the full account of Abraham's own voice about before and after God's urging him to live a life of diaspora, of stranger, of foreigner, of outsider, of being "cut off from the consolations of consensus and community, from the common sense of the *sensus communis*, stripped down to the madness of solitude,"[64] it implies that the life experience of diaspora, the homeless, the life of the "nonhistory of absolute beginnings,"[65] has made Abram Abraham. Jesus, the primary reference of Christianity, declares that he himself is homeless: "Foxes have lairs, the birds of the sky have nests, but the Chosen One has nowhere to rest" (Luke 9:58, *The Inclusive Bible*). The life without home is a life in interstitial space, liminal space, that helps one to invent a new mode of seeing, of listening, of relating, of caring without claiming any kind of ownership, as with Jesus the homeless.

I have no desire, however, to romanticize one's diasporic life—whether it be physical, metaphorical, or intellectual. Despite some fashionable portrayals of displacement and dislocation, one's diasporic life can always be a lifelong struggle of anxiety and existential anguish about fragmented life, a constant search for home, nonbelonging, and a painful negotiating process between home and away. Just as Edward Said describes his diasporic experience through his life in exile as "strangely compelling to think about but terrible to experience,"[66] one's real diasporic life can be always already a life

---

64. John D. Caputo, *The Prayers and Tears of Jacques Derrida: Religion without Religion* (Bloomington: Indiana University Press, 1997), 199.
65. Jacques Derrida, *The Gift of Death*, trans. David Willis (Chicago: University of Chicago Press, 1995 [1992]), 80.
66. Said, *Reflections on Exile*, 173.

of pain, loneliness, and nonbelonging. Adorno illustrates the life of émigrés:

> The past life of emigres is, as we know, annulled. Earlier it was the warrant of arrest, today it is intellectual experience, that is declared non-transferable and unnatualizable. Anything that is not reified, cannot be counted and measured, ceases to exist. Not satisfied with this, however, reification spreads to its own opposite, the life that cannot be directly actualized; anything that lives on merely as thought and recollection. For this a special rubric has been invented. It is called 'background' and appears on the questionnaire as an appendix, after sex, age and profession. To complete its violation, life is dragged along on the triumphal automobile of the united statisticians, and even the past is no longer safe from the present, whose remembrance of it consigns it a second time to oblivion.[67]

What I am articulating is a feminist theological discourse that sees a source of creativity in the diasporic consciousness that would create a space of transformation, reconciliation, hospitality, worldliness, and border-traversing. In diasporic discourse, a sense of homelessness is one of the key themes. In her essay "We Refugees," Hannah Arendt, a diaspora, a pariah herself, makes painful remarks of loss on the diasporic condition of homelessness: "We lost our home, which means the familiarity of daily life. We lost our occupation, which means the confidence that we are of some use in this world. We lost our language, which means the naturalness of reactions, the simplicity of gestures, the unaffected expression of feelings."[68] Here, one should note that the condition of homelessness of the displaced diaspora, however, is not just about the loss of a physical, geographical home but about the loss of language, a linguistic homelessness. Gilles Deleuze and Felix Guattari raise a significant,

---

67. Adorno, *Minima Moralia*, 46–47.
68. Hannah Arendt, "We Refugees," in *The Jew as Pariah: Jewish Identity and Politics in the Modern Age,* ed. Ron H. Feldman (New York: Random House, 1978), 55–56.

but often neglected, question: "How many people today live in a language that is not their own? . . . This is the problem of immigrants, and especially of their children, the problem of minorities, the problem of a minor literature, but also a problem for all of us."[69] The linguistic homelessness makes a tremendous impact on the lives of diaspora. Gloria Anzaldua, a diaspora in multiple senses as a Chicana, a feminist, a lesbian living and writing in the United States, illustrates the destructive nature of the loss of her own language in her use of the term "linguistic terrorism" and goes on to claim, "I am my language."[70] In this sense, Anzaldua asks: "Who is to say that robbing a people of its language is less violent than war?"[71]

When people do not affirm one's heart language, the loss of one's heart language and the need to use the acquired language become a constant reminder of one's diasporic location and the life of marginality. Here, marginality denotes "not being simply at home in the world."[72] However, the state of not-being-at-home can turn into a site of inventive engagement with the world because the person of marginality can become deliberate in seeking, cultivating, and constructing a space of relationship with others and society. Those who are always at home in the world take for granted whatever is out there without any intentionality or inventive engagement with others and the world. In this sense, Arendt contends: " I'm still a stateless person. . . . I'm more than ever of the opinion that a decent human existence is possible today only on the fringes of society, where one then runs the risk of starving or being stoned to death."[73]

---

69. Gilles Deleuze and Felix Guattari, "What Is a Minor Literature?," in *Out There: Marginalization and Contemporary Cultures*, ed. Russell Ferguson, Martha Gever, Trinh T. Minh-ha, and Cornel West (New York: The New Museum of Contemporary Art/Cambridge: MIT Press, 1990), 61.
70. Gloria Anzaldua, *Borderlands/La Frontera: The New Mestiza* (San Francisco: Aunt Lute, 1987), 58, 59.
71. Ray Gwyn Smith, *Moorland Is Gold Country*, unpub. book, cited in ibid., 53.
72. Lisa Jane Disch, *Hannah Arendt and the Limits of Philosophy* (Ithaca: Cornell University Press, 1994), 173.

Diasporic homelessness is a condition of critical understanding of the world but not a "form of theoretical tourism . . . where the margin becomes a linguistic or critical vacation, a new poetics of the exotic."[74] The diasporic mentality of homelessness can offer theological grounds of radical hospitality, responsibility, and critical engagements with the life of living together, the potential site for a radical solidarity without a sense of claiming the ownership of a unitary *we*. The homelessness, the nonbelonging makes possible for creating a condition of doing theology with "a sense of being unwilling to accept easy formulas, or ready-made clichés, or the smooth, ever-so-accommodating confirmations of what the powerful or conventional have to say, and what they do," which requires "maintaining a state of *constant alertness*."[75] Diasporic homelessness is a critical condition for doing feminist theology that crosses exclusive borders and breaks discriminatory barriers of discourse, practice, system, and institution.

Diasporic Feminist Theology:
The Inventive Engagement in Living Together

An anonymous author offers a popular definition of feminism: *feminism is a radical notion that women are people*. This definition of feminism indicates the ultimate goal of feminism is to achieve the state in which people admit women to the ranks of universal humanity. Accepting women as people means granting their equality

---

73. Hannah Arendt and Karl Jaspers, *Correspondence: 1926–1969*, ed. Lotte Kohler and Hans Saner, trans. Robert Kimber and Rita Kimber (New York: Harcourt Brace Jovanovich, 1992 [1985]), 29.
74. Caren Kaplan, "Deterritorializations: The Rewriting of Home and Exile in Western Feminist Discourse," in JanMohamed and Lloyd, ed., *Nature and Context of Minority Discourse*, 361.
75. Edward Said, *Representations of the Intellectual*, The 1993 Reith Lectures (New York: Vintage, 1996 [1994]), 23.

and dignity as human beings, not only spiritually but also institutionally, socioeconomically, structurally, politically, and discursively as well. The precondition for doing feminist theology means to have a critical understanding of the world, and its ultimate goal is to claim justice and equality for every individual human being—a fellow citizen of the universal humanity regardless of one's gender, race, class, ability, or sexuality. Remaining critical requires an intentional distance from the world. Those who feel always at home in the world would hardly be able to achieve an appropriate distance from the world, which would make them easily blind—epistemologically, geopolitically, and theologically—to the issues of power, exclusion, and oppression. In this context, being on the fringes, on the margins, means residing in a state of not being simply at home, but being homeless. The homelessness is in between wordlessness and being too much at home.[76]

In her essay "Choosing the Margin as a Space of Radical Openness," bell hooks rightly argues for the need for choosing to be on the margin: "As a radical standpoint, perspective, position, 'the politics of location' necessarily calls those of us who would participate in the formation of counter-hegemonic cultural practice to identify the spaces where we begin the process of re-vision."[77] The politics of location, the questions as to how and where one locates oneself in the world and how such an act of locating would function, are always already theopolitical decisions that have significant theoethical implications. I would define feminist theology, in a broad sense, as theopolitical and theoethical discourses that offer new configurations of communities of believers and nonbelievers and new visions for a world in which people treat every individual human being as equal to everyone else, regardless of one's gender, race, ethnicity,

76. Disch, *Hannah Arendt and the Limits of Philosophy*, 176.
77. bell hooks, *Yearning: Race, Gender, and Cultural Politics* (Boston: South End Press, 1990), 145.

ability, sexuality, class, citizenship, religion, and so forth—a messianic envisioning of the approximate world of the *kindom* of God. In order to work on the feminist theopolitical envisioning of the kindom, feminist theologians need to maintain their distance from the existing world and not feel at home in the world-as-it-is.

The primary vocation of feminist theology is to dismantle the patriarchal and androcentric construction of discourses and practices in religion and society. Furthermore, it must offer counterhegemonic discourses and alternative ways of reading, thinking, seeing, judging, and acting to promote the materialized justice that pertains to the issues of gender, race and ethnicity, class, sexuality, ability, and so forth. Taking the feminist theological vocation seriously requires one to choose the margin, the diasporic location. However, choosing to locate oneself in a diasporic space, on the fringes, does not mean to live in a state of absolute outsidership but to live as a being with critical marginality as a conscious pariah, a conscious diaspora. To live as a diaspora is to live always on the fringe. bell hooks articulates: "To be in the margin is to be part of the whole but outside the main body. . . . Living as we did—on the edge—we developed a particular way of seeing reality. We looked both from the outside in and from the inside out. We focused our attention on the center as well as the margin. We understand both. This mode of seeing reminded us of the existence of a whole universe, a main body made up of both margin and center."[78]

In this context, two types of marginality can exist in human reality: marginality by imposition and marginality by choice—critical marginality. It is important to note that the two types or conditions of marginality can often get intertwined in the sense that one could make a decisive shift from the marginality by imposition to a critical

---

78. bell hooks, *Feminist Theory: From Margin to Center* (Boston: South End Press, 2000), xvi.

marginality, as in the case of conscious pariah, Lazare, in Arendt's illustration of four types of pariahs. The diasporic location of critical marginality takes one's marginality not simply as a location of exclusion, deprivation, or absolute outsidership but as a critical site of radical contestation, resistance, deconstruction, deterritorialization, and border-traversing. Whereas the absolute outsidership is an imposed marginality, the critical marginality of the diasporic location is a marginality one decisively and consciously chooses as a transformative site of counterhegemonic discourse and practice for a more just world, a world of living together in its radical sense. This site of critical marginality, where one chooses not to be at home in the world, can be a space of pain, suffering, and loneliness. At the same time, however, the site of critical, diasporic marginality is a space of possibility of the impossible and of transformation not only in an individual and collective life but also in systems, discourses, and practices. The conscious diaspora, the conscious homeless, is the one who becomes politically conscious about his or her marginality by imposition and turns it to an experience of critical marginality as a site of resistance to any form of an unjust totalization, oppression, and exclusion.

Here, one of the most urgent issues that we face in our time can be how to live together. "Living is always 'living together,'" [79] Jacques Derrida reminds us. However, the issue of living together becomes increasingly complex, especially in an era of displacement in various forms. I do not mean to refer to a romanticized, apoliticized, self-contained, self-protective, naturalized, or exclusive perception of living together. Before one attempts to respond the question of how to live together, one must think about "*Who* addresses *whom* in asking 'how to live together'?"[80] A togetherness, a gathering,

79. Derrida, "Avowing—The Impossible," 19–20.
80. Ibid., 20 (italics mine).

or an ensemble in the living together-ness is neither a mechanical cohabitation, coexistence, nor does it refer to a "totality of a natural, biological, or genetic ensemble, to the cohesiveness of an organism or of some social body (family, ethnic group, nation) that would be measured with this organic metaphor."[81] Instead, a living together means "living *well* together," which requires an ethics of living together. The ethics of living together, Derrida contends, "supposes accord beyond any statutory condition, not necessarily in contradiction with it, but beyond and across the normality of a legal, political, and state-controlled bond between two or more than one (male or female) who are not only spouses, co-citizens, co-countrymen, congeners, or coreligionist individuals, but remain strangers, (from) others and radically other."[82]

In this sense, the issue of living together is, I would argue, one of the most significant theopolitical and theoethical issues that any form of theological discourse and practice must address to make itself relevant in the world. The mandate of living together is manifest in Jesus' teaching on the final judgment (Matt. 25:31-46) and his parable on a true neighbor (Luke 10:25-37), for instance. I believe the peace of living together is the core of Jesus' teaching and therefore constitutes what it means to be a Christian, a Jesus follower. Here, the peace of living together, Derrida contends, "exceeds the juridical, even the political, at any rate, the political as determined by the state, by the sovereignty of the state,"[83] and he further illustrates the mandate of living together:

> One cannot not "live together" even if one does not know how or with whom, with God, with gods, men [sic], animals, with one's own, with one's close ones, neighbors, family, or friends, with one's fellow citizens or countrymen but also with the most distant strangers, with

81. Ibid., 26.
82. Ibid.
83. Ibid.

one's enemies, with oneself, with one's contemporaries, with those who are no longer so or will never be so, so many names that I draw from daily language and of which I do not yet presume that we know what they designate.[84]

One should also note that the living together, in its radical sense, with oneself, with both close and distant others, with neighbors and non-neighbors, with nationals and non-nationals, with the divine, with the marginalized on various grounds, with humanity, or with animals and other living beings, means one's plural belonging to various sites of living together. The plural belonging further requires a condition of nonbelonging. When one is unable to locate oneself in a state of nonbelonging that symbolizes and implies a diasporic condition, it is impossible to have an endlessly plural belonging because the "plural belonging" is possible "only through the experience of nonbelonging" of "separations, rejections, ruptures, exclusions."[85] A radical sense of living together has to be against two distorted and limited ways of living together: first, against racist, sexist, classist, homophobic, or xenophobic living together; and second, against the "conservative and self-protective" way of living together.[86]

When feminism first touched my life, I attempted to go to a lot of feminist discussion groups and meetings. At that time, while I enjoyed the feminist conviviality and camaraderie as women, I also found myself having somewhat unsettling, uncomfortable experiences, often leaving the meetings wondering how these feminists ended up in the same room with each other. While I appreciated the mutual understanding and support, I nevertheless thought that they were overlooking the oppressive realities of race, class, sexuality, or national and religious citizenship that matter to

84. Ibid., 24.
85. Ibid., 27.
86. Ibid., 28.

so many people—both men and women. When one's discourse and practice of feminist living together becomes self-protective and self-contained, one must leave the site of self-contained living together, the space of exclusive belonging, and locate oneself in a diasporic space of nonbelonging in order to live one's life in the plural belonging. If a feminist is the one who believes and wants to live up to the claim that "feminism is a radical notion that women are people," he or she must to be able to claim not only that women are people but also that X are people, moving beyond the gender-protective confinement of living together toward a living together-ness of plural belonging to various Xs, which requires a diasporic sense of nonbelonging.

Using an adjective for one's own work, such as *diasporic* or *feminist*, indicates the author's minority locationality, and thus the work remains as a minority discourse. White-male theologians, for instance, do not need to use any adjective such as *feminist* in the titles of their works, whereas white-feminist theologians often use only one adjective, *feminist*. Ethnic and feminist theologians, however, use double adjectives to indicate polyvocality. Minority discourses reveal the polyvocality of minority voices, provoking and invoking the perception of human beings as being-with-others, which always already implies sociopolitical and theoethical meaning of one's existence, one's identity.

> The one/the other is neither "by," nor "for," nor "in," nor "despite," but rather "with." This "with" is at once both more and less than "relation" or "bond" . . . the "with" is the exact contemporary of its terms; it is, in fact, their contemporaneity. "With" is the sharing of time-space; it is the at-the-same-time-in-the-same-place as itself, in itself, shattered. It is the instant scaling back of the principle of identity. Being is at the same time in the same place only on the condition of the spacing of an infinite plurality of singularities. Being is with Beings; it does not ever recover itself, but it is near to itself, beside itself; in touch with itself, its very self,

in the paradox of that proximity where distancing and strangeness are revealed.[87]

Feminist theologians are those who have read, speak, and write in the interstitial, liminal space of patriarchal culture and religion, moving back and forth between the two spaces: the space of mainstream languages, expression, and symbol systems and the space of the feminist experiences of marginality and, at the same time, the new alternative languages, metaphors, and symbols for the world to come. In a similar vein, those men and women who become dislocated and relocated between different cultures where the configuration of language, meaning, and powers function differently come to possess diasporic consciousness that make them to be able to read, speak, and write from multiple angles and gazes.

The diasporic consciousness and subject destabilizes and deterritorializes the conventions and traditions that people fix in a way to maintain the status quo. The term *deterritorialization* denotes the displacement of fixed identities, ownership of knowledge and meanings. Feminist theologians have attempted to deterritorialize the religious traditions, discourses, and practices that have justified and perpetuated patriarchy in the every sector of human reality. When feminist theologians embody diasporic subjectivity that make them reside at the margin or outside the conventional community, this diasporic location can offer them an inventive possibility "to express another possible community and to forge the means for another consciousness and another sensibility."[88] One of the paradoxical aspects of the diasporic consciousness is to leave home and to look for home. However, the other possible community or home they look for and refashion is a different kind of home that is revolutionary in its deterritorializing attitude and radically affirming and open

---

87. Nancy, *Being Singular Plural*, 34–35.
88. Deleuze and Guattari, "What Is a Minor Literature?," 60.

to alterity and differences. Deterritorialization can enable diasporic feminist theologians' creative imagination, a double mode of seeing and writing, even though it may also bring alienation, despair, hopelessness, and exile.

The significant meaning of the diasporic consciousness in feminist theological discourse lies in the paradoxical movement between home and away, a refusal to permanently reside in one space as final, fixed, or static. The diasporic positionality will offer feminist theology a new angle through which it can construct theological discourse and practices with hypersensitivity to the complex issues of margin and center in various intersectional contexts of gender, languages, race, citizenship, sexuality, ability, and so on. The diasporic feminist theological location has the potential for critical reconfiguration of religious practices, institutions, and theological discourse, although it is always possible in reality to be the site of despair and isolation. The diasporic location is in the midst of creating, inventing, embracing multiple gatherings of the marginalized, as Homi Bhabha poetically and metaphorically articulates: "Gatherings of exiles and émigrés and refugees; gatherings on the edge of 'foreign' cultures; gathering at the frontiers; gatherings in the ghettos or cafes of city centres; gathering in the half-life, half-light of foreign tongues, or in the uncanny fluency of another's language; gathering the signs of approval and acceptance, degrees, discourses, disciplines; gathering the memories of underdevelopment, of other worlds lived retroactively; gathering the past in a ritual of revival; gathering the present."[89]

Feminist discourse takes gender as a primary point of entry, but this does not necessarily mean that gender should be the point of arrival as well. The complexity of human reality in which one's gender, class,

---

89. Homi K. Bhabha, "DissemiNation: Time, Narrative and the Margins of the Modern Nation," in *Location of Culture*, 199.

race and ethnicity, ability, sexuality, religion, physical appearance, or age intersects with one another requires feminist theologians to utilize multiples lenses even to analyze and locate gender in a specific context. Doing feminist theology in the twenty-first century requires a constant movement between the microdimensional and the macrodimensional of human lives and the world. Here, doing feminist theology means an "inventive engagement in the transaction that suspends the safe horizons and criteria, the existing norms and rules, but also has the ability—intelligently—to analyze, to criticize, to deconstruct them" and one should never "lose sight of the macrodimensional perspective, not in a sense of dogmatic ideas of globalization."[90]

Diasporic feminist theology can be a theopolitical discourse that radicalizes, reenergizes transformative theories and practices, which postcolonial, feminist, queer, Marxist, and critical race discourses have invoked. The diasporic feminist theology, adopting contemporary invocation of diaspora, quests for ever-embracing discourses and practices of theology of living together, and constructs theology of *Mitsein* ("being-with"). The initial step to cultivate, activate, and sustain the discourses and practices of theology of *Mitsein* is always to resist and "remain rebellious to totalization"[91] and multiple forms of colonization. The diasporic mode of seeing enables one to realize that a sense of compassion and hospitality are the most significant components of our living together because diasporas in their interstitial consciousness deterritorialize unnecessary boundaries and do not claim any sense of ownership of mainstream sociocultural spaces. Human equality, Hannah Arendt critically points out, is "the result of human organization insofar as it is guided by the principle

---

90. Jacques Derrida, *Paper Machine*, trans. Rachel Bowlby (Stanford: Stanford University Press, 2005 [2001]), 38–39.
91. Derrida, "Avowing—The Impossible," 35.

of justice" that requires human solidarity and commitment to justice and equality. Arendt goes on to argue: "*We are not born equal; we become equal* as members of a group on the strength of our decision to guarantee ourselves mutually equal rights. Our political life rests on the assumption that we can produce equality through organization, because man [sic] can act in and change and build a common world, together with his equals and only with his equals."[92]

Arendt's claim that equality does not come automatically but can be possible only when we are committed to becoming equal and organize ourselves into a polity presents significant theopolitical and theoethical tasks of doing theology. Numerous scholars have tried to respond to the question, What is a religion? Taking Jan Patocka as his interlocutor, who connects the sacred to responsibility and the demonic to irresponsibility, Derrida lucidly offers his answer to the question: "Religion is responsibility or it is nothing at all."[93] In this sense, the demonic has something to do with "irresponsibility" or "nonresponsibility" and an authentic religion can be possible only when the "marriage of responsibility and faith"[94] takes place. In this sense, the significant task of theologians today is "'inventive engagements' with the question of how to live together in a world in which the de-localizing and uprooting forces evoked by the term 'globalization.'"[95]

Doing feminist theology with diasporic consciousness means defending, representing, articulating the need to work together in multiple and interstitial gatherings of living together for the justice for and peace of each and every individual human being who is at the margin and who cannot find home in the world. In this

---

92. Hannah Arendt, *The Origins of Totalitarianism* (New York: Schocken, 2004 [1951]), 382 (italics mine).
93. Derrida, *Gift of Death*, 2.
94. Ibid., 3, 6.
95. Elizabeth Weber, "Introduction," in Weber, ed., *Living Together*, 3.

sense, doing diasporic feminist theologies means to live as the critic on the fringes, taking the responsibility for radical living together and making a constant movement between home and away, the center and the margin, roots and routes, macrodimensional reality and microdimensional reality, the world of already and the world to come.

2

Identity, *Différance*, and Alterity

Deconstructive Mediation of the Identity Politics

Ethnic identity is twin skin to linguistic identity—I am my language.
Until I can take pride in my language, I cannot take pride in myself.
—Gloria Anzaldua[1]

Gender is a complexity whose totality is permanently deferred, never
fully what it is at any given juncture in time.
—Judith Butler[2]

Identity, like God in negative theology, is not *what one is* but rather *what
one is not.*
—Dmitri M. Slivniak[3]

---

1. Gloria Anzaldua, *Borderlands/La Frontera: The New Mestiza* (San Francisco: Aunt Lute Books, 1987), 59.
2. Judith Butler, "Subjects of Sex/Gender/Desire," in *Feminist Theory: A Philosophical Anthology*, Blackwell Philosophy Anthologies, ed. Ann Cudd and Robin Andreasen (Malden, MA: Wiley-Blackwell, 2005), 151.
3. Dmitri M. Slivniak, "The Book of Esther: The Making and Unmaking of Jewish Identity," in *Derrida's Bible (Reading a Page of Scripture with a Little Help from Derrida)*, ed. Yvonne Sherwood (New York: Palgrave, 2004), 135 (italics mine).

> Identity—who we are, where we come from, what we are—is difficult to maintain in exile . . . we are the 'other,' an opposite. . . .
> —Edward Said[4]

The Double Bind of Identity Politics:
Necessity and Impossibility

The question of self-identity, Who am I?, is an enduring theme in human reality. When one connects this question of Who am I? to the question of Who are we?, one forms a politics of identity. The question as to how and where people as groups construct and express the identity that holds them together is more complex than it appears on the surface. Identity politics has made tremendous contributions for the marginalized groups: raising self-awareness and self-dignity; challenging through politicization the mainstream claim to hegemonic power; providing spaces to claim their voices and experiences as legitimate; and empowering both an individual and the group. At the same time, the limits of the identity politics are as follows: we–they binarism, essentialization, homogenization, suppression of heterogeneity, exoticization and idealization, ghettoization, oversimplification of the complexity of power and privilege, overlooking the intersectionality of oppressions, and so forth.

The dilemma, therefore, is that one cannot fully constitute or fix the identity itself, whether it is based on gender, race, ethnicity, class, or sexuality. One's identification with the group based on a particular gender, race, ethnicity, class, or sexuality cannot be simply reducible to one's identity through either radical affirmation or radical differentiation. One's identity in the world has to deal with both

4. Edward Said, *After the Last Sky* (New York: Columbia University Press, 1998), 16–17.

interiority and exteriority, which are inextricably intertwined and entangled but not identical. One can make a clear distinction between *difference* and *alterity* as follows: one's *difference* always requires a constitutive other to make its claim for being different, whereas *alterity* can exist on its own without a constitutive other for comparison. In this sense, the limit of the identity politics of difference can be twofold: the necessity of the constitutive other from which one differentiates oneself and the multiple, often contradicting, axes of differences that one needs to re/present.

Since the 1960s, identity politics has played a significant role in politicizing the experiences of a variety of marginalized groups. "Identity politics" refers to the act of constructing a claim in the name of a particular group that presupposes group membership and certain political positionalities. For various groups, identity politics covers a number of complex and diverse theoretical positions and discourses, which have evolved around questions of subjectivity, representation, culture, difference, struggle, and liberation. Based on various grounds, such as gender, race, ethnicity, religion, ability, or sexuality, identity politics has become one of the more powerful commonsense constructions marginalized groups have developed. Questions of identity increasingly become interlaced with the issues of power and representation. The battle for the rights of and justice for new social groups dominates the current political, cultural, ideological, and theological landscape.

Although the question of one's identity in a broad sense is not new, the emergence of identity politics since the 1960s has a unique meaning in terms of how each marginalized group's self-affirmed and self-claimed nature functions differently from the identity that the dominant group ascribes to them. Furthermore, identity politics has functioned as a discourse of counterhegemony and created spaces of self-affirmation and allegiance among the various marginalized groups. Questions of gender, race, ethnicity, class, culture, ability, or sexuality inevitably become intertwined with the complex issues of representation, locationality, authenticity, power, and identity. Constructing one's identity is a process of shaping the meaning of one's existence in the world in terms of a self-perception about who one is as an individual and as part of a group to which one belongs.

Those in the mainstream usually are not concerned about their identity in given societies, as they tend to perceive themselves as part of the normative group who do not need from others any particular recognition of or affirmation for who/what they are. In contrast, the marginalized need to claim their identity in an affirmative way to reverse the existing negative images of who they are and, further, to produce counterdiscourses and movements to dismantle the politics of domination and subjugation. This context creates an inevitable necessity for an identity politics in every movement to change and raise the self-esteem of marginal groups. Such groups use identity politics as a form of resistance to contest the negative images and perceptions about who or what they are and also form their identity by transforming negative images to positive. Therefore, every movement for social change by a marginalized group needs identity politics both externally and internally. Here, the difference of the marginalized group from the dominant group, which people once perceived as inferior, deviant, abnormal, or inauthentic, becomes a source of affirmation and positive self-image. One's difference from others becomes a significant site both of self-affirmation and empowerment as well as for appealing to rights, justice, and equality in society.

However, appealing to difference can also function as a way of establishing a rigid differentiation and block any criticism from others who do not share the same ethnic or gender identification. By using an ethnic identity marker combined with gender, such as

"Asian women," discursively runs the risk of being geographically deterministic and culturally essentialist, thus heavily ethnicizing gender. The fundamental dilemma of this ethnic-gender identity politics lies in the fact that the description of what people have in common as Asian women hardly reveals and captures the *actual* Asian women who are inextricably heterogeneous, complex, and indefinable. In this context, those at the margin on various grounds come to encounter the necessity, contradiction, dilemma, or irony of identity politics, what Jacques Derrida describes as the *double bind* (a term coined by Gregory Bateson).[5]

On the one hand, the *necessity* of identity politics seems clear and obvious. One only needs to recognize the urgent need to construct an affirmative identity, whether personal or collective. Every movement for social change and claims for human rights, justice, and equality begins with the marginalized claiming an affirmative group identity based on gender, race, ethnicity, sexuality, ability, and so forth. Those formerly objectified try to subjectivize themselves by claiming an identity of affirmation. On the other hand, one needs to recognize the impossibility of identity politics. Any type of identity is always provisional, partial, unstable, and elusive because in one's unique singularity one is never static, comprehensible, and fixable. At the same time, no form of identity politics can avoid becoming a homogenizing and totalizing discourse as soon as people fix the identity label as such on an individual person or a group. Without a process of homogenization, the constitution of identity politics is impossible at the outset. One forms an identity politics through the constitution of the fixed *we*, and the constitution of we requires a kind of homogenization of the we—a politics of sameness.

5. Cf. Gregory Bateson, *Steps to an Ecology of Mind* (New York: Chandler, 1972), 206–207.

Operated by the politics of sameness, the we-rhetoric, such as *we* Asians, *we* African Americans, *we* women, *we* Latinas/os, *we* Muslims, *we* gay, *we* Christians, and so forth, becomes a necessary precondition for the constitution of identity politics. In the process of differentiating *we* from *they* by appealing to *our* difference from *them*, identity politics comes to suppress the difference and heterogeneity among and within *we*. So any identity politics bears an internal contradictory claim both for difference, on the one hand, and for sameness, on the other, which functions ironically as homogenizing the heterogeneity among we in claiming a difference from they, grounded in the sameness of we. The we here becomes "the mark of the plural,"[6] the identifier that identity politics criticizes as the dominant group's colonizing act. As Stuart Hall contends, the primary functions of the collective identities can be: "they give us a good night's rest. Because what they tell us is that there is a kind of stable, only very slowly-changing ground inside the hectic upsets, discontinuities and ruptures of history. Around us history is constantly breaking in unpredictable ways but we, somehow, go on being the same." However, this politics of fixed, stable, unchanging identity is "for good or ill, finished."[7]

One needs to apply hypersensitivity to the standardization, centralization, and authenticization of identity by those who have the power to produce identity discourse and practice. Various social movements that call for social change have heavily relied on the politics of identity. However, the dilemma is that one cannot fully constitute or fix the identity itself as such. One's identification with the group of a particular gender, race, ethnicity, class, or sexuality

6. Albert Memmi, *The Colonizer and the Colonized* (Boston: Beacon, 1967), 85.
7. Stuart Hall, "Old and New Identities, Old and New Ethnicities," in *Culture, Globalization, and the World-System: Contemporary Conditions for the Representation of Identity*, ed. Anthony King (Minneapolis: University of Minnesota Press, 1997), 42–43.

cannot be simply reducible to such monolithic identity in its comprehensive sense. No single identity marker can fully capture who one is in a comprehensive way, because one is always already becoming in one's absolute singularity. As soon as people use the identity specifier on a person, this act establishes a binary logic of we–they and functions as fixing and confining a person to a homogeneous, unitary entity as such. Here, for instance, the discursive specifier "Asian women" becomes the mark of the plural, the refusal to see one's absolute singularity in terms of being an individual person, her/his irreplaceability, irreducibility, and, at the same time, the "indefinite plurality of singularities."[8] As a result, such an identity politics based on one's ethnicity, race, gender, religion, sexuality, and so forth becomes more confining than liberating. For such identity markers perpetuate the gaze through which one sees the person: that is, with an identity marker not as an individual person with unique features but simply as a part of an anonymous and undifferentiated collectivity. Through this undifferentiated identity marker, all Asian women with their ethnic-gender identity marker look alike, carrying the mark of the plural. In this sense, identity politics is impossible to shape and operate due to the endless heterogeneity among and within the same ethnic gender and the plurality of the very individual person within the same category of identity politics because, as Jean-Luc Nancy argues, "the One is more than one; it is not that 'it divides itself,' . . . 'one' cannot be counted without counting more than one."[9]

Another impossibility of identity politics lies in its fundamental dilemma of the epistemological disparity between the ethnic/gendered and the nonethnic/nongendered. Needless to say,

---

8. Jean-Luc Nancy, *Being Singular Plural*, trans. Robert D. Richardson and Anne E. O'Byrne (Stanford: Stanford University Press, 2000 [1996]), 35.
9. Ibid., 39.

everybody has his or her gender, sexuality, race, or ethnicity. However, certain groups of people do not use any ethnic, racial, sexual, or gendered markers. The act of using the identity category in identity politics ends up, against the will of the user of such an identity marker, normativizing and standardizing the nonethnic, nonracial, or nongendered people: the ethnically European, the racially white, sexually heterosexual, or the biologically male, for example. By absenting the identity marker, those nonethnic, nonracial, nonsexual, or nongendered groups of people continue to maintain the normative, standard, heterogeneous, universal subjectivity, while this dynamic continues to push groups with certain identity markers toward becoming homogeneous objects.

While recognizing the complexity of one's discursive specifier of *as* (for instance, *as* women, *as* Asian, *as* African American, or *as* gay) one should note that one cannot touch the issue of identity politics without addressing its fundamental dilemma: the double bind—the necessity and impossibility. In this sense, addressing and engaging in identity politics should mean negotiating between these two poles of necessity and impossibility and making all the necessary decisions, allegiances, and responsibilities between them. One must also note that simply dismissing identity politics because of its dilemmas and problems is dangerous because "in order to deconstruct the subject one must first have gained the right to speak as one; in order to de-mystify meta-discourse one must first have access to a place of enunciation."[10] The ongoing question that one must wrestle with, while acknowledging the double bind of identity politics, would be: How can we offer a theological discourse that helps us build a

---

10. Rosi Braidotti, "Patterns of Dissonance: Women and/in Philosophy," in *Feministische Philosophie*, ed. Herta Nagl-Docekal (Vienna/Munich: R. Oldenburg, 1990), 119–20, quoted by Seyla Benhabib, "Feminism and Postmodernism: An Uneasy Alliance," in *Feminist Contentions: A Philosophical Exchange*, ed. Linda Nicholson (New York: Routledge, 1995), 32.

we without labels and without repressing alterity, and promote a spirit of solidarity with, without, and beyond identity markers, which requires a constant epistemological and ontological traversing?

Identity Politics as a Spatial Practice

Any act of mapping identity politics runs the risk of overgeneralization and oversimplification, given that feminists, queer theorists, cultural critics, postmodern critics, postcolonial critics, and critics of race and ethnicity have all influenced its construction In trying to do such mapping, I know I run the risk of falling into the danger of homogenizing heterogeneous streams of identity politics. However, it is worth taking a risk of mapping to see approximate patterns of identity politics from diverse marginal groups so that one can complexify and diversify their discourse and practice. Dominant groups rarely adopt identity politics, and therefore identity politics is about the marginal groups who seek their own spaces of empowerment, rights, affirmation, coalition, and epistemological, theopolitical, geopolitical transformation in a given society and its institutions.

Understanding the geopolitics of ethnic-gender identity such as Asian women is not just thinking about gender with the particular ethnic, cultural, or geographical tie but locating gender in a geopolitical context. Discourse on ethnic-gender identity is therefore a spatial practice[11] that requires borders and border crossings between Asia and non-Asia, women and men, home and away, rootedness and rootlessness, sameness and *différance*, identity and alterity, and so

---

11. James Clifford also adopts the term *spatial practice* in his work. James Clifford, "Spatial Practices," in *Routes: Travel and Translation in the Late Twentieth Century* (Cambridge: Harvard University Press, 1997), 52–91.

forth. Distinguishing space from place, Michel de Certeau contends that "space is composed of intersections of mobile elements. . . . *space is a practiced place*," whereas place is the order and implies an indication of stability, which "excludes the possibility of two things being in the same location."[12] He goes on to affirm, "'space is existential' and 'existence is spatial.'" Therefore, one seeks one's identity through "spatial stories" because "every story is a travel story—a spatial practice."[13] The space of identity of those from the margins is often multivalent and paradoxical.

Space is especially significant in examining identity politics. Identity politics reveals how and where marginalized individuals and groups locate themselves in the world. Constructing identity politics means, therefore, crafting a spatial map of identification, belonging, and agency: *spatial practice*. How one forms and locates one's sense of identity, belonging, power, and agency as a member of a group is inextricably intertwined with the territorialized or deterritorialized spaces. Michel Foucault rightly argues: "A whole history remains to be written of *spaces*—which would at the same time be the history of *powers* (both these terms in the plural)—from the great strategies of geo-politics to the little tactics of the habitat, institutional architecture from the classroom to the design of hospitals, passing via economic and political installations. It is surprising how long the problem of space took to emerge as a historico-political problem."[14]

Any type of identity politics needs to carefully address the double edges of the politics. On the one hand, one needs to recognize the urgent political need of construction of identity in a society of inequality and exclusion based on one's physical appearance, social

12. Michel de Certeau, *The Practice of Everyday Life*, trans. Steven F. Rendall (Berkeley: University of California Press, 1984), 117 (italics original).
13. Ibid., 115.
14. Michel Foucault, *Power/Knowledge: Selected Interviews & Other Writings 1972–1977*, ed. Colin Gordon, trans. Colin Gordon, et al. (New York: Pantheon, 1980), 149.

status, or sexual orientation. On the other hand, however, one also needs to apply a critical hypersensitivity to issues of standardization, centralization, and authenticization of identity by those who have the power to produce the very totalizing identity discourse and practice. Exercising the power of authenticization and consensus of identity is a form of violence and of constituting a "hegemonic center" within the group. Derrida rightly points out:

> Double injunction: *on the one hand* . . . cultural identity cannot be dispersed (and when I say "cannot," this should also be taken as "must not"—and this double state of affairs is at the heart of the difficulty). . . . But, *on the other hand*, it cannot and must not accept the capital of a centralizing authority which . . . would control and standardize. . . . For my reconstituting places of an easy consensus, places of a demagogical and "salable" consensus. . . such normalization would establish a cultural capital at any place and at all times. It would establish a hegemonic center.[15]

Forms of identity can vary depending on what angles one adopts to look into the nature and constitution of identity. One can categorize forms of identity thus: (1) *legitimating identity*, (2) *resistance identity*, and (3) *project identity*.[16] The dominant body and institution produces *legitimating identity*, often manifested in a form of exclusive nationalism or ethnocentrism, to maintain, justify, perpetuate, normativize, and normalize its dominating authority and power. On the other hand, the oppressed and the marginalized groups construct *resistance identity* as an act of contesting and reversing their negative portrayal by the dominant group. This form of resistance identity can be both positive, as in various forms of social movements based on race, gender, or sexuality, and negative, as in various types of religious fundamentalisms, for instance. Progressive groups such as

---

15. Jacques Derrida, *Other Heading*, trans. Pascale-Anne Brault and Michael B. Naas (Bloomington: Indiana University Press, 1992), 38–40 (italics original).
16. Manuel Castells, *The Power of Identity* (Oxford: Blackwell, 1997), 8.

feminists and liberationists take a further step to challenge the patriarchal, racist, ethnocentric, or homophobic sociopolitical structures and value systems, and envision an alternative society by constructing *project identity*. Each form of identity has its different motifs, objectives, and consequences. In this sense, identity politics persists in social movements that seek transformation of the sociocultural, economic, political, and religious relations of the individuals in a given society. It is again important, however, to acknowledge the double bind of identity politics to see the complex aspects of the constitution of one's identity. We should neither simply defend nor dismiss identity politics. Instead, we need to constantly contest, diversify, and complexify the discourses of identity in order to attain appropriate political strategies for changes. In the end, identity politics is not merely a discursive matter but more about political strategy and vision for a better world.

Identity Politics of Affirmation:
Shifting the Negative to the Positive

Since the late 1960s, when identity politics began emerging, contesting the negative and distorted images of marginal groups and replaced these with positive and affirmative ones has been the primary struggle. Women and African Americans, for example, have tried to construct authentic identities that society has negatively framed. Black liberation theologians such as James H. Cone argue, "What is needed is not integration but a sense of worth in being black, and only black people can teach that. Black consciousness is the key to the Black man's emancipation from his distorted self-image."[17] Here the motto "I'm Black and I'm Proud" and its extension to "symbolic

17. James H. Cone, *Black Theology and Black Power* (New York: HarperCollins, 1969), 19.

blackness"[18] became significant in constructing black liberation theological discourse and practice in the initial stage of the theopolitical development of liberation theology.

In the postcolonial movements, the dire urge to discover and construct an affirmative identity centers these movements among the colonized. Such a desire for an identity is, Franz Fanon contends, "directed by the secret hope of discovering beyond the misery of today, beyond self-contempt, resignation and abjuration, some very beautiful and splendid era whose existence rehabilitates us both in regard to ourselves and in regard to others."[19] Feminist movements in their initial stage also began with their claim for a self-achieved identity politics of affirmation, portraying women as caring, nurturing, life-giving, biophilic, and peace-loving, while picturing men as aggressive, violent, necrophilic, and power-driven. Here the traits traditionally assigned as inferior became reversed as superior in the identity politics of affirmation: the *transvaluation of values*.

Any social movement for change requires a radical affirmation of a sense of worth in people being who they are as women, as black, as gay or lesbian, in order to move beyond the existing negative images and to claim for their own affirming identity. This first form of identity politics by the marginal group is significant because it is not what others ascribed/imposed to them but what they themselves achieved/claimed about who they are. The identity politics of affirmation primarily offers the marginal groups a positive self-esteem and a critical passion and strength for working for resistance and change in the existing system of exclusion and marginalization based on gender, race and ethnicity, sexuality, ability, or religion. It also provides "a standpoint from which to criticize prevailing institutions

18. James H. Cone, *A Black Theology of Liberation* (Maryknoll, NY: Orbis, 1991 [1970]), 25, 7.
19. Franz Fanon, *The Wretched of the Earth*, trans. Constance Farrington (New York: Grove, 1963), 210.

and norms."[20] Those marginalized groups try to retrieve the beauty and virtue of their tradition and descent, and idealize these traits as X (i.e., as women, as Asian, and so forth), but not without knowing the limits of their attempts:

> Herkunft is the equivalent of stock or descent; it is the ancient affiliation to a group, sustained by the bonds of blood, tradition, or social class. The analysis of Herkunft often involves a consideration of race or social type. But the traits it attempts to identify are not the exclusive generic characteristics of an individual, a sentiment, or an idea, which permit us to qualify them as "Greek" or "English"; rather, it seeks the subtle, singular, and subindividual marks that might possibly intersect in them to form a network that is difficult to unravel.[21]

In the beginning of social movements, appealing to one's gender (as women), race (as black), ethnicity (as Latin American), sexuality (as gay) as a unitary, homogeneous group, for instance, seems in a way a necessary practice and point of entry. It is, therefore, important to note that various social movements that call for social change have heavily relied on the politics of identity of affirmation. The identity politics of affirmation grounds its identity claim in a fixed, distinct, homogeneous entity of a marginal group, which often falls into an essentialist position, and the limit of this identity of affirmation lies in its tendency to cling to a fixed, separate, unitary identity of a group.

20. Seyla Benhabib, "The Generalized and the Concrete Other," in *Feminism as Critique*, ed. Seyla Benhabib and Drucilla Cornell (Minneapolis: University of Minnesota Press, 1987), 87.
21. Michel Foucault, *Language, Counter-Memory, Practice: Selected Essays and Interviews*, trans. Donald F. Bouchard and Sherry Simon (Ithaca: Cornell University Press, 1977), 145 (italics original).

Identity Politics of Difference:
Identity-in-Differential

The identity politics of difference primarily focuses on the difference of a marginal group from others and its representational function. It constitutes its being by that difference, in which one's identity is constructed through a formula of X-is-not-Y. It is an *identity-in-differential*, as Stuart Hall points out: "when you know what everybody else is, then you are what they are not. Identity is always, in that sense, a structured representation which only achieves its positive through the narrow eye of the negative. It has to go through the eye of the needle of the other before it can construct itself. It produces a very Manichean set of opposites."[22] To claim who-one-is is to know who the constitutive other is and to locate oneself in relation to who-the-other-is-*not*. Here the constitutive other can be the colonizer or those in the mainstream based on various categories, for the various types of identity politics have emerged only from the marginal groups. It is important to note the distinction between difference and alterity in discourses of identity politics. Difference in identity politics depends on identity being constructed based on one's difference from they, whereas alterity in identity politics affirms that one exists in one's own place, without any specific relation to they.

The rejection of single identity in identity politics of affirmation and the emphasis on differences by the identity politics of difference highlight the need to create a space in which to connect the contesting fragments and a possibility of theorizing the intersectionality of race/ethnicity, gender, class, ability, sexuality, and so forth. Julia Kristeva illustrates:

Believing oneself "a woman" is almost as absurd and obscurantist as

---

22. Stuart Hall, "The Local and the Global: Globalization and Ethnicity," in *Culture, Globalization and the World-System*, ed. Anthony King (London: Macmillan, 1991), 21.

believing oneself "a man." I say almost because there are still things to be got for women: freedom of abortion and contraception, childcare facilities, recognition of work, etc. Therefore, "we are women" should still be kept as a slogan, for demands and publicity. But more fundamentally, women cannot *be*: the category woman is even that which does not fit in to *being*. From there, women's practice can only be negative, in opposition to that which exists, to say that "this is not it" and "it is not yet." What I mean by "woman" is that which is not represented, that which is unspoken, that which is left out of namings and ideologies.[23]

The challenge in the identity politics of difference is to theorize more than one difference at once between one's race, ethnicity, gender, sexuality, ability, religion, and so forth. In this process of differentiation, whiteness, maleness, straightness, middle–upper-classness, and abledness continue to remain normative in society as unmarked terms, remaining abstract and invisible from discourses of identity politics. Gayatri Chakravorty Spivak points out the dilemma of identity politics when she says, "Identitarianism can be as dangerous as it is powerful."[24]

Whenever I am invited to speak, I always wonder to whom they want to listen. If the invitation is from academia, especially in the United States, what the audience wants to hear is primarily my voice of marginality, a voice of difference as a woman or an Asian. One of the dilemmas is when the academy wants to hold on to the identity politics of difference, even with good intentions, and when marginality becomes a catchword. One cannot claim one's pure marginality simply based on one's specific gender, class, race, ethnicity, or sexuality, as it is impossible to put oneself into such a single box; one is not just a single thing. There seems, however, no way that we can do without labels. What kind of label shall I

23. Julia Kristeva, "Interview—1974," trans. Claire Pajaczkowska, *m/f* 5/6 (1981): 166. Quoted in *The Postmodern Bible*, George Aichele, et al. (New Haven: Yale University Press, 1995), 214.
24. Gayatri Chakravorty Spivak, *Outside in the Teaching Machine* (New York: Routledge, 1993), 54.

then carry in order to inspire others to listen to me? Who can speak without label? Who will listen to the speakers without label but with the color of physical marginality? So Trinh T. Minh-ha relevantly remarks:

> Now, i am not only given the permission to open up and talk, i am also encouraged to express my difference. My audience expects and demands it; otherwise people would feel as if they have been cheated: We did not come to hear a Third World member speak about the First (?) World, We came to listen to that voice of difference likely to bring us *what we can't have* and to divert us from the monotony of sameness.[25]

The questions as to how people come up with new terms and how such new terms continue to function in personal and institutional epistemologies and lives are extremely significant because language shapes, needless to say, the ethos and value systems of people and institutions. Many of the terms that I have frequently encountered since I began my life in the United States are terms of color: people of color, students of color, women of color, faculty of color, scholars of color.[26] When I came across these terms for the first time in U.S. academia, having relocated from Germany as a doctoral student, I found it extremely interesting because I suddenly found myself being categorized into a color box such that I had hardly thought of before. It has become clear to me that if I resided in my physical place of birth or if I did not happen to live and work in a place like the United States where, consciously or unconsciously, "white" is still regarded as the norm and the center, people would never

---

25. Trinh T. Minh-ha, *Woman, Native, Other: Writing Postcoloniality and Feminism* (Bloomington: Indiana University Press, 1989), 88 (italics original).
26. For the terms of color, see the following works: G. Gay, "Navigating Marginality En Route to the Professoriate: Graduate Students of Color Learning and Living in Academia," *International Journal of Qualitative Studies in Education*, 17, no. 2 (2004): 265–88; C. S. V. Turner, "Women of Color in Academia: Living with Multiple Marginality," *The Journal of Higher Education*, 73, no. 1 (2002): 74–93; C. S. V. Turner, et al., "Faculty of Color in Academia: What 20 Years of Literature Tells Us," *Journal of Diversity in Higher Education*, 1, no. 3 (2008): 139–68.

categorize me into such a collective color group regardless of my desire or intentionality. In this context, Trinh T. Minh-ha contends, "'difference' is essentially 'division'. . . . It is no more than a tool of self-defense and conquest. . . . It is as if everywhere we go, we become Someone's private zoo,"[27] words that reflect Spivak's remarks on her experience in a symposium: "the maids upstairs in the guest quarters were women of color."[28]

Regardless of the intentionality of those who use and adopt such terms in their speeches and writings, this adoption uncritically continues to perpetuate the status quo where whites remain as the norm and the center of every sector of society. Here, we need to scrutinize critically the functionality of such taxonomies, because uncritical uses can be an act of endorsing the normativization of whites, thereby totalizing and homogenizing nonwhites. Needless to say, white is also a color. However, applying such terms of color in our speeches and writings only to nonwhites, as if whites are natural, tends to function as endorsing, both wittingly and unwittingly, the false presupposition that whites have no color and do not need *names*.

Absenting the white (or the male in a patriarchal society) from its own naming has been one of the ways white hegemony maintains and sustains its power. Here, whiteness serves itself as a universalized marker for being normative, civilized, rationalized, and advanced. The moment that one adopts such taxonomies for whatever intention, good or ill, people of color turn into an objectified, collectivized, particularized, and totalized group, whereas whites—the people of noncolor—remain as speaking subjects, individualized, universalized, and normativized human beings. Regardless of one's intention, whether nonwhite people use this

---

27. Trinh T. Minh-ha, *Woman, Native, Other*, 82.
28. Gayatry Chakravorty Spivak, "The Politics of Interpretation," in *In Other Worlds: Essays in Cultural Politics* (New York: Routledge, 1988), 133.

taxonomy to claim their rights and identities or whether white people adopt it to attend to the issue of imbalanced representation in their institutions/communities, one's uncritical use of it functions as an act of othering the others who are outsiders to the mainstream. As numerous postcolonial theorists point out, one important tactic that colonizers adopt is to use the "mark of the plural" for the colonized, removing the unique singularity as an individual human being from the faces of the colonized, as if they think, look, behave alike.

In their introduction to *Feminists Theorize the Political*, volume editors Judith Butler and Joan W. Scott introduce fifteen questions that they posed to the book contributors. One of the questions asks: "What are the points of convergence between 1) poststructuralist criticisms of identity and b) recent theory by women of color that critically exposes the unified or coherent subject as a prerogative of white theory? How do we theorize the split or multiple 'subject' of feminism?" [29] Here Butler and Scott unwittingly segregate women of color from poststructuralists, as if nonwhite women are a unitary entity who cannot be poststructuralists like themselves—the women of noncolor. Paula Moya criticizes the use of the term "women of color" in the volume because such terms can "enact an un-self-critical enlistment of the 'women of color,' the 'subaltern,' and the 'cultural minority' to serve as legitimators of the project entailed in 'postmodern' or poststructuralist criticisms of identity." [30] By continuously using such taxonomies as people of color, students of color, faculty of color, women of color, or scholars of color in one's personal and institutional lives, regardless of contexts, one can easily end up particularizing those groups of people (often including

29. Judith Butler and Joan W. Scott, eds., "Introduction," in *Feminists Theorize the Political* (New York: Routledge, 1992), xiv–xv.
30. Paula M. Moya, "Postmodernism, 'Realism,' and the Politics of Identity: Cherríe Moraga and Chicana Feminism," in *Feminist Genealogies, Colonial Legacies, Democratic Futures*, ed. M. Jacqui Alexander and Chandra Talpade Mohanty (New York: Routledge, 1997), 379–80.

oneself) while universalizing the white. As a result, the singularity of the so-called people of color with a unique face collapses into a collective "they," perpetuating their sociopolitical destiny as the other. The big question then is: When someone speaks as a scholar of color and when the person's singularity is already collapsed into the collective confinement of a color line, *who* exactly is speaking?

Our world has become much more complex than ever. One's race, ethnicity, citizenship, nationality, religion, gender, class, and sexuality intersect with context-specific issues, agendas, and urgency. Every term that people have coined comes into being from a particular context. However, critical examination as to whether or not such a context-specific term continues to have its meaning, legitimacy, and relevance in a general sense is a significant task that lies before scholars in academia—a space where people constantly construct, scrutinize, contest, disseminate, and archive knowledge. Inventing an alternative language means inventing a new ethos and new perspectives, value systems, and epistemologies as to what kind of world-to-come one envisions in one's personal and institutional life.

The identity politics of difference, regardless who adopts it, can function both to liberate and to confine the marginalized subjects in complex ways; moreover, its essentialized portrayal of the marginalized can mislead and distort the actual lived experience of the marginalized. In the preface to his book *The Black Atlantic*, Paul Gilroy criticizes the "dangerous obsessions" with pure identity and further suggests an alternative:

> There are two aspirations that I would like to share with readers. . . . The first is my hope that the contents of this book are unified by a concern to repudiate the dangerous obsessions with "racial" purity which are circulating inside and outside black politics. It is after all, essentially an essay about the inescapable hybridity and intermixture of ideas. The

second is my desire that the book's heartfelt plea against the closure of the categories with which we conduct our political lives will not go unheard. The history of the black Atlantic yields a course of lessons as to the instability and mutability of identities which are always unfinished, always being remade.[31]

The identity politics of difference has a strong tendency toward cultural, ethnic, gender, or racial essentialism. The cultural essentialist rhetoric, for instance, replicates essentialist perception of cultural differences between the West and Asia in its construction of Asian discourse, which sometimes results in what Gilroy calls an "ethnic absolutism."[32]

Furthermore, people heavily tie the cultural essentialism to gender essentialism when it comes to ethnic-gender discourse, such as Asian women. In this context, the "[s]eemingly *universal* essentialist generalizations about 'all women' are replaced by *culture-specific* essentialist generalizations that depend on totalizing categories such as 'Western culture,' 'Non-western cultures,' 'Western women,' 'Third World women,' and so forth."[33]

Using the label "Asian women" as a specifier signals a discursive attention to two identity locations: ethnic/cultural identity and gender identity. When one uses such ethnic and gender markers, one's discursive positionality tends to ground itself in a double essentialism and this very doubleness makes Asian women look more victimized, static, fixed, and unchanging than just "Asian" in general. Any discursive specifier requires some form of identity claim—whether ascribed or achieved.[34] Unlike the *ascribed identity*, a

31. Paul Gilroy, *The Black Atlantic: Modernity and Double Consciousness* (Cambridge: Harvard University Press, 1993), xi.
32. Gilroy, "The Black Atlantic as a Counterculture of Modernity," in ibid., 1–40.
33. Uma Narayan, "Essence of Culture and a Sense of History: A Feminist Critique of Cultural Essentialism," in Uma Narayan and Sandra Harding, eds., *Decentering the Center: Philosophy for a Multicultural, Postcolonial, and Feminist World* (Bloomington: Indiana University Press, 2000), 81 (italics original).

struggle against those persons and practices that exclude people due to their differences based on gender, race, ethnicity, class, ability, or sexuality has motivated in part the *achieved identity* politics. In this context, the achieved or self-affirmed identity politics has provided the marginalized a standpoint from which to criticize prevailing institutions and norms that discriminates against people of difference. Once one establishes ethnic-gender identity as such, the identity building becomes itself totalized, essentialized, and ghettoized. Here the following question emerges: "How do we negotiate an intellectually charged space for experience in a way that is not totalizing and essentializing—a space that acknowledges the constructedess of and the differences within our lived experiences while at the same time attending to the inclining, rather than declining, significance of race, class, culture, and gender?"[35]

Articulating the relationship among identities is neither easy nor simple. Although identity politics has played a central role in politicizing the marginalized group, challenging the mainstream hegemonic power, and providing spaces for the marginalized groups to claim their voices and experiences as legitimate, it often fails to move beyond a fixed notion of difference and clings to the polarizing we–they binarism. In doing so, identity politics structures an uncritical appeal to a discourse of essentialized authenticity. The politics of identity has grounded itself in an essentialism that denotes:

> There is a single woman's, or Black person's, or any other group's experience that can be described independently from other aspects of the person—that there is an "essence" to that experience. An essentialist outlook assumes that the experience of being a member of the group under discussion is a stable one, one with a clear meaning, a meaning

34. For the terms *ascribed* and *achieved* identity, see Jodi Dean, *Solidarity of Strangers: Feminism after Identity Politics* (Berkeley: University of California Press, 1996), 42.

35. Ann duCille, "The Occult of True Black Womanhood: Critical Demeanor and Black Feminist Studies," *Signs: Journal of Women in Culture and Society* 19, no. 3 (1994): 607.

constant through time, space, and different historical, social, political, and personal contexts.[36]

Is it possible simply to be an antiessentialist? The critique of essentialism is, Spivak argues, itself predicated upon essentialism and she admits that she is "an essentialist from time to time,"[37] but strategically. However, Spivak's position about essentialism is ambivalent when she also states that "I am fundamentally concerned with that heterogeneity," and that "my search is not a search for coherence."[38] She goes on to express that "[i]f there's one thing I totally distrust, in fact, more than distrust, despise and have contempt for, it is people looking for roots."[39]

Who does want to claim identity in a sociopolitical context? Mostly those who are on the margin want to claim and reclaim their identity as such. Those who are in the center usually do not need to claim any identity because they are the normative, unless they want to invent legitimating identity to normalize their dominating power and authority, as one sees in an exclusive national identity building. What they need to do is only to recognize the labels/markers that the marginalized use. Here, the politics of identity turns to a politics of recognition. The question, "Recognized by whom?," is hidden in the politics of identity because the labels in the politics of identity seem only self-claimed rather than imposed. One's marginality becomes a subject and issue of teaching, writing, and speaking. What happens when one's life becomes an issue/subject? The marginality tends to become homogenized, generalized, essentialized, stereotyped, and naturalized. The identity politics becomes then not only powerful in

36. Trina Grillo, "Anti-Essentialism and Intersectionality: Tools to Dismantle the Master's House," *Berkeley Women's Law Journal* 10, no. 1 (1995): 19.
37. Gayatri Chakravorty Spivak, *The Postcolonial Critic: Interviews, Strategies, Dialogues*, ed. Sarah Harasym (New York: Routledge, 1990), 11.
38. Ibid.
39. Ibid., 91.

its construction of subjecthood of the marginalized but at the same time dangerous in its function of otherizing the marginalized. Here we must ask: Whose interest does the identity claim serve? What need does the identity satisfy? Who does give a proper name, not just a common name, to the marginalized? Spivak rightly points out that "neocolonialism is fabricating its allies by proposing a share of the center in a seemingly new way (not a rupture but a displacement): disciplinary support for the conviction of authentic marginality by the (aspiring) elite."[40]

Deconstructive Mediation:
Master Identity and the Identity of Singularity

Every identity politics often deals with the issue of the binary of normal–abnormal. Those in the mainstream regard the marginalized as abnormal or subnormal. People have simplified one's race, gender, class, sexual orientation, physical appearance, ability, ethnicity, nationality, citizenship, or language in the name of power of binary categorization of normal–abnormal (or subnormal). Perpetrators have justified and perpetuated the witch-hunts, holocaust, colonization, racism, sexism, homosexism, classism, ableism, linguistic terrorism,[41]immigration policies, hate crimes against sexual minority people, racial and ethnic cleansing, and warfare in human history through the destructive binarism of normal–abnormal, good–evil, superior–inferior.

People construct an ethnic-gender identity such as Asian women in a non-Asian, patriarchal world against the binary lens of inferior–superior, normal–subnormal. Identity based on race, gender,

---

40. Spivak, *Outside in the Teaching Machine*, 57.
41. For the term "linguistic terrorism," see Anzaldua, *Borderlands/La Frontera*, 58.

ethnicity, class, or sexuality becomes a master identity[42] for the group. The perennial dilemma of this master identity is in seeking for an identity in this context, the universal humanhood of the "I" as the being of singularity becomes ethnicized, particularized, and genderized, while nonethnic, nongendered groups of people maintain their universal humanhood. The gendered-ethnicization of the I in the process of claiming one's humanhood against the destructive binary lens of inferior–superior is an ironic consequence of ethnic-gender identity. Paul Brass asserts that an ethnic group is "any group of people dissimilar from other peoples in terms of objective cultural criteria [language or dialect, distinctive dress or diet or customs, religion or race] and containing within its membership."[43] Furthermore, the ethnic identity is "itself a variable, rather than a fixed or 'given' disposition."[44] People formulate ethnicity from two sources—language and race—and "most often the two operate together, for only their complementarity makes it possible for the 'people' to be represented as an absolutely autonomous unit."[45] If one defines an ethnic group as a culturally similar group that shares a common language, then Asians do not fit that category of an ethnic group simply because Asians do not share a language nor a race. Asia, as the largest continent in the world, consists of Central Asia, East Asia, North Asia, South Asia, Southeast Asia, and West Asia, from which have sprung countlessly different ethnic groups. Sixty percent of the world's population resides in the Asian continent. In this sense, portraying Asian as one ethnic group does not reflect the reality but is what people have imagined, constructed, and invented. In this context, "ethnicity is something

---

42. Paul du Gay, Jessica Evans, and Peter Redman, eds., *Identity: A Reader* (London: Sage, 2000), 1.
43. Paul R. Brass, *Ethnicity and Nationalism: Theory and Comparison* (London: Sage, 1991), 19
44. Ibid, 13.
45. Etienne Balibar and Immanuel Wallerstein, *Race, Nation, Class: Ambiguous Identities* (London: Verso, 1991), 96.

reinvented and reinterpreted in each generation by each individual, something over which he or she lacks control"[46] and one can regard "the search or struggle for a sense of ethnic identity as a (re-) invention"[47]

The master identity for any sociocultural group based on gender, race, and ethnicity, class, sexuality, or religion becomes a serious question when it comes to the human singularity and the unfixable, ever-evolving nature of human subjecthood. In the master identity that presupposes the unchanging, fixable *we* as such, the *I* in its infinite singularity becomes inevitably dissolved into the collective, master *we* that does not allow the radical heterogeneity of the *I*. As Judith Butler contends in this chapter's epigraph, "Gender is a complexity whose totality is permanently deferred, never fully what it is at any given juncture in time,"[48] and therefore taking gender in constructing a master identity, for instance, is always already at stake. At the same time, it is important to note that gender is not the only category that is a complexity. Race, ethnicity, class, ability, or sexuality is also a complexity that one cannot offer any totalizing master identity. In this sense, "identity is not as transparent or unproblematic as we think. . . . we should think, instead, of identity as a 'production', which is never complete, always in process, and always constituted within, not outside, representation."[49]

The first view of group-based grand, master identity emphasizes an *imaginary oneness* of the group and envisions for the better world where people finally dismantle marginalization, oppression, or colonization. One should not simply dismiss the critical function and

---

46. Michael J. Fischer, "Ethnicity and the Post-Modern Arts of Memory," in *Writing Culture: The Poetics and Politics of Ethnography*, ed. James Clifford and George E. Marcus (Berkeley: University of California Press, 1986), 195.
47. Ibid., 196.
48. Butler, "Subjects of Sex/Gender/Desire," 151.
49. Hall, "Cultural Identity and Diaspora," 222.

significant political commitment of the master identity in the history of emancipation, liberation, or postcolonization. The imagery of oneness as X (as women, as gay, as Asian, as African, as Muslim, and so forth) can be significant recourses for stimulating and maintaining the passion for liberation and resistance, and for constructing one's identity both on a personal and collective level. However, one should also look at another view of master identity. This second view acknowledges not only social similarity and common denominator as X but also the *enormous difference* in the constitution of X. It is impossible to permanently cling to the grand experience and grand identity as X as stable and frozen in a certain time and space, and fixed to an unchanging essence as such. Spivak critically points out: "'Becoming minor' is not a question of essence (as the stereotypes of minorities in dominant ideology would want us to believe), but a question of position: a subject-position that in the final analysis can be defined only in 'political' terms—that is, in terms of the effects of economic exploitation, political disenfranchisement, social manipulation, and ideological domination on the cultural formation of minority subjects and discourses." [50]

The discontinuity, ruptures, alterity, and heterogeneity also constitute what X is. Furthermore, no one is purely, simply just X, and the X is also a part of Y, both of which are often in contradiction. At the same time, the individual member of the X is not a fixed being. Simply because they share one external component of X does not mean to justify one's overlooking the significant fact that an individual person is always an evolving and becoming being. Therefore, it is impossible to hold on to the first view of master identity as X as homogeneous, unitary, essential oneness. One's being as such and becoming as singular plural is in a spiral relationship

50. Abdul R. JanMohamed and David Lloyd, eds., *The Nature and Context of Minority Discourse* (New York: Oxford University Press, 1990), 9.

that does not have a fine divided line in a binary way. As Jean-Luc Nancy puts it: "From now on, *we, we others* are charged with this truth—it is more *ours* than ever—the truth of this paradoxical 'the first-person plural' which makes sense of the world as the spacing and intertwining of so many worlds (earths, skies, histories) that there is a taking place of meaning, or the crossing-through of presence. 'We' says (and 'we say') the unique event whose uniqueness and unity consist in multiplicity."[51]

The multiple dimensions of our existence reveal: we are X, in terms of the social categorization to a certain group; we share the cosmic oneness as fellow humanity; and at the same time we consist of individuals of endless singularities with uniqueness, irreducibility, and irreplaceability, as in one's birth and death. The existence of the repetition of human birth and death does not mean that one's individual birth and death is replaceable or repeatable. Like each and every birth/death, an individual human being is in its own unique singularity. Emmanuel Lévinas eloquently illustrates the infinite singularity of a human being:

> The alterity, the radical heterogeneity of the other, is possible only if the other is other with respect to a term whose essence is to remain at the point of departure, to serve as entry into the relation, to be the same not relatively but absolutely. *A term can remain absolutely at the point of departure of relationship only as I.* . . . The I is not a being that always remains the same, but is the being whose existing consists in identifying itself, in recovering its identity throughout all that happens to it. It is the primal identity, the primordial work of identification.[52]

In this sense, one's identity is an *event*, what happens, which is always evolving. Here, the term *identity* comes to take on different

51. Nancy, *Being Singular Plural*, 5.
52. Emmanuel Lévinas, *Totality and Infinity: An Essay on Exteriority*, trans. Alphonso Lingis (Pittsburgh: Duquesne University Press, 1969 [1961]), 36 (italics original).

connotations. On the one hand, if one perceives one's identity as what happens, as an event, identity is always *under erasure* in a deconstructive concept. On the other hand, if one traces back to where and why the grand identity from the marginalized group has emerged, one can see that the issues of affirmation, representation, agency, solidarity, allegiance, and sociopolitical change are at the centrality of the emergence of the identity politics.

Here a deconstructive mediation of identity is necessary to make an infinite negotiation between the group-based master identity, on the one hand, and the individual identity of singularity, of alterity, or identity as an ever-evolving event, on the other. Deconstructive mediation can take place not through an either–or binary approach but through a radical reconceptualization of the master identity, because the dilemma that one faces is the core issue of the ongoing spiral relationship between subjectivity and intersubjectivity, of an individual person and sociopolitical and religious community. What deconstructive mediation makes possible is a call for an ongoing radical historicization and contextualization of the very master identity politics without dismissing or overlooking the heterogeneity and singularity of the members of the group. The radical historicization and contextualization are necessary for two reasons: first, each member of the group is located, situated, and positioned in a specific time, space, and context; and second, each member of the group X is always already evolving as being singular plural, as being of radical singularity. The first reason has to do with the *exteriority* of one's existence, whereas the second reason with the *interiority*.

The deconstructive reconstitution of identity begins with a realization that it is impossible to have a final formula of master identity because one's identity is always already in process, evolving and drawing distinctions in time, or what Derrida calls *différance*. Some scholars dismiss the political implications of deconstruction in terms of its suspension of normative claims by calling it the "politics of the ineffable,"[53] a claim with which I do not concur. The deconstructive mediation of identity is not merely a different way of reading but, more fundamentally, of constituting the world and humans in it in a more politically transformative way: "They [deconstructive readings and writings] are not simply analyses of discourse. . . . They are also effective or active (as one says) interventions, in particular political and institutional interventions that transform contexts without limiting themselves to theoretical or constantive utterances even though they must also produce such utterances."[54] Living is always "living together,"[55] which substantially entails the political implications of deconstructive mediation of identity.

One's identity, whether it is a personal or a collective, is not about "an essence but a *positioning*."[56] Positioning oneself as being-with-others in the world is the ground of solidarity, coalition, and compassion with others, not one's essence that is unchanging, fixed, framed, unitary. Suppressing *différance* is a form of violence and "desire for pure identity and ideal meaning sets into motion an entire economy of violence."[57] Mediating and negotiating between the two poles of continuity, commonality and discontinuity—that is, ruptures, alterity, *différance* in articulating and forming who I am and who we are—is like a spiral dancing that does not have a rigid binary line

53. Cf. Thomas McCarthy, "The Politics of Ineffable," *The Philosophic Forum* 21 (Fall-Winter 1989–90): 146–68.
54. Jacques Derrida, "Critical Response: But, beyond . . . (Open Letter to Anne McClintock and Rob Nixon)," *Critical Inquiry* 13, no. 1 (Autumn 1996): 168.
55. Jacques Derrida, "Avowing—The Impossible: 'Returns,' Repentance, and Reconciliation," in *Living Together: Jacques Derrida's Communities of Violence and Peace*, ed. Elisabeth Weber (New York: Fordham University Press, 2013), 18.
56. Stuart Hall, "Cultural Identity and Diaspora," in *Identity: Community, Culture, Difference*, ed. Jonathan Rutherford (London: Lawrence and Wishart, 1990), 226 (italics original).
57. Nicholas Dungey, "(Re)Turning Derrida to Heidegger: Being-with-Others as Primordial Politics," *Polity* 33, no. 3 (Spring 2001): 467.

to draw. *Différance*, in its differing and deferring function, always already underlies the constitution of one's identity, in and alongside sameness, similarity, and continuity. In this sense, it is possible to say that one is both X and not-X, depending on the discursive and political context in which one locates oneself. Remaining suspended between differing and deferring, one can form one's identity in a hyperaffirmative mode, instead of merely getting "a good night's rest"[58] with fixity, stability, and certainty.

Therefore, a deconstructive mediation of identity politics opens up a site of identity that embraces and encourages ambivalence, discontinuity from, alongside the identity: one is X but always already more than X and beyond X, both inside and outside X. Forming mobilizing identity and community of X is possible not by claiming the genuineness and sameness of X, but by embracing heterogeneities, disunities, multiple positionalities and locationalities in histories and contexts of oneself. Deconstructive mediation of identity is therefore not destroying but resituating, reconstituting, reaffirming, reconfiguring the subject. In this context, one's identity is *diasporic* in the sense that it constantly constructs and reconstructs oneself anew through *différance* and transformation. Deconstructive mediation makes possible for one to have a provisional and arbitrary closure constructed across differences and alterity, which makes it possible to form a sense of we without any fixed, binary identity marker. In this context, identity, whether collective or personal, is "temporary and arbitrary" and a "syncretism,"[59] constantly mixing through a deconstructive mediation of sameness, difference, and alterity.

58. Stuart Hall, "Old and New Identities, Old and New Ethnicities," in *Culture, Globalization, and the World-System: Contemporary Conditions for the Representation of Identity*, ed. Anthony King (Minneapolis: University of Minnesota Press, 1997), 42–43.
59. Lawrence Grossberg, "Cultural Studies and/in New Worlds," *Critical Studies in Mass Communication* 10, no. 1 (March 1993): 11.

Identity politics that gears itself to a politics of solidarity has to be always context specific, strategic, and positional. Identity-grounded action for social change has its own limit because when one's identity becomes the ground of collective action of solidarity for human freedom, justice, and peace, it easily comes to encounter its epistemological contradiction with multiple paradoxical, ambivalent identities between and among groups. What we need to look for is not so much a grand master identity but the potential sites of politicization, mobilization, coalition, and transformation to work together across difference, heterogeneity, undecidability, and discontinuity. One master identity that would be true to hold on to is the identity as a human being, which is the ground of the prime notion of crime against humanity, not just crime against women, against gays, against Muslims, and so forth. Whatever unjustly happens to others, it is a violation of human rights and justice. One can take one's particular identity as a point of entry into a political community of action, engagement, compassion, and solidarity with and for the marginalized, but not necessarily always as a point of arrival. Identity politics for action is about political strategies, context-specific positions, and border-crossing coalitions between and among different constituencies of society.

3

Asia as Theopolitical Imagination

A Postcolonial Theological Reading of Orientalism and Neo-Orientalism

'The West' is a historical, not a geographical, construct. . . . 'The West' is therefore also an idea, a concept.
—Stuart Hall[1]

Asia the East as a Historical Invention:
The Rest to the West

People use the term *invention* in many different ways. Once people used the term only for technological advances and innovations; gradually, it came to be used to reveal, criticize, or reappraise diverse phenomena. My use of the term *invention* is to denaturalize and deessentialize the category of Asia or Asian women. The fundamental

---

1. Stuart Hall, "The West and the Rest: Discourse and Power," in *Formations of Modernity*, ed. Stuart Hall and Bram Gieben (Cambridge, UK: Polity, 1992), 277.

dangers and problems in this naturalized and essentialized category of Asia or Asian women lie in its mode of seeing: fixed, homogenized, and unchanging. The term *invention* further calls for close scrutiny of the geopolitical constructedness of Asia and Asian women as genderized ethnicity and ethnicized gender. James Clifford argues that ethnographic writings are "composed of *inventions* rather than observed facts" and "can properly be called *fictions* in the sense of *'something made or fashioned.'*"[2] In his *Imagined Communities*, Benedict Anderson analyzes the conditions under which people have invented or imagined modern national and ethnic groups,[3] citing Ernest Gellner: "Nationalism is not the awakening of nations to self-consciousness; it invents nations where they do not exist."[4] In this context, Asia is an "open-ended imaginary space,"[5] and Asia as a singular entity is actually an "imaginative geography"[6] and a discursively invented site.

Nowadays, one cannot discuss Asia the East without referring to the West. In public discourse, Europeans, not Asians themselves, have constructed the perception of Asia. The notion of the West first emerged in Western Europe. In the contemporary world, however, the idea of the West has expanded to include the United States, even though it is not geographically located in Europe, whereas people have hardly regarded Eastern European countries as the West. In this sense, the West is "a *historical*, not a geographical, construct."[7] In order to construct the West, it was necessary for the Westerners

---

2. James Clifford, "Introduction: Partial Truths," in James Clifford and George E. Marcus, eds., *Writing Culture: The Poetics and Politics of Ethnography* (Berkeley: University of California Press, 1986), 5, 6 (italics mine).

3. Benedict Anderson, *Imagined Communities: Reflections of the Origins and Spread of Nationalism* (London: Verso, 1985 [1983]), 62.

4. Ernest Gellner, *Thought and Change* (London: Weidenfeld and Nicholson, 1964), 169.

5. Kuan-Hsing Chen, *Asia as Method: Toward Deimperialization* (Durham: Duke University Press, 2010), 282.

6. Cf. Edward W. Said, *Orientalism* (New York: Vintage, 1978), 49–72.

7. Hall, "West and the Rest," 277.

to distinguish the West from the rest of the world. The discourse of "the West" and "the Rest" emerged especially in a historical time of Western expansion, thus necessitating the homogenization and essentialization of these two worlds.

It is, however, impossible to draw the border between the West and the East. The questions involving where exactly the East begins and the West ends on a geographical map are hard to answer. Whereas Asia, as the East to the West, appears on the map, the West does not occupy its territory on the map as clearly. As long as people perceive Asia as the East to the West, the West becomes the point of entry for discourses on the Rest—"the non-West." Furthermore, if one moves from geography to culture, the question of boundary between the West and the East becomes even more difficult to answer today, when the influence of the West has permeated every sector of reality of people everywhere in the world through politics, economy, culture, technology, educational system, lifestyle, religion, and so forth.

Whenever I go to conferences where theologians from the West and the East gather together, most of the time an unchallenged rhetoric dominates the floor: an ethnic, cultural essentialism. Both groups—the Westerners and the Easterners—tend to presuppose that the East is and should be completely different from the West and that native Asians should claim their essential difference as a unique virtue that Westerners do not possess. For nonnative Westerners, respect and encouragement for the presumably unique virtues of the East seem to function as nonimperialist sentiments in engaging with the non-West. For the native Easterners, on the other hand, their ethnic essentialist position often functions as a form of survival technique that makes their voice heard in a world of neoimperialism where the West (especially Western Europe and the USA) still dominates every sector of reality. Furthermore, such cultural essentialism often functions as a "culturalist alibi" that works "within a basically elitist culture industry, insisting on the continuity of a native tradition untouched by a Westernization,"[8] which Asians use to block any criticism on patriarchal and hierarchal aspects of Asian culture and tradition. The adoption of an ethnic essentialist rhetoric, by both natives and non-natives, keeps the West at the universal center of knowledge and the discursive norm, whereas the non-West remains as the particularized, ethnicized, often exoticized, and idealized margin in the world of knowledge production, archiving, and dissemination. Here both natives and non-natives, regardless of their intentionality, end up homogenizing the heterogeneity of the East and suppressing the critical difference within the East and among its people in different nation-states based on their respective geopolitical power, economic status, social class, religion, gender, or other axis of oppression and discrimination.

The rhetoric of geographical determinism and ethnic/cultural essentialism also functions as orientalism, a "transcultural phenomenon"[9] that dehistoricizes the rapidly changing history and its society of the East and ahistoricizes the daily experience of the actual people in the East, who live and experience both as victims and victimizers and oppressed and oppressors in their own specific contexts. Here *orientalism*, a "transcultural phenomenon,"[10] becomes applicable not only to the Middle East but also to the other Asia as well. When native Asians do not show the so-called ethnic distinctiveness but present political issues in their works, Western scholars criticize them, accusing them of wanting "to *sell oneself abroad* by what an international audience, hungry for political virtue,

---

8. Gayatri Chakravorty Spivak, "Who Claims Alterity?" in *Remaking History*, ed. Barbara Kruger and Phil Marian (Seattle: Bay Press, 1989), 281.
9. Rey Chow, *Writing Diaspora: Tactics of Intervention in Contemporary Cultural Studies* (Bloomington: Indiana University Press, 1993), 3.
10. Ibid.

which is always in short supply, finds touching."[11] Stephen Owen, a Sinologist, analyzes a Chinese poet, Bei Dao, who does not seem to show uniquely local aspects of Chinese history, culture, and the past; Owen harshly criticizes Bei Dao for selling himself abroad, not celebrating his indigenous cultural heritage. Owen also indicates his suspicion about the originality of the universal tone of the poetry and says the world poetries "have often been formed by reading Western poetry in translations, sometimes in very poor translations."[12] Here poetry without any adjective constitutes the poetry in the West, whereas *world poetry* indicates poetries from the non-Western worlds. So in the world of poets, people operate in a geopolitical hierarchy of poetry. When a poet from Asia such as Bei Dao does not show an exotic, particular, or essentialized cultural tone but presents a universal spirit, scholars regard him or her as inauthentic. However, this poem by Bei Dao captures, from my perspective, a cosmopolitan ethos by moving beyond his nationalist confinement toward a cosmopolitan consciousness:

Spring has no nationality,
Clouds are citizens of the world.

Become friends again with mankind [sic].
My song.[13]

However, Owen criticizes Bei Dao by taking this poem as an example and argues: "This may aspire to be an international poetry that sails over boundaries, but it does have *local* origins, origins that are not *Chinese*. . . . 'my song,' is as alien to traditional Chinese poetry

11. Stephen Owen, "The Anxiety of Global Influence: What Is World Poetry?" *The New Republic* 203, no. 21 (November 19, 1990): 29 (italics mine).
12. Ibid.
13. Bei Dao, "True," in *The August Sleepwalker,*" trans. Bonnie S. McDougall (London: New Directions, 1990), 22, quoted in ibid., 31.

as it is familiar in the Western poetic tradition."[14] Owen's "moralistic indictment of the other's infidelity"[15] to a poet's own traditions and cultural origins reveals his patronizing and orientalist attitude toward the East in the name of respecting the diversity, beauty, and virtue of the East, which perpetuates, in fact, the superiority of the Western norm and language, especially English and French, according to his article. Furthermore, Owen's argument that a sense of individuality in the phrase of "*my* song" is not Chinese reveals a stereotypical orientalist, essentialist perception of the East as the place of absence of the individuality under the virtue of communitarian we-ness. Owen invalidates, in a patronizing and judgmental tone, the poetry by an Asian poet that conveys the poet's universalist consciousness and longing for a cosmopolitan world where every being, like clouds, are fellow citizens of the world, where one's nationality does not have any specific confinement, as it is now. Owen bases his critique on a geographical determinism, orientalism, and ethnic, cultural essentialism, arguing that a Chinese poet *must* reveal something uniquely local and Chinese. Owen is right when he indicates: "to write in the dominant language of the age is to have the luxury of writing with unshaken faith in the permanence of a culture's hegemony. But poets in many other countries and languages must . . . dream of being translated."[16] He is also aware that "cultural power is not evenly distributed, and the poet writing in English (or French) can work in blithe self-confidence regarding the universal adequacy of his or her linguistic community."[17] However, from Owen's essentialist perspective, Bei Dao, a Chinese poet in exile, is an *inauthentic* Chinese and the cultural hegemony he mentions operates

---

14. Owen, "Anxiety of Global Influence," 31 (italics mine).
15. Chow, *Writing Diaspora*, 4.
16. Owen, "Anxiety of Global Influence," 28.
17. Stephen Owen, "Stepping Forward and Back: Issues and Possibilities for 'World' Poetry," *Modern Philology* 100, no. 4 (May 2003): 533.

in his own assessment of a native Asian, being "uneasy at seeing 'natives' who have gone 'civilized' or who, . . . have taken up the active task of shaping their own culture."[18] When the native Asians do not stay in their stereotyped frames, both non-native Westerners and native Asians label those unconventional Asians as inauthentic.

Asian feminists run the risk of being labeled as *inauthentic* Asians, as being too Westernized, or as being unappreciative of their own culture if they do not use traditional Asian cultural resources for their feminist theological construction. Even among feminist groups, when a feminist uses an ethnic marker such as Asian, a general expectation among feminist groups, both from the West or Asia, is to see a presentation of their victimhood as pure victim or to retrieve their theological ground from rather exotic Asian resources, often using their vernacular languages that are untranslatable into Western languages, such as *han* or *minjung*. Both natives and non-natives expect Asians, whether they are patriarchal or feminist, universalist or exclusive nationalist, to remain in stereotyped frames that the West has constructed, based on its Orientalist attitude toward the East. One can find orientalist sentiments both in native Asians and nonnatives alike, but each with a different motive and functionality.

Here one should note that universalism and particularism inextricably intertwine. Being an Asian does not preclude one's universalist inclination, especially in a world where the West and the East deeply intersect, where the universal and the particular feed into one another, and where everything gets entangled with everything else. When an Asian poet like Bei Dao shows not his particular local color but a universal color, such a native Asian is criticized as being too Westernized, losing his or her national, cultural, or ethnic heritage and identity. In this context, native Asians also criticize

18. Chow, *Writing Diaspora*, 28.

those who are critical about the unexamined ethnic essentialist presupposition as being too Westernized, if the critics are fellow natives, or as being too imperialistic, if they are non-native Westerners. Interestingly, Westerners often regard those critics as lacking their own national, ethnic, cultural pride, which they should hold on to as unique virtues/beauties of their own indigenous roots. The common presupposition that interplays in the binary scheme of West and East is in fact the binary between universalism and particularism: people attach the West to universalism, and the East to particularism. In this context, the West subjugates the non-West and the standardization and normativization of the West remain intact. In reality, however, one can hardly dissociate universalism from particularism and vice versa. Instead, the two poles are inseparable and inextricably intertwined. However, the orientalist essentialism that both natives and non-natives adopt perpetuates normativizing and universalizing the West while particularizing and provincializing the East.

Another issue at stake in this orientalist rhetoric is an issue of contextualization. An author of a theological discourse, wherever that author comes from, grounds such discourse in his or her context. However, people often use the phrase "contextual theology" or "indigenous theology" only for works by non-Western theologians, which presupposes that contextualization is necessary only for those non-Westerners but not for Western theologians. Often, under the name of contextualization, the non-Western culture and people become essentialized, particularized, and, thereby, provincialized. Contextualizing and essentializing are completely different matters, but when it comes to non-Western persons, people often get confused, contextualizing and essentializing them based on their culture, geography, race and ethnicity, gender, or sexuality. In the process of exploring cultural difference, the West always is absent from the stage of cultural diversity and its absence becomes a significant mechanism in maintaining the West as the universalized center and the non-West as the provincialized margin.

The Rise of Postcolonial Sensibility:
Theopolitical Critique of Epistemic Hegemony

Whoever travels across Asia soon notices that one cannot categorize Asia into a single homogeneous group. Cultural, religious, historical, economic, and sociopolitical contexts vary extremely from country to country. Asia is the largest of the earth's seven continents. Its people account for three-fifths of the world's population. Therefore, one cannot define Asia as a monolithic, unified entity. Furthermore, in the contemporary postindustrial world, one requires cross-national and cross-cultural analyses in order to understand various Asian countries according to their own internal features and socioeconomic conditions. Asia can no longer be defined by the same geographical contours and boundaries as before.

Charting the ground for a discourse on Asian theology thus is not an easy task. First, one needs to respond to the following questions: Who/what is Asian? Do Asians make up any kind of a constituency? On what basis? Can we assume that Asians' theological constructions are necessarily Asian? Second, one also needs to respond to questions about contexts for exploring and formulating Asian theological discourses: Which/whose history do we draw on to chart this map of Asian theologians' engagement with the construction of Asian theology? Who has produced knowledge about Asians and their authentic experiences, and from what space/location? What are the disciplinary parameters of this knowledge? What are the methods used to locate and chart Asians' experience and context? I do not assume that the current versions of Asian theology and its articulation of what "Asian" is are the ultimate form of Asian theological discourse. I consider theological construction in Asia to be an unfinished project, in the sense that one needs to clarify, refine, and develop theopolitical foundations, principles, resources, representations, and institutional devices in praxis.

Theology has undergone major changes in the last four decades. The changes concern what theology is; who does theology; the issues that theology considers; the cultural, political, and philosophical contexts of theology. Especially those marginalized from the mainstream of theological construction—namely women, African Americans, and the so-called Third World—have begun to raise fundamental questions that have brought changes in doing theology. In contemporary theology, one could call the change discursive shifts, which have fundamentally altered the ways in which theologians formulate their theological reflection. One of the discursive shifts is the rise of postcolonial sensibility, which made Asian theologians examine how the West constructed its superiority and how Christianity in the West supported such West-centrism through Christian beliefs and practices. Asian theologians associated their theological discourse with the world process of decolonization after World War II.[19] A sense of anti-West-centrism was predominant in Asian theological discourse. Asian theologians have related Western systems of knowledge and representation to the long history of the West's material and political subordination of the non-Western world. In this colonizing process of knowledge construction, theological discourse is no exception.

---

19. The "World War" itself is the very product of West-centrism. It is quite obvious that the so-called World Wars I and II were not, in fact, "world" wars, because, geographically speaking, the wars did not break out worldwide.

Many Asian theologians have developed their theological discourse with the spirit of postcolonialism, undermining the prevalence of West-centeredness in most traditional theological discourse. One of the powerful arguments emerging from the first generation of Asian theology is that traditional Western theology is limited because it falsely universalizes on the basis of limited perspectives, which are the perspectives of white, middle-class men of North America and Western Europe. They go on to argue that traditional theologies left out Asian resources and experiences, while positively employing Western cultural and religious resources. It is natural, therefore, for Asian theologians to try to break the general assumption of the superiority of Western theology and culture at the primary stage of constructing their own theological discourse. They harshly criticize Western theologians for being part of a Constantinian captivity of the faith and instead try to construct Asian theology on the basis of Asian culture and resources. In this process, the issue of identity as Asian becomes very urgent and significant in formulating Asian theology.

Edward Said's 1978 book *Orientalism* initiated contemporary postcolonial discourse, becoming the catalyst and reference for postcolonialism and the founding text through which "the marginal can speak and be spoken, even spoken for."[20] Said elaborates a unique understanding of imperialism/colonialism as an epistemological and cultural attitude, illustrating it as "a Western style for dominating, restructuring, and having authority over the Orient"[21] and

> [A] *distribution* of geographical awareness into aesthetic, scholarly, economic, sociological, historical, and philosophical texts; it is an *elaboration* not only of a basic geographical distinction (the world is made up of two unequal halves, Orient and Occident) but also of a

---

20. Gayatri Chakravorty Spivak, *Outside in the Teaching Machine* (New York: Routledge, 1993), 56.
21. Said, *Orientalism*, 3.

whole series of "interest" which, by such means as scholarly discovery, philosophical reconstruction, it not only creates but also maintains; it *is*, rather than expresses, a certain *will* or *intention* to understand, in some cases to control, manipulate, even to incorporate, what is a manifestly different (or alternative and novel) world.[22]

The typical image of the Orient conceptualized by orientalism focuses on its strangeness, difference, exotic sensuousness, eccentricity, backwardness, silent indifference, feminine penetrability, uncivilized nature, and so forth.[23] The image of the Orient tends to be static, frozen, and fixed eternally, so people deny the possibility of transformation and development in the Orient. Moreover, both Western and Asian people sometimes glorify, mystify, and idealize those frozen characteristics of the Orient as the wisdom of the East. According to this orientalist perspective, the West is the knowing agent, whereas Asia is the object to be known. At a deeper level, the West's desire to establish its own identity motivated orientalism, the West's self-identity being the historical agent that created that modern spirit and civilization. To establish this identity, the West needed Asia the Orient as the other. Asia must be the negative background against which the West presents its own positive figure. In other words, orientalism is an epistemological device for guaranteeing Western hegemony over Asia. Although Said's primary concern is with the Western perception of the Islamic world in the Middle and Near East, his analysis and critique of orientalism are relevant to Asia in general. The Hegelian perception of Asian ahistorical stagnancy still remains true in various discourses on Asia.[24]

22. Ibid., 12.
23. Ibid., 206–207.
24. Cf. G. W. F. Hegel, *Lectures on the Philosophy of World History*, trans. H. B. Nisbet (London: Cambridge University Press, 1975). In his notorious foreword for the chapter on China, Hegel places China and India outside the scope of world history on the grounds that these countries experience no dialectical change whatever but merely repeat the same pattern.

Asian theologians who critique Western epistemic hegemony aim to undermine the orientalist dogma. In this process, Asian theologians reversely claim Asian superiority and deny universal validity to Western culture and knowledge. For these theologians, Asia, as the orientalists see it, is essentially different from the West. Asserting Asian cultural uniqueness, based on the old dualism of Asia as the Orient and Euro-American countries as the Occident, becomes the core of Asian theological discourse. Reclaiming their own Asianness is one of the Asian theologians' tasks, along with "theological responsibility with fellow Asians."[25] They go on to argue that "we are all under the power of the culture into which we are born. Our cultural heritage makes us what we are. Our views on life and the world are formed under the direct and indirect influence of our cultural tradition."[26] In this claim, theologians operate with a strong we–they binarism of we-Asian and they-Western, and they do not show how different and diverse the Asian cultures actually are. Because the West as a homogeneous whole exists only in the imagination, Asia as a homogeneous whole exists only in the imagination as well. When one dichotomizes Asia–West into we–they contrasts, one then essentializes the resultant other, the constitutive other.

One should further note that this dualist assumption itself is the product of the Western intellectual imperialist construct referred to as orientalism, the product of the West-centrism that Asian theologians themselves criticize. When Asian theologians reject traditional theology as being specifically Western and culturally inadequate to the Asian context, they ironically ascribe the same homogeneous cultural essence to Asia that orientalists utilize to contrast Asia with

25. Choan-Seng Song, "Freedom of Christian Theology for Asian Cultures: Celebrating the Inauguration of the Programme for Theology and Cultures in Asia," *Asian Journal of Theology* 1, no. 3 (1989): 87.
26. Choan-Seng Song, *Third-Eye Theology* (Maryknoll, NY: Orbis, 1979), 6.

the West's self-portrait. They change the evaluative connotation of this essence from negative to positive but keep its cognitive content unchanged. For an Asian identity they look to the stereotype that orientalists imposed on Asia to establish a superior Western identity. In favor of a kind of unity as Asian against the West, Asian theologians themselves tend to disregard, trivialize, and erase the diversity and complexity of Asian peoples and cultures and to overlook the very fact that the West is as heterogeneous and hybrid as Asia.

As a result, Asian theologians unwittingly readopt and internalize the orientalist view of monolithic Asia that they criticize, and at the same time create occidentalism in the same manner, though this occidentalism does not have a hegemonic power over the West as orientalism does over Asia.[27] This attitude is ironic but understandable. It is the same mechanism found in practices of social discrimination. When people deeply hold the discriminatory stereotype, people induce the groups against whom they discriminate to convert that stereotype into a basis for self-esteem. This transvaluation of the stereotype occurs not because, given its persistence, it is strategically easier to turn it to one's own advantage rather than destroy it. Rather, the conversion strategy promises to heal a people's wounded self-respect more powerfully than does the strategy of destroying the stereotype. As "'the once-colonized others' insisting on taking their place as historical subjects," they begin to expose their own hidden voices in terms of essential difference from the colonizer on the basis of culture, ethnicity, race, or gender. Gayatri Chakravorty Spivak explains this with the expression, "strategic choices of essentialism."[28]

---

27. For more discussion on occidentalism, see, Xiaomei Chen, *Occidentalism* (New York: Oxford University Press, 1995).

Who are Asian Women?
Invention of Ethnicized Gender, Gendered Ethnicity

The strategy that Spivak describes is, in a way, a natural response for those discriminated against who want to disassociate themselves from the presumption of cultural inferiority that the practice of discrimination imposes on them. They positively affirm their Asian identity, because to detach their identity from being Asian in order to prove their equal status with the Western would make them accomplices to the presumption of inferiority. To the deep-seated orientalist prejudice, the Asian theologians seeking to increase their self-esteem offer an analogous response: *Asia is beautiful.* This rhetoric has a healing effect on people's self-esteem. Their legitimate claim to equal respect with the West turns into an ironic affirmation of the imposed Asian identity.

Although understandable and effective, this reverse use of the imposed Asian identity is false and dangerous, for Asian identity will easily turn into a tyrannical imposition of the authentic ways of being Asian and of the authentic image of Asia. Moreover, it represses the recognition of Asia's internal diversity and potential for endogenous transformation, and tempts one to discourage and even to oppress and dismiss Asian demands for emancipatory movements, for instance, women's liberation movements or movement for sexual minority rights, based on their foreign origin. This politics of essentialized/nativist identity in Asian theological discourse will then reinforce not just the orientalist prejudice that Asian culture is inadequate for a universal theological discourse, but also cultural/geographical

---

28. Cf. Gayatri Chakravorty Spivak, "Criticism, Feminism, and the Institution," in Sarah Harasym, ed., *The Post-colonial Critic: Interviews, Strategies, Dialogues* (New York: Routledge, 1990), 11–13.

essentialism: Asians are only Asians just as women are only women. The epistemic hegemony critique enables us to get out of this trap of Asian essentialized identity by dissolving the orientalist dualism internalized in Asian theological discourse. This critique undermines the assumption of a monolithic Asian cultural essence. The polarizing drive of orientalist dualism traps the West and Asia in a distorted perception of self-identity. The critique of epistemic hegemony enables us to direct both Asia and the West away from the cage of their deceptively polarized identities.

Asian theologians characterize Asia by its overwhelming poverty and multifaceted religiosity. According to Aloysius Pieris, poverty constitutes a common denominator shared with the rest of the so-called Third World, and multifaceted religiosity refers to the specific character of Asia.[29] Following this argument, one's own identity as Asian requires being poor, and some Asian people do not qualify as Asian if they are not extremely poor. Choan-Seng Song even argues that the poor Asia is "the Asia betrayed by the prosperous Hong Kong, the orderly Singapore, the industrialized Japan, and by pseudo-democracy in most Asian countries."[30] Although one can find poverty and poor people everywhere in the world, even in the so-called First World, the reality of poverty in Asia is more striking. More than three-quarters of the world's poor live in Asia. Moreover, poverty is normally closely interwoven with the religiosity of the people. Being Asian, according to Asian theologians, means living in poverty and with multifaceted religiosity. The Asian church must be, therefore, "humble enough to be baptized in the Jordan of Asian *religiosity* and bold enough to be crucified on the cross of Asian

---

29. Aloysius Pieris, "Towards an Asian Theology of Liberation: Some Religio-Cultural Guidelines," in *Asia's Struggle for Full Humanity: Towards a Relevant Theology*, ed. Virginia Fabella, Papers from the Asian Theological Conference (Wennappuwa, Sri Lanka) (Maryknoll, NY: Orbis, 1980).

30. Choan-Seng Song, *Jesus, the Crucified People* (New York: Crossroad, 1990), 8.

poverty. . . . our desperate search for the Asian face of Christ can find fulfillment only if we participate in Asia's own search for it in the unfathomable abyss where religion and poverty seem to have the same common source: God . . ."[31] Poor Asia is in this respect fundamentally different from the wealthy West and, furthermore, the source of Asian poverty is God. Theology, according to Asian theologians, must arise from the Asian poor, and "a truly liberating theology must ultimately be the work of the Asian poor."[32]

Although this kind of monolithic understanding of Asia by Asian theologians can be appealing and carries a partial truth, such an understanding tends to suppress the diversity among people of different social/cultural strata within Asian countries, as if Asians were classless, genderless, stateless, raceless. The degree and experience of poverty vary extremely, and the notion of being poor is itself a relative and complex one. So, the question, Who are Asians?, is complicated and elusive. Asian identity cannot be comprehended by such a grand concept as poverty. It is so obvious that the process of finding one's identity, whether it be personal, national, regional, or universal, is an ongoing process that one cannot fix by grand concepts such as poverty or multifaceted religiosity. Formulating Asian identity only as difference from the Westernness ignores the complexity among Asian issues and the overlapping dimensions with the West. The root causes of various forms of oppression tend to blur.

In most Asian theological discourse, theologians have a strong tendency to posit an essential Asianness, which is entirely different from Westernness, in which all Asians have and share in common despite the racial, class, gender, religious, ethnic, and cultural differences among Asians: anonymous collectivity. This tendency carries the mark of the plural,[33] obscures the heterogeneity of Asians,

---

31. Pieris, "Towards an Asian Theology," 93–94.
32. "Final Statement," in Fabella, ed., *Asia's Struggle*, 157.

and eventually cuts off examination of the significance of such heterogeneity for contemporary construction of Asian theology. Here, all Asians look alike. In Asian feminist theological discourse, for example, theologians often present Asian women as either pure victims or heroic figures who transcend all the pain and suffering with an amazing liberating power. The typical images of Asian women portrayed in writings by Asian feminist theologians are victims of starvation, rape, and poverty, and theologians have glorified them as being able to liberate themselves with heroic power.

> Asian women share the domestic, economic, political, and religious oppression that their sisters all over the world suffer. . . . Asian women have also been raped, tortured, imprisoned, and killed for their political beliefs. . . . Asian women are struggling against, and in the process of the struggle they are giving birth to a spirituality that is particularly *woman's* and specifically *Asian*.[34]

> Asian women's theology has emerged from Asian women's cries and screams, from the extreme suffering in their everyday lives. They have shouted from pain when their own and their children's bodies collapsed from starvation, rape, and battering. . . . Asian women's theology is very "Third World" because their reality is marked by poverty and oppression. . . . Asian women's theology is "very Asian." . . . Asian women's theology is also "very women." . . . Asian women are oppressed economically, socially, politically, religiously, and culturally in specific ways just because they are women.[35]

Here one needs to raise some fundamental questions: What is *very women* and *very Asian*? Who are Asian women anyway? Do Asian women make up any kind of a constituency? On what basis? Who defines Asian women as an entity? Just as one cannot define Western

33. Albert Memmi, *The Colonizer and the Colonized* (Boston: Beacon, 1967), 85.
34. Virginia Fabella and Mercy Amba, eds., *With Passion and Compassion: Third World Women Doing Theology* (Maryknoll, NY: Orbis, 1990), 78–79 (emphasis added).
35. Chung Hyun Kyung, *Struggle to Be the Sun Again: Introducing Asian Women's Theology* (Maryknoll, NY: Orbis, 1990), 22–24.

women as a unitary entity, one cannot also conceptualize Asian women as a homogeneous, monolithic, unitary group. If Asian theologians continue to portray Asians as an entity, Asian theology, like Asian discourse and movement, will lose its accountability to the concrete transformation by under- or misrepresenting the tremendously diverse reality of Asian people.

In the primary stage of liberation from Western theological imperialism and of its own theological formulation, asserting "Asian" as an entity and essentialized identity "as Asian" is impossible to avoid. If the notion of Asianness becomes fixed, however, Asian identity will more and more constrain rather than liberate Asians. Those images of Asian women as *minjung* of the *minjung*, or poor among the poor, for example, cannot embrace the diversity of Asian women because many women are not *minjung*, *dalit*, or poor, and others are, for instance, politicians, professors, teachers, doctors, lawyers, businesswomen, upper-middle-class women, or affluent housewives. A large number of Asian people do not fit into these romanticized/oppressed images of Asians. In this context, Asian women's experience in general is impossible to construct, including the experiences of oppression and liberation. What is possible is only historically circumscribed experience in a particular time and space, which people differently experience based on their particular context of social class, race, education, individual difference, religion, culture, and so forth. It is difficult for Koreans, for example, to understand multiracial countries such as Malaysia or Indonesia, because racial and cultural homogeneity has been central to Korean nationalism. It is also not easy for Koreans to understand the long history of other Asian countries. For example, Pakistan and Korea, or China and India, or New Zealand and Sri Lanka have hardly anything in common. In this context, it is either arrogant or ignorant to define Asian as a single, unitary entity and as having one face. The reification of Asian women as slaves of slaves, *minjung* of the *minjung*,[36] or poor among the poor, is a typical essentialization of the nature of Asian women. Through these essentialized portrayals, theologians constitute Asian women unilaterally as *absolute victims* and deny any historical cultural specificity.

In fact, the category of women is much broader than that of *minjung*. Defining women as *minjung* among *minjung* minimizes the range of women's issues because of its limited scope of analysis. While *minjung* are those marginalized and oppressed people, based primarily on their socioeconomic status, this oppression is not always due to patriarchal institutions and social values. Women in every social stratum, from the lower class to upper middle class, from the factory workers even to the first lady, have experienced patriarchy in different forms and intensity. To identify the upper-middle-class women as *minjung* of the *minjung* simply because they are biologically female is to overgeneralize, for doing so can blur the root causes of oppression both of *minjung* and of women as well. Moreover, the category of *minjung* is not static, while that of women is, because while the *minjung* can transcend their *minjung*-ness through socioeconomic advancement, women cannot change their being biologically women no matter what.

In this sense, fundamental questions as to what and who constitute Asian women become significant theopolitical questions with which Asian feminist theologians need to wrestle. My first encounter with the label "Asian woman" took place in a graduate seminar on women and religion during my doctorate study in the United States. One day during our discussion, I found myself being labeled and categorized as an Asian woman, expected to talk about Asian women as a native

36. Letty Russell, "Minjung Theology in Women's Prospective," in *An Emerging Theology in World Perspective*, ed. Jung Young Lee (Mystic, CT: Twenty-Third Publications, 1988), 83.

informant, as if "Asian woman" were another proper name. At first, I felt perplexed, puzzled, annoyed, and betrayed as being segregated from my peer students without any persuasive, explanatory process of mutual agreement over this categorization. It seemed to me, at that time, that my being became the only nonuniversal ethnic, while their universal humanity remained intact. They, including the professor, did not have an ethnic category. At that time, preoccupied with all existentialist philosophical questions, I did not know what role they expected me to play and what stories they wanted to hear from me as "Asian woman," although I sensed that they expected me to play a particular role and to tell particular stories in front of my non-Asian, mostly white fellow students and professor—the universal, nonethnic human beings. In this context, "ethnicity is something reinvented and reinterpreted in each generation by each individual" and "is often something quite puzzling to the individual, something over which he or she lacks control."[37] I also noticed that Asians in general, regardless of their gender, became feminized in relation to the Western and that Asian women become more ethnicized than Asian men. I am not overlooking the fact that transforming "Asian" into a singular entity can suggest potential alliances and collaborations across divisive boundaries in Asian countries. However, one cannot avoid a great danger in projecting "Asian" as an entity and in postulating Asian women only as victims, for it cannot sufficiently present a dynamic, historically specific view of the oppression and struggles of Asians of different times and contexts.

---

37. Michael J. Fischer, "Ethnicity and the Post-Modern Arts of Memory," in Clifford and Marcus, eds., *Writing Culture*, 195.

Dangerous Trap of Neo-Orientalism:
Asians-in-Differential

In her article "Under Western Eyes," Chandra Talpade Mohanty analyzes the issue of the representation of Third-World women, objectified by First-World feminists. She shows how Western feminism created Third-World women as a single category, and how this produces "discursive homogenization and systematization of the oppression of women in the Third World."[38] First-World feminists regard Third-World women as different from Western women, and present them as existing as a "coherent group with identical interests and desires, regardless of class, ethnic, or racial location."[39] Also, this "homogeneous notion of the oppression of women as a group" produces "the image of an average third world woman."[40] Their specific context, in fact, does not matter because they are all alike. They are welcome only when they present themselves as different from Western women.

> Now, i am not only given the permission to open up and talk, i am also encouraged to express my difference. My audience expects and demands it; otherwise people would feel as if they have been cheated: We did not come to hear a Third World member speak about the First (?) World, We came to listen to that voice of difference likely to bring us *what we can't have* and to divert us from the monotony of sameness. . . . the Third World representative the modern sophisticated public ideally seeks is the *unspoiled* African, Asian, or Native American, who remains more preoccupied with her/his image of the real native—the *truly different*—than with the issues of hegemony, racism, feminism, and social change.[41]

---

38. Chandra Talpade Mohanty, "Under Western Eyes: Feminist Scholarship and Colonial Discources," in *Third World Women and the Politics of Feminism*, ed. Chandra Talpade Mohanty, Ann Russo, and Lourdes Torres (Bloomington: Indiana University Press, 1991), 54.
39. Ibid., 55.
40. Ibid., 56.
41. Minh-ha T. Trinh, *Woman Native Other: Writing Postcoloniality and Feminism* (Bloomington: Indiana University Press, 1989), 88.

First-World feminists expect Asian women to speak and write only as Asian, otherwise, they are not authentic enough. Then, Asians have to overgeneralize themselves, to make themselves representative, to distance themselves from Western feminists. So, in fact, "for the person who does the *speaking as* something, it is a problem of distancing from one's self" but "the hegemonic people, the dominant people, talk about listening to someone 'speaking as' something or the other . . . *there* one encounters a problem. When *they* want to hear an Indian speaking as an Indian, a Third World woman speaking as a Third World woman, they cover over the fact of the ignorance that they are allowed to possess, into a kind of homogenization."[42]

When they want to cover non-Western theological discourse in their work, homogenizing and tokenizing and ghettoizing are part of the process. Rosemary Radford Ruether, for instance, covers Asian feminist theology in her book *Women and Redemption*.[43] Reading this book, one can easily find a kind of inconsistency in each chapter. Comparing chapters 6, 7, and 8, for example, one can see how Ruether tries to avoid the trap of generalization when she introduces feminist theologies in the West by mentioning various individual feminist theologians in chapters 6 and 7, even though there still remains the question of what the disciplinary parameters of this selection are and what the standards used to select these representative figures are in feminist theological discourse in the West. Biographical narratives about those feminist theologians show that they are singular individuals, not a collective group of people. But in chapter 8, Ruether shows a methodological inconsistency. The names of individual theologians disappear from the content of the book and,

---

42. Spivak, "Question of Multi-culturalism," in Harasym, ed., *The Post-colonial Critic*, 60 (italics original).
43. Rosemary Radford Ruether, *Women and Redemption: A Theological History* (Minneapolis: Fortress Press, 1998).

instead, Ruether deals with such a vast region within one chapter by using a grand categorization: Latin America, Africa, and Asia. Since she does not have knowledge of the vernacular languages of each region, I suppose, she must have been unable to access enormously various resources written in these vernacular languages. Here, overgeneralization, oversimplification, and homogenization become a method of representation, and by doing so, Ruether ends up suppressing, despite her good intentions, the diversity, complexity, and historicity of the feminist theological discourse of those regions. Spivak's critique of Kristiva's *About Chinese Women*,[44]a book based on a short trip to China, helps us to see the critique of contemporary Western feminism of modern androcentric humanism. However, western feminists lose their insistence on heterogeneity of women, when Western feminist theology faces the non-Western.

Even though I acknowledge the informative value of Ruether's writings on feminist theology(ies) in the non-Western regions, it is not possible, nor should she try, to treat a couple of particular figures or meetings from such a vast region as the representative voice. In *covering* Asia, Africa, and Latin America in her book through the *average women's issue* of the non-Western regions, she is not only practicing a discursive hegemonic power but also *tokenizing* and therefore *ghettoizing* non-Western feminist theological discourse. Such a manner produces the idea that women in non-Western regions are just a collective entity, and such an idea makes the analysis of specific historical, cultural, societal, and personal differences within/among such women impossible. Ruether also ignores the variety of disciplines and standpoints and methodologies for doing feminist theologies within a region and among feminist theologians

---

44. Cf. Gayatri Chakravorty Spivak, "French Feminism in an International Frame," in *In Other Worlds: Essays in Cultural Politics* (New York: Methuen, 1987) and Julia Kristeva, *About Chinese Women*, trans. Anita Barrows (London: Marion Boyars, 1977).

of the region. In this way, feminists with good intention freeze and fix those non-Western women into a certain image of victimization and oppression, and fundamentally deny their historical specificity. They are native, indigenous, exotic, nonstate, nonclass. This homogenizing of non-Western feminist theological discourse is an act of *othering* the women in Africa, Latin America, and Asia: non-Western women are somehow *others*, fundamentally different from Western feminist theologians.

While othered objects—here Asian/Latin American/African feminist theologians—do not have the power to include or exclude feminist theologians in the West, the othering subjects—here, feminist theologians in the West like Ruether—have a discursive power to make a decision whether to include or exclude feminist theologians in non-Western regions. So, they sometimes include feminist theologians in Asia as women (on the ground of the biological sameness) and other times exclude and segregate these women as Asians (on the ground of the geographical/cultural difference). Asia is itself infinite layers, and one can hardly convey its complexity and diversity through such a monolithic description and analysis as in Ruether's book. Homogenizing Asian feminist theology is a kind of *epistemic violence* because people represent Asian women identically in feminist theological discourse regardless of their historicity and specific physicality. Ruether does not use terms like "North American feminist theology" as she does for other parts of the world. If she were to use it, she would immediately receive harsh critique from her fellow feminist theologians for generalizing and homogenizing the extreme diversity of feminist theologies in North America.

We should therefore ask, Who is homogenizing? and What discursive connotation does it have? When those who have a discursive hegemonic power practice homogenization, they are practicing a form of *neo-orientalism*. It is a type of re-forming and distribution of geographical awareness into theological texts: "It not only creates but also maintains; it *is*, rather than expresses, a certain *will* or *intention* to understand, in some cases to control. . . . what is a manifestly different world."[45] When I am asked to speak as an Asian woman, I am aware that this can be both complimentary and complementary, leaving a serious lack behind to be filled. This makes me feel I am special in the sense that I should/must be different from those who make this request. However, in the process of tokenizing, homogenizing, and eventually ghettoizing, the multiple I's disappear. There remains only the mark of the plural—the collective identity.

Discursive hegemony is extremely subtle, much more pernicious than blatant discrimination and colonization. Claiming a collective identity is a necessary process for the once-discriminated-against to politicize themselves. But when those who have discursive power re-form the collective identity, it is a way of practicing discursive hegemonic power. Power, according to Michel Foucault, constructs a pastoral regime through which it seeks to control its subjects by re-forming them, and the key instrument of power is knowledge. Discourse, as in discourse *on* Asian feminist theology by Western feminist theologians like Ruether, "produces reality; it produces domains of objects and rituals of truth."[46] As Edward Said contends, the regime of disciplinary power inscribed in orientalism transforms the real East into a discursive Orient. When I read the chapter on Asian feminist theologies in *Women and Redemption*, I felt that the *real* me had been re-formed into the *discursive* me—Asian/Korean women, the plural, lacking my physicality, historicity, and personality as an individual. In explaining what *Han* is, Ruether

45. Said, *Orientalism*, 12.
46. Michel Foucault, *Discipline and Punish: The Birth of the Prison*, trans. Alan Sheridan (Harmondsworth, UK: Peregrine, 1979), 194.

explains, citing from Korean *minjung* theology: "Han is not simply the experiences of individuals. It is collective and transmitted from generation to generation."[47] In this homogenized discourse on Asian feminist theology, I, as an Asian woman, hardly feel she fairly/ properly represents me, an Asian woman. She chooses what parts she wants to hear, and she chooses what she does with that material, and she then thinks she has covered the issue. She doesn't seem to apply her critical analysis to this universal claim about the so-called Korean women's experience in general. Instead, she capitalizes the word *Han*—usually lowercased—which suggests that she does not question whether her notion of *Han* is really as comprehensive as some theologians claim.

In this context, Ruether's notion of *Han* and its description in relation to Korean women's experience in general romanticize and essentialize Korean women's experience, as if historical change and dynamics do not matter to Korean women's everyday lives. Even though I am well aware of Korean women's experience under the patriarchal system and institutions in Korea, I could not and would not claim that I am a *han*-ridden person and that the previous generation has transmitted the *han* to me, simply on the ground of my being a Korean woman. As is true of other women in the world, various life conditions, such as economic status, educational/religious background, professional and marital status, divide Korean women. Korean women are not just pure victims—*han*-ridden people. They can be both victims in one sense and victimizers in another. Such a thing as Korean/Asian women's *Han*-in-general is impossible to capture. Furthermore, one cannot transmit Korean women's suffering or anger or sorrow from generation to generation because suffering or anger is always context-specific and a historical product

47. Ruether, *Women and Redemption*, 270.

of one's specific time and location. Claiming *Han* as Korean women's collective experience is, in a way, a product of fictive ethnicity—an invention of ethnicity. It may sound very exotic and interesting for Westerners, but it does not convey or represent what the *real* Asian/Korean women of today are. Instead, it produces and reinforces the false assumption that the meaning of gender identity and the experience of sexism are the same for all Korean/Asian women as women, and the false assumption that gender identity exists in isolation from class, sexuality, race, ability, religion, and so forth. Even within a single society like Korea, not to mention Asia generally, the definitions, expectations, and experiences of what it means to be a woman vary tremendously. The experience of sexism by female factory owners, for instance, cannot be the same as the experience of female factory workers. Gender identity deeply intermingles with other kind of identities.

Just as one can never univocally define women, one can never univocally define Asian due to its cultural, political, economic, societal, and religious diversities. Asia is utterly hybrid/heterogeneous and never can be homogeneous. Either undervaluing/devaluing or overvaluing Asia distorts the real Asia. Claiming one's identity only in differential, claimed by either Asians themselves or non-Asians, essentializes the multiple/hybrid identities of Asia and the West through a binarism of representations in the realm of stereotype, with the aim of fixating the sense of difference between Western and Asian parts of the world. Trinh Minh-ha rightly points out that

> . . . difference as uniqueness or special identity is both limiting and deceiving. If identity refers to the whole pattern of sameness within a human life, the style of a continuing me that permeates all the changes undergone, then difference remains within the boundary of that which distinguishes one identity from another . . . claiming a female/ethnic identity/difference is commonly tantamount to reviving a kind of naïve "male-tinted" romanticism.[48]

The dilemma of "speaking as" lies in the fact that when it is practiced by the marginalized themselves, it might have an effect of making their voices heard, but when dominant people, hegemonic people strongly expect this practice, it becomes a process of generalizing, homogenizing, and tokenizing oneself. Moreover, it becomes a process of distancing from oneself, for one has to make oneself a representative. When people ask Asian women to present themselves *as* Asian-women theologians, people usually expect them to present Asian ancient folklore, rites, shamanistic symbols and rituals, dance, emotional *han*-ridden storytelling. Otherwise, they don't listen because it bores them. Fellow Asians also accuse us of being Westernized. We have to be born and continuously to live only in the past. However, "like it or not, the past can in no way guide me in the present moment," and we Asian theologians, whether by choice or by discursive force, are becoming more and more "the slave of the past"[49] in the name of indigenization, of self-identity, of multiculturalism, of celebrating/respecting difference. We are more and more frozen into the past because *we*-the East are/must be different from *them*-the West.

People frequently ask why I don't do Korean/Asian feminist theology but do just feminist theology when I teach or deliver a lecture. The major reason for such a question is the fact that I don't adopt Asian folklore and ancient or exotic stories into my theological construction but deal with the current issues that Korean/Asian women face. For those who ask such questions, the *real* Korean/Asian theology should have something to do with the past—the premodern era, not with the twenty-first century. Surprisingly, for many people, either Asians or non-Asians, they solely relate something genuine/ authentic Korean/Asian to the unpolluted past—the past that remains

48. Trinh, *Woman Native Other*, 95–96.
49. Franz Fanon, *Black Skin, White Masks* (New York: Grove Press, 1952), 225.

intact from Western influence. However, like it or not, no such unpolluted, unspoiled, past exists. It seems also improper when non-Western women's stories become the means for Western feminist theologians, even well-meaning ones, to cover their own academic works, thus extending their academic authority to transnational contexts. A problem of representation deals with whether one can truly represent less privileged others. As Spivak contends, the authentic feelings of the subaltern once named will be misrepresented, because of the multiple mediations of more powerful groups and institutions, both local and global. The privileged must unlearn one's privilege, "[so] that, not only does one become able to listen to that other constituency, but one learns to speak in such a way that one will be taken seriously by that other constituency."[50]

Asia as Theopolitical Imagination:
Feminist Hybridized Intersubjectivity in the Third Space

If we criticize orientalism for its universalizing overtones, then the idea of Asia as a distinct historical entity is itself the other side of orientalism. It is a bitter truth that today Asia does not stand outside the West. Even the so-called Asianness is already implicated in the ubiquitous West. Orientalism and particularism like nativism are two sides of the same coin, and one cannot criticize one without criticizing the other. The nativist use of culture leads to what Spivak calls a "new culturalist alibi,"[51] by which some seek to avoid the pitfalls of the earlier orientalism simply by particularizing their inquiries as meticulously as possible by way of class, gender, race, nation, and geographical locale. One can see this nativist attitude in

50. Spivak, "Strategy, Identity, Writing," in Harasym, ed., *The Post-colonial Critic*, 42.
51. Spivak, "Who Claims Alterity?," 281.

term constructions in English writings such as *Han, Han-pu-ri,* or *minjung.* The use of "Korean" as a specifier signals a new kind of care and a new kind of attentiveness to the discursive imperatives of cultural pluralism. In the name of investigating "theological/cultural difference" from the West, these vernacular terms such as "Korean" in English writings easily become a method of differentiation that precisely blocks criticism from its critical task. A scholarly nativism that functions squarely within the orientalist dynamic and that continues to imprison other cultures within entirely conventional disciplinary boundaries thus remains intact. It is clear that a postcolonial position alone does not guarantee that we can or will convey the truth.

Being most recently associated with the work of Homi K. Bhabha, the term *hybridity* helps us Asians to overcome the exoticism of cultural identity. Bhabha argues that people construct all cultural statements and systems in a space that he calls the "Third Space of enunciation."[52] Bhabha contends: "It is significant that the productive capacities of this Third Space have a colonial or postcolonial provenance. For a willingness to descend into that alien territory . . . may open the way to conceptualizing an *inter*national culture, based not on the exoticism of multiculturalism or the *diversity* of cultures, but on the inscription and articulation of culture's *hybridity.*"[53] Here, the Third Space is not a fixed space, but an indeterminate one, which occurs with cultural hybridity. All forms of culture are, Bhabha points out, continually in a process of hybridity, and hybridity is the Third Space that enables other positions to emerge. It seems very useful to employ Bhabha's notion of hybridity in Asian theologians' search for an identity as Asian because "the process of cultural hybridity gives rise to something different, something new and unrecognizable, a

52. Homi K. Bhabha, *The Location of Culture* (New York: Routledge, 2006 [1994]), 37.
53. Ibid., 38.

new area of negotiation of meaning and representation."[54] One can resituate the monolithic categories of gender, class, race, sexuality, or ethnicity in terms of borderline crossings, and in-between spaces—the Third Space of hybridity. The Third Space as an extended concept of hybridity and, as the chosen marginality, is a space of resistance in the postcolonial world, as well as a strategy that will reinscribe the past culture and other neighboring culture. Much of Asian theological discourse has been about Asia as a distinct territory with a distinct history. This type of discourse is, I would argue, geographically deterministic and hence culturally essentialist.

We have moved into a new period of theological reflection. A large number of theologians adopt and create various methods and diverse programs in doing theology today. People also experience a drastic change in the Asian context, which is quite different from the past industrial age. We have entered the Internet age, in which geographical borders are blurred and the confluence of cultures is a daily reality. Discourses such as postcolonialism, postmodernism, and feminism, furthermore, began to single out grand narrativity, a reorientalizing tendency, and a patriarchal ethos within Asian theological discourse, and to present the importance of local narratives, postpatriarchality, and the hybridity of Asianness in Asian theological discourse. Postcolonialism and feminism are methodologically useful for creating conditions for cross-cutting coalitions that challenge totalizing discourses in the name of culture, race, ethnicity, and nation in Asian theological construction. The new situation is cross-cultural, multiple, and hybrid. It pulls theologians in a new direction for constructing Asian theology that reflects the current situation. Thus, exploring the continuity and discontinuity of the new situation relative to the old means that

---

54. Homi K. Bhabha, ed., *Nation and Narration* (New York: Routledge, 1990), 211.

we must also articulate the implications of this exploration for constructing Asian theological discourse today. In this process, one should note what Edward Said relevantly remarks, "All cultures are involved in one another; none is single and pure, all are hybrid, heterogeneous, extraordinarily differentiated, and unmonolithic . . ."[55] He continues,

> No one today is purely one thing. Labels like Indian, or woman, or Muslim, an American are not more than starting points. . . . Imperialism consolidated the mixture of cultures and identities on a global scale. But its worst and most paradoxical gift was to allow people to believe that they were only, mainly, exclusively, white, or Black, or Western, or Oriental. . . . but there seems no reason except fear and prejudices to keep insisting on their separation and distinctiveness, as if that was all human life was about. Survival in fact is about the connections between things.[56]

It is clear today that whatever isolates itself—whether Asian theology or Western theology—petrifies, and whatever petrifies dies. Theologians and scholars often disguise orientalist dualism as an empirical generalization, but in fact it is a transcendental scheme for interpreting data that justifies the observer in disregarding any counterexample as a meaningless anomaly and thus blinds one to the internal diversity and dynamic potential. It is an epistemological device for guaranteeing Western hegemony over Asia. Although both Asians and Westerners are not free from the spell of orientalism, as we have seen, one can say that Asians might be in a better position to break it, because it is easier for the targets of stereotypes to destroy them than for their perpetrators. By breaking this spell of orientalism and neo-orientalism, Asian theologies can communicate that the West no more can be complacent about its own record in constructing theology today.

55. Edward W. Said, *Culture and Imperialism* (New York: Vintage, 1993), xxv.
56. Ibid., 336.

Asian theologians today face an inevitable question: Will Asian theology be recognizable on a global context if it doesn't talk about Asian "as Asian," if it doesn't focus on essentialized ethnic identity in isolation from the other elements of identity, and if it doesn't try to describe the situation of Asians in general? Although this question is difficult to answer, theologians have to struggle regarding the definition of Asian or to grapple with the significance of differences/similarities among Asians and between Asia and the West. When such struggles come to constitute Asian theological discourse, theological discourses will thrive on such struggles. Through these struggles, Asian theology with a postcolonial perspective will create conditions for cross-cutting coalitions that challenge totalizing discourse in the name of culture, race, ethnicity, and nation. Postcolonial theological anthropology must reject the search for the unchanging, culturally essential core of Asians/Asianness. The hybrid self, decentering any foundational notion of Asian, can be a Christian ideal of losing oneself to find oneself. Then in a postcolonial approach to Asian theology, the question, *What is the Asian?* yields to the question, *Who is the Asian?* While the *What* question is the search for the unchanging, essential core of the Asian, the *Who* question is the search for the ever-changing nature of the Asian as the hybrid, decentered, multiple selves. This postcolonial theological anthropology will invite us to live in critical and radical openness to the cultural hybridity of our time, and to have a constant sensitivity to the other in various forms, not reducing the other to the totality of the same in a hybridized intersubjectivity that invites us to a *Third Space* of alliances and solidarity with both the close and distant others.

4

———

Radical Border-Traversing

Postcolonial Feminist Theology

The subaltern as female is even more deeply in shadow.
—Gayatri Chakravorty Spivak[1]

The task facing the Christian world today is the recovery of its universalizing function without any colonial, imperialist, or Eurocentric implications.
—Gianni Vattimo[2]

All culture is originarily colonial. . . . Every culture institutes itself through the unilateral imposition of some "politics" of language. Mastery begins . . . through the power of naming, of imposing and legitimating appellations.
—Jacques Derrida[3]

1. Gayatri Chakravorty Spivak, "Can the Subaltern Speak?," in *Colonial Discourse and Post-colonial Theory: A Reader*, ed. Patrick Williams and Laura Chrisman (New York: Columbia University Press, 1994), 83.
2. Gianni Vattimo, *After Christianity*, trans. Luca D'Isanto (New York: Columbia University Press, 2002), 101.
3. Jacques Derrida, *Monolingualism of the Other; or, The Prosthesis of Origin*, trans. Patrick Mensah, (Stanford: Stanford University Press, 1998), 39.

Colonialism under Disguise

Postcolonialism has emerged as one of the major critical discourses in academia since its development in the 1980s. Defining postcolonialism is, however, not easy due to its complexity and the variety of its implications. Postcolonial scholars tend to split over the question as to whether postcolonialism implies certain *historicality*, pertaining to a specific time and space, or if it entails *transhistoricality*.[4] That scholars write the term in two ways, *post-colonialism* and *postcolonialism*, further reveals the multiple understandings and perceptions of postcolonialism itself.[5] Some scholars use the two terms interchangeably without making a distinction between them. Scholars who emphasize the historical, chronological aspect of postcolonial discourse hyphenate the words, whereas those who wish to denote the transhistoricality of postcolonial discourse use the unhyphenated spelling. Some, especially political scientists and economists, use the hyphenated version to refer to the period after colonialism. Others, since the late 1970s, have adopted the unhyphenated spelling to indicate still more wide-ranging understandings.[6] I use postcolonialism without the hyphen because I do not heavily rely on a chronological implication of colonialism, but do adopt it as a critical discourse of resistance and liberation in various realms of reality.

The usage of *postcolonialism* that I adopt here is "the discourse of oppositionality which colonialism brings into being,"[7] and it

---

4. One can see these two different positions of postcolonial scholars in such collections of essays on postcolonialism as Bill Ashcroft, Gareth Griffiths, and Helen Tiffin, eds., *The Post-Colonial Studies Reader* (New York: Routledge, 1995).

5. Bill Ashcroft, Gareth Griffiths, and Helen Tiffin, eds., *Key Concepts in Post-colonial Studies:* (New York: Routledge, 1998), 186–92.

6. Ibid.

7. "Postmodernism and Post-colonialism: Introduction," in Ashcroft, et al., eds., *Post-Colonial Studies Reader*, 117.

functions as the discourse of critical resistance to and liberation from colonial confinement and oppression. *Colonialism* or *colonial mentality* is about various kinds of socio-political, economic, symbolic, or religious oppression, domination, power, and control, which do not necessarily pertain to a specific historical context. Although postcolonial scholars often base their discourses primarily in the specific historical context of Western colonialism and imperialism, the postcolonialism that I employ, as a discursive analytical tool, entails *transhistoricality* in that it does not refer only to specific *historicality*, without excluding it. One can say that postcolonialism as a concept is "like the concept of patriarchy in feminism"[8]—a *universal* concept, although one's experience of patriarchy varies according to one's socio-cultural and historical location.

Postcolonial discourse offers a critical analytical tool to dismantle implicit or explicit colonial mentality and practice. Therefore, scholars and practitioners in various disciplines adopt postcolonial discourse to deal with issues such as representation, identity, migration, oppression and resistance, difference, race, gender, place, and responses to the grand discourses of the imperial West such as theology, philosophy, history, linguistics, and so forth.[9] Postcolonial perspective offers an analytical lens through which to approach issues of power, domination and subjugation, or marginalization and resistance in a critically sophisticated way, which is extremely significant for creating an alternative world of justice, equality, and peace for all living beings. Furthermore, postcolonial discourses, along with feminist and postmodern discourses, help people see the tyranny of the colonial mentality of domination and control. Colonial mentality runs through interpersonal relations, international

8. Stephen Slemon, "The Scramble for Post-colonialism," in Ashcroft, et al., eds., *Post-Colonial Studies Reader*, 50.
9. Cf. "General Introduction," in Ashcroft, et al., eds., *Post-Colonial Studies Reader*, 1–11.

or intercontinental relations, or interreligious relations. People can construct, legitimize, justify, perpetuate, and disseminate the colonial mentality with the logic of domination based on one's gender, race and ethnicity, class, age, religion, birth origin, sexuality, nationality, citizenship, familial or educational background, physical or mental ability, and so forth.

Ashis Nandy contends that the carriers of "the second wave of colonialism," such as Christian, humanitarian, social, and medical missions, "were people who, unlike the rapacious first generation of bandit-kings who conquered the colonies, sought to be helpful," and those carriers of the second wave of colonialism were "well-meaning, hard-working, middle-class missionaries, liberals, modernists, and believers in science, equality and progress," yet, they "released forces within the colonized societies to alter their cultural priorities once and for all."[10] Christian missionaries were and still mostly play the role of well-meaning carriers of the second wave of colonialism and look like what Albert Memmi describes:

> We sometimes enjoy picturing the colonizer as a tall man, bronzed by the sun, wearing Wellington boots, proudly leaning on a shovel—as he rivets his gaze far away on the horizon of his land. When not engaged in battles against nature, we think of him laboring selflessly for mankind [sic], attending the sick, and spreading culture to the nonliterate. In other words, his pose is one of a noble adventurer, a righteous pioneer.[11]

The reason we still concern ourselves about colonialism and its residue in theological discourse and practice when the era of colonialism seems over is that the colonial mentality resides in the very act of well-meaning mission, charity, or philanthropy. Even though the modern form of colonialism, which required a territorial

10. Ashis Nandy, *The Intimate Enemy: Loss and Recovery of Self Under Colonialism* (New York: Oxford University Press, 1988), x–xi.
11. Albert Memmi, *The Colonizer and the Colonized* (Boston: Beacon, 1967), 3.

occupation by the colonizer, mostly ended after the Second World War, a new form of colonialism, a *neocolonialism*, has emerged and permeates every sector of our life in the world, without having to invade the colony's physical territory. In this sense, the neocolonialism that people experience today is formless, forceless, and thereby invisible. The residue of colonialism strongly influences the construction of theological discourses and praxes, education, language, culture, geopolitics and economy, and so forth. As long as people try to patronize, dominate, and control others, whether on the basis of gender, race and ethnicity, sexuality, religion, nationality and citizenship, age, or social class, the colonial mentality permeates and operates in the very well-meaning act. Therefore, I adopt the notion of colonial mentality in a critically broad way in terms of its application and connotation in the life of Christianity, as it involves not only a socio- or geopolitical realm but also an interpersonal, institutional, or theological realm of discourse and practice.

Through the very act of naming, the construction of the colonized other becomes materialized. According to Memmi, the colonizer always perceives the colonized as *not*, that is, as lacking the qualities the colonizer possesses.[12] In this sense, the term "the *non-West*" exemplifies how the West becomes placed discursively and politically at the center and the non-West on the periphery, perceived as *not*. One can apply the dichotomous distinction of *A* and *Not-A* to various sociopolitical relations of gender, race, religion, or sexuality, and "all dichotomous distinctions are not necessarily phrased as A/Not-A."[13] The problem in this dichotomous distinction between the West (A) and the non-West (Not-A) is that it portrays the non-West as the lesser West.

---

12. Ibid., 83.
13. Nancy Jay, "Gender and Dichotomy," *Feminist Studies* 7, no. 1 (Spring 1981): 44.

If I apply the A and Not-A distinction as Asia and non-Asia to denote the entire world, as in the West and the non-West, the political implication of the power differential between Asia and Non-Asia does not have the same effect with the West and the non-West. In mission discourse and practice, such dichotomous distinction as Christians and non-Christians precisely captures the implication of the dichotomous distinction of A and Not-A. It renders non-Christians as those who are lacking some valued qualities that Christians have and therefore they become lesser human beings. The very naming of the religious neighbors as non-Christians perpetuates a Christian-centric worldview and resembles the colonial mentality of superiority over the colonized other. Constructing a postcolonial mission in the contemporary world requires a fundamental change in the language that the Christian mission discourse has uncritically adopted and used. The non-Christians are simply the religious neighbors in the faith journey. Therefore, it is extremely important critically and constantly to create alternatives to the colonial way of naming and constructing the other.

In the eyes of the Christian missionaries, the religious and cultural others in the non-Western countries are an anonymous collectivity, carrying the mark of the plural.[14] In this context, Jean-Paul Sartre states, "the European has only been able to become a man [sic] through creating slaves and monsters," who belong to a "race of less-than-humans."[15] Revisiting the history of Christian discourse and practice from a postcolonial feminist perspective requires scrutinizing colonial mentality and practice because the initial Christian missionary movement in world Christianity cannot separate itself from compliance with the European colonialism and its mindset.

14. Memmi, *Colonizer and the Colonized*, 85.
15. Jean-Paul Sartre, "Preface," in Franz Fanon, *The Wretched of the Earth*, trans. Constance Farrington (New York: Grove Weidenfeld, 1963), 26.

In this context, how Christianity would respond to the following remarks by Franz Fanon is a theopolitical matter: "The well-being and the progress of Europe have been built up with the sweat and the dead bodies of Negroes, Arabs, Indians, and the yellow races. . . . Europe is literally the creation of the Third World. The wealth which smothers her is that which was stolen from the underdeveloped peoples."[16]

One cannot dissociate the history of colonialism in the West from the history of global design in Christianity. Walter Mignolo contends, "the global design of Christianity was part of the European Renaissance and was constitutive of modernity and of its darker side, coloniality."[17] However, I do not limit my use of postcolonial discourse to such a historically specific context. Whereas the use of postcolonialism as a historical discourse takes primarily a specific historico-political context as its discursive ground, the adoption of postcolonialism as a transhistorical discourse does not limit itself to a specific historical context of colonization. Postcolonialism as a transhistorical discourse and practice intends to move beyond the colonialism in its multiple forms and continues to remain relevant in analyzing multiple, complex contexts of domination and subjugation, and power and knowledge, which are indivisible from and irreducible to one another. Although the specific historical context of colonialism can function as a significant reference, my use of postcolonialism as a transhistorical discourse and movement requires moving beyond the historical specificity of colonialism, "like the concept of patriarchy in feminism,"[18] though not precluding it. The *post* in postcolonialism here therefore signifies not a chronological "after" but, rather, a critical, resistant "beyond." The beyondness

---

16. Fanon, *Wretched of the Earth*, 96, 102.
17. Walter Mignolo, "The Many Faces of Cosmo-polis: Border Thinking and Critical Cosmopolitanism," *Public Culture* 12, no. 3 (Fall 2000): 722.
18. Slemon, "Scramble for Post-colonialism," 50.

embodies, Homi Bhabha argues, "its restless and revisionary energy."[19]

Postcolonial discourse makes it clear that one can no longer so easily position the old, simplistic binary of men–women, the West–the Rest, white–color, rich–poor, right–left, or center–margin in terms of oppressor–oppressed, victimizer–victim, or colonizer–colonized due to the intersecting, complex nature of various forms of oppression and discrimination. Today, the issue of marginalization and oppression is becoming more and more complex and disputatious than ever. The complex and elusive nature of the two poles—the *center-colonizer-oppressor* and the *margin-colonized-oppressed*—requires one to deconstruct the problematic binary of center and margin, colonizer and colonized, inclusion and exclusion, powerful and powerless based on rigid lines of gender, race, class, sexuality, and so forth.

Nowadays, it is hard to pinpoint who "we" and "they" are because of the entanglement of the axes of oppression and colonization. The "we" as a singular-monolithic identity becomes impossible, problematic, and even dangerous because it tends to distort re/presentations of we-ness. For a singular-monolithic identity, whether individual or collective, cannot capture the heterogeneous and heteronomous intersectionality of gender, race, ethnicity, class, sexuality, ability, nationality, citizenship, religion, and so forth. We are living in a world where the center, the colonizer, the oppressor is often invisible and disguised. Utilizing the discourses of postcolonialism and feminism helps one become aware of the multiple axes of colonization and oppression. Furthermore, postcolonialism and feminism bring the geopolitical axis into sharp focus on hypersensitivity not only to ethnocentrism and geocentrism

---

19. Homi K. Bhabha, *The Location of Culture* (New York: Routledge, 2006 [1994]), 6.

but also to androcentrism and heterocentrism in politics, economics, cultures, and theological and religious discourses and practices.

Entanglement of Colonialism, Gender, and Religion

Generally speaking, colonialism or colonial mentality is about power and ruling, and thereby about domination and subjugation. The colonial mentality is firmly grounded on the logic of power and domination. Christians have perceived Christianity in an exclusive way as the only true religion in the world and portray God as the Emperor of the world. Theopolitically speaking, how one perceives God provides a ground for Christians' self-understanding in the world. In this sense, Christian theological construction of God as, for instance, Father, Lord, or King conveys the colonial image of an Emperor with an untouchable absolute authority. For those who perceive God in an exclusive, militant, hierarchical way, Christian mission always means dominating and colonizing the religious or cultural others and the heathen in foreign land. As well, within this paradigm it is inevitable that Jesus Christ also be seen as King or Emperor of the world because he is the very incarnation of God.

Although Christians have claimed that God is beyond human attributions such as gender, race, sexuality, or age and beyond human comprehension, it is hard to deny that people shape and mediate the symbol for God by the values inherent in a social matrix, in which the values of patriarchy, hierarchy, or colonial mentality prevail. As Paul Tillich posits, "God is a symbol for God."[20] However, some Christian theologians and practitioners confuse symbol with fact, and use the masculine symbol for God as a divine ground for men's superiority over women. After analyzing 328 hymns, Brian Wren concluded:

20. Paul Tillich, *Dynamics of Faith* (New York: Harper & Brothers, 1957), 46.

> If male and female humans were really believed to be created as an equal partnership in the divine image, one would expect to find both feminine and masculine pronouns chosen for divine action. This is not so. In the 177 texts carrying pronouns, there are 1,423 pronouns for the divine. One is neuter, none are feminine, and 1,422 are masculine. . . . We know that human languages (like our own) draw on the experience of their speakers and blow powerful uprights or downrights on thought and behavior. The fact that the genderless Trinity is prayed to and depicted in exclusively male images and pronouns must give humans a hooded or one-eyed vision of God.[21]

The literal and factual association of God with maleness has prevailed in Christian tradition and churches and it has bequeathed a distorted perception of God as male.

Furthermore, the problematic notion of God is not exclusively gender related, but also *race* related. In the history of Christianity, people have conceived God not only as male, but also as white. In her novel *The Color Purple*, womanist writer Alice Walker depicts a black woman who perceives God as male, white, and old, even when she has suffered her entire life from the oppression of white and males:

> Tell me what God look like, Celie. . . . *He* big and *old* and tall and graybeard and *white*. *He* wear white robes and go barefooted. Blu eyes? She ast. Soft of bluish-gray. Cool. Big though. White lashes, I say. . . . Then she tell me this *old white man* is the same God in church, Celie, she say, that's who is bound to show up, cause that's where *he* live. . . . When I found out I thought God was white, and a man, I lost interest.[22]

This exchange of "God-talk" between two black women reveals how the perception of God that many people usually have is not divinely given but, rather, has been shaped in the image of those who have

---

21. Brian Wren, *What Language Shall I Borrow? God-Talk in Worship: A Male Response to Feminist Theology* (New York: Crossroad, 1991), 118.

22. Alice Walker, *The Color Purple* (London: The Women's Press, 1983 [1982]), 165–66 (italics mine).

"power," reflecting the sociocultural milieu and value systems in which they are located and positioned.

The perception of God as male, white, and King is too easily compatible with sexism, racism, and imperialism, which has formed a conceptual framework of Christian colonial mentality of various types. In this sense, Christianity as a missionary religion "has legitimated the exploitation and dehumanization of colonialism and imperialism, i.e. through the portrayal of an all-knowing, all-seeing, bearded, white, male deity 'from far'" and some churches "have largely ignored social issues in order to proclaim a white, male, supremacist deity who offers eternal life in the next world."[23] If one portrays God in an anthropomorphic way, that is, depicts God's gender as male or God's race as white, then one has to answer to question, What then would be God's sexuality—heterosexual, homosexual, bisexual, transgender, or transsexual?

Needless to say, the anthropomorphic construction of the knowledge of God has been closely linked to power, and power and knowledge are two indivisible foundations of colonial mentality. Constructing theological discourses that justify and perpetuate the superiorism and expansionism of the colonizer and dissemination of the colonizer's religion, culture, language, literature, education, or customs is the foundation of maintaining the colonial power. As Michel Foucault rightly points out, the centers of power and knowledge overlap, and "truth isn't outside power or lacking power."[24] When theological discourse resides in the colonial mentality of domination and control on various grounds, Christian doctrines and institutions establish their authority through their differentiation of religious identity from non-Christians, and then

---

23. Leo G. Perdue, *Reconstructing Old Testament Theology: After the Collapse of History* (Minneapolis: Fortress Press, 2005), 280, 281.
24. Michel Foucault, *Power/Knowledge: Selected Interviews and Other Writings 1972–1977*, ed. Colin Gordon, trans. Colin Gordon, et al. (New York: Pantheon, 1980 [1972]), 131.

Christians use their religious difference to legitimize their own superior position and colonial mentality in the world.

When the dominant knowledge about God takes a form of superiority of one group over the other, whether based on gender, culture, race, sexuality, or religion, power as a dominating and controlling force emerges and operates in every aspect of Christian theological discourse and practice. The dominant Christian doctrines and practices have silenced the voices of the powerless and the marginalized. In this sense, the main task of postcolonial feminist theology today is "to listen to the voices of those who are silent and silenced" in the Bible, in the church, and in society, such as the poor, the uneducated, women, racial others, religious others, or sexual others (lesbian, gay, bisexual, transgender, and so forth) and "to take that experience, that life, that story, as a crucial source for reflection."[25]

Here, the inextricable interconnection of the issues of gender and colonialism with religion becomes obvious. Religion, colonialism, and gender are critical sites where domination and subjugation, and power asymmetry take place in the world today. People often use the binaries of the colonizer–the colonized or domination–subjugation to analyze the power differential between male and female, and others also use religion as a sacred sanction of such a power asymmetry. In this sense, one can use gender as a metaphor for the colonial power differential and asymmetries in terms of domination and subjugation. Feminist scholars often criticize male postcolonial theorists for their failure to address gender issues in their theoretical offerings. At the same time, feminists in the West often exercise the colonial paradigm of domination and subjugation in relation to Third-World women,

---

25. Steve de Gruchy, "Human Being in Christ: Resources for an Inclusive Anthropology," in *Aliens in the Household of God: Homosexuality and Christian Faith in South Africa*, ed. Paul Germond and Steve de Gruchy (Cape Town: David Philip, 1997), 235.

albeit with good intentions. Postcolonialism as a transhistorical discourse reveals how *discursive colonization* functions as a process of "discursive homogenization and systematization of the oppression of women in the third world that power is exercised in much of recent Western feminist discourse."[26]

Since one experiences multiple axes of oppression and colonization in one's reality, one must acknowledge that the center of the imperial powers is often invisible and elusive and that one must resist any simplistic binary definition of who the colonizer, the privileged, the oppressor is, especially when women from the global South are standing at the crossroads of gender, race, ethnicity, class, sexuality, and nation. Postcolonialism and feminism offer significant discursive tools with which one can critically analyze how oppression by the multiple imperial and colonizing powers affects the concrete lives of the colonized—the minority groups. A monolithic, simple classification can use different names to hide, or make invisible, the colonial center since one can be in a position of power/privilege due to one's economic position while remaining marginal because of one's race, sexuality, ability, or gender. The following reveals the complexity of power privilege and the intersectionality of gender, race and ethnicity, class, and nation:

> Not all Third World women are "women of color"—if by this concept we mean exclusively "non-white." And not all women of color are really Third World—if this term is used in reference to underdeveloped or developing societies. . . . Yet if we extend the concept of Third World to include internally "colonised" racial and ethnic minority groups in this country, so many different kinds of groups could conceivably be included, that the crucial issue of social and institutional racism and its historic tie to slavery in the U.S. could get diluted, lost in the shuffle. . . . Things begin to get even more complicated when I begin to

26. Chandra Talpade Mohanty, "Under Western Eyes: Feminist Scholarship and Colonial Discourses," in *Third World Women and the Politics of Feminism*, ed. Chandra Talpade Mohanty, Ann Russo, and Lourdes Torres (Bloomington: Indiana University Press, 1991), 54.

consider that many of us who identify as "Third World" or "Women of Color," have grown up as or are fast becoming "middle class" and highly educated, and therefore more privileged than many of our white, poor, working class sisters.[27]

The colonizer, as the knowing subject, has produced, institutionalized, disseminated, and archived knowledge in a way that makes the West—the global North, the male, Christians, middle-class, English-speaking, heterosexual—as the norm and the center of the world. From both postcolonial and feminist theories, one can surface the epistemological limits of the Euro/US-centric view in Western feminist scholarship and the androcentric view in the postcolonial discourses of male scholars in raising the voices of Third-World women, the colonized, minority groups on various grounds. Chandra T. Mohanty, for instance, critically points out, "Western feminist writing on women in the third world must be considered in the context of the global hegemony of Western scholarship—i.e., the production, publication, distribution, and consumption of information and ideas."[28]

Postcolonialism and feminism, as theological analytical tools, offer strategies of resistance to and critique of imperial powers of state, geopolitics, socioculture, and of various communities of believers as to how they have justified, perpetuated, and sacralized the oppressions through their theologies, doctrines, and institutional systems, and how power can complicate religion. At the same time, postcolonial and feminist discourses also scrutinize how the marginalized, oppressed, colonized people come to internalize the oppressive values and systems and often give their consent to such hegemonic colonial powers. In this sense, liberation from colonial powers in multiple

27. Mirthat Quintanales, "I Paid Very Hard for My Immigrant Ignorance," in *This Bridge Called My Back: Writings by Radical Women of Color*, ed. Cherrie Moraga and Gloria Anzaldua (New York: Kitchen Table, Women of Color Press, 1983), 151.
28. Mohanty, "Under Western Eyes," 55.

forms should begin both internally and externally and require not only the change of the objective condition but also the transformation of the subjectivity of the colonized/marginalized themselves through a theological "pedagogy of the oppressed."[29] Postcolonial feminist discourse therefore questions and interrogates cultural, theopolitical, discursive hegemony and its domination. The colonizing paradigm repeats itself through the discursive exercise of surveillance, otherization, homogenization, stereotypization, naturalization, classification, debasement, and the distorted idealization/romanticization of the colonized, women, or minority groups. However, resisting multiple forms of hegemonic systems of knowledge, thoughts, and symbolic power means not simply adopting a strategy of rigid binarism of the colonizer and colonized. Instead, postcolonial feminism challenges the colonial powers in multiple forms, and explores ambiguities, contradictions, intersectionalities, and paradoxes, because locating the center or the margin is as complex and elusive as ever today. The center from which people exercise colonizing powers seems to be in a hidden place.

Doing Theology with Discursive Tools of Postcolonialism and Feminism

Postcolonialism and feminism are discourses and practices of resistance to and liberation from various types of domination and subjugation, and are relevant, necessary, and useful analytical tools. As Gilles Deleuze says, "theory is exactly like a box of tools."[30]

---

29. Paulo Freire, *Pedagogy of the Oppressed*, 30th anniversary ed. (New York: Continuum, 2000).
30. Michel Foucault and Gilles Deleuze, "Intellectuals and Power: A Conversation between Michel Foucault and Gilles Deleuze," in Michel Foucault, *Language, Counter-Memory, Practice: Selected Essays and Interviews* (Ithaca: Cornell University Press, 1993 [1977]), 208.

Utilizing postcolonialism and feminism as analytical tools helps one construct theological discourse and practice with critical sensitivity to the issues of representation, identity, epistemic violence, intersectionality of gender, race, class, sexuality and its colonizing paradigms, power differential between differences, and so forth. I offer five key issues that postcolonial and feminist theological discourse must address.

First, postcolonial and feminist discourses must urge *the deconstruction of the Western construction of binary fixity.* One of the main critiques that both postcolonial and feminist discourse make is the modern construction of fixed, unified, and essentialized identity, whether it is the identity of the colonized, gender identity, racial and ethnic identity, or religious identity. The modern construction of identity as sameness, for instance, produces an exclusive binary of men–women, reason–emotion, normal–abnormal, pure–impure, subject–object, normative–deviant, spirit–body, we–they, heterosexual–homosexual, abled–disabled, human–nonhuman, civilized–primitive, Christian–non-Christian, First World–Third World, the West–the Rest, and so forth. Postcolonial and feminist discourses aim their deconstructive and critical glances "not specifically at the putative identity of the two poles in a binary opposition, but at the hidden ethico-political agenda that drives the differentiation between the two."[31]

No one can be just one thing, as in the unifying, fixed, and essentialized identity of both the colonizer and the colonized themselves. As Edward Said rightly points out, imperialism's "worst and most paradoxical gift, was to allow people to believe that they were only, mainly, exclusively, white or Black, or Western, or Oriental."[32] Colonial discourse depends on such fixity, Homi Bhabha

---

31. Gayatri Chakravorty Spivak, *Critique of Postcolonial Reason: Toward a History of the Vanishing Present* (Cambridge: Harvard University Press, 1999), 332.

contends, in its ideological construction of the others. As a result, fixity becomes the "sign of cultural/historical/racial difference in the discourse of colonialism" and "the major discursive strategy" of colonial discourse.[33]

Postcolonial and feminist identities move beyond this essentialized identity toward an identity of interstitial subjectivity, a hybrid identity, or a liminal identity that one provisionally builds in-between spaces of borderlands, crossroads, interstices. The in-between space is not only a space of critical resistance to the imperial powers but also a significant space of creative transformation and liberation from the colonizing systems and values. When the colonized/marginalized/oppressed people find their authentic identity not in a unified, fixed, essentialized space but in a space of multiple, contradicting, paradoxical, hybrid positions, possibilities, and potentialities, liberation as an event can take place. The metaphor of hybridity is also significant in Christianity because Christianity is grounded in the divine identity of hybridity: divine incarnation into Jesus Christ as the hybrid of both the divine and the human. The issue of the complex hybrid and hyphenated identity becomes significant and is emerging especially among the marginalized, oppressed, colonized, who are not in the mainstream. However, one must note that the emphasis on hybrid identity is not to celebrate blindly hybridity itself but to recognize hybridity as a significant space for resistance to the unitary fixity of colonial paradigm and discourse.

Second, one of the tasks of postcolonial and feminist theological discourse is *decentering (Euro/US) ethnocentrism, (global northern) geocentrism, androcentrism, and heterocentrism in the construction of theological power/knowledge.* I am not proposing, however, simply to reverse the positionality of the center by a "desire for postcolonial

32. Edward Said, *Culture and Imperialism* (New York: Vintage, 1993), 336.
33. Bhabha, *Location of Culture*, 94–95.

revenge"[34] or feminist revenge. Replacing Euro/US theological interlocutors with those from Asia, or male with female, for instance, does not mean decentering the colonizing center. Decentering these various forms of centrism would mean questioning theological norms and standards, regardless of the regional or biological origins of signifiers of such norms that inferiorize the power/knowledge of the other—racialized other, gendered other, sexualized other, and so on. Here I am not denying the reality that it is impossible to construct theological discourse anywhere in the world without engaging or invoking the intellectual genealogies and theological traditions of Europe. Such significant concepts as legal equality, sociopolitical justice, individual freedom, human rights, democracy, rationality, and so on have come from Europe.

Here, one must acknowledge that wherever one lives, one needs to engage the intellectual and theological tradition of Europe, affirmatively or critically, because "this [European] heritage is now global."[35] *Minjung* theology in Korea and liberation theology in Latin America, for instance, owe a great debt to Marxist thought from Europe, whereas feminist theologies and theories owe a debt to the Enlightenment legacy of freedom and equality of individual human beings, in spite of the epistemological and sociopolitical limits in the Enlightenment. The very vision of human beings in the theological and intellectual tradition of Europe laid the significant ground of theological discourse of justice and equality, although it has failed in practice through the colonization of the other, denying its own vision of humans as free and equal fellows. Franz Fanon, a postcolonial thinker, acknowledges that the Enlightenment idea of the human being has become a part of the universal, global heritage:

---

34. Leela Gandi, *Postcolonial Theory: An Introduction* (Sydney: Allen and Unwin, 1998), x.
35. Dipesh Chakrabarty, *Provincializing Europe: Postcolonial Thought and Historical Difference* (Princeton: Princeton University Press, 2000), 4.

"All the elements of a solution to the great problems of humanity have, at different times, existed in European thought. But the action of European men has not carried out the mission which fell to them. . . . Europe has done what she set out to do and on the whole she has done it well; let us stop blaming her."[36] As a non-Euro/ US philosopher-theologian, I, too, live, think, teach, or write from within and beyond this European heritage. Postcolonial and feminist theological scholarship engages the universals of justice, equality, freedom, human rights, but the universals that postcolonial and feminist theological scholarship invoke and recover are without any form of centrism, "without any colonial, imperialist, or Eurocentric implications."[37]

Third, postcolonial and feminist theological discourses should promote a *hypersensitivity to the marginalized*. Jesus' parable on the last judgment (Matt. 25:31-46) clearly indicates that being a person of faith requires a hypersensitivity to the marginalized, colonized, imprisoned, and the poor:

> The ruler will say to those on the right,
> 'Come, you blessed of my Abba God!
> Inherit the kindom prepared for you from the creation of the world!
>
> For I was hungry and you fed me;
> I was thirsty and you gave me drink;
> I was a stranger and you gave me no welcome;
> I was a stranger and you welcomed me;
> naked and you clothed me.
> I was ill and you comforted me;
> in prison and you came to visit me.
>
> . . . .
>
> The truth is, every time you did this

36. Fanon, *Wretched of the Earth*, 314.
37. Vattimo, *After Christianity*, 101.

for the least of my sisters and brothers,
you did it for me (Matt. 25:35-46, *The Inclusive Bible*).

Discerning who the hungry, the thirsty, the stranger, the naked, the sick, the imprisoned would be in the contemporary world of neoimperialism requires postcolonial, geopolitical, and feminist sensitivity. With a hypersensitivity to the marginalized, postcolonial and feminist theological discourses try to reinvent universals for and with the marginalized on various grounds. In this sense, what we need to do is think *with* and *beyond* the Euro-America characterized by a colonizing paradigm. Furthermore, utilizing the analytical tools of postcolonialism and feminism helps one to develop a double mode of seeing. The double mode of seeing is to place one's gaze not only upon the center but also upon the margin. The double mode of seeing helps one to see the asymmetric power-differential between people of difference and also to maintain one's hypersensitivity to the marginalized, and the sensitivity to the complexity and intersectionality of multiple forms of colonization.

Fourth, postcolonial and feminist theological discourses must seek *radical affirmation of the others, regardless*. Awareness of and claiming one's locations in the world play a constitutive function in shaping frames of theological reference within which we develop our projects not only in constructing our theological discourse but also positioning our institutional and religious affiliations, as well as the grain of daily life. One's locationality, whether socially ascribed or consciously achieved, becomes the site of one's intervention, questions, commitments, passion, and functions as the site of one's accountability and relevance, both personally and institutionally. Postcolonial and feminist discourses affirm that there are overlapping spaces between the seemingly oppositional two poles such as men–women, West–East, white–non-white, Christians–non-

Christians, heterosexual–homosexual, and so forth, despite the uneven relations and discrepant spaces of power and privilege. Affirming others as who or what they are is what religious discourse and practice must promote in every sector of human life, stimulating a theology of hospitality, responsibility, and solidarity.

Fifth, postcolonial and feminist theological discourses should construct theological discourses for *reinstating the colonized/ marginalized/oppressed in the imago Dei*. Postcolonial and feminist theology works within and against/beyond the religious heritage—scripture, tradition, doctrine, creed, and the like—to preserve the liberating heritage and at the same time deconstruct, dismantle, debunk the heritages that produce, perpetuate, justify, and sacralize imperial power over the grain of everyday life, both visibly and invisibly, internally and externally, personally and institutionally. The first creation story of Genesis lucidly declares the ontological equality of every being as the image of the divine. The ontological equality of every individual human being that Genesis reveals has no conditionality, no boundaries. Michel Foucault offers an interesting concept of international citizenship that in fact resembles the notion of the human being as *imago Dei* and can form the ground of shared citizenship of dignity, rights, justice, and equality. He contends: "There exists an *international citizenship* that has its rights and its duties and that obliges one to speak out against every abuse of power, whoever its author, whoever its victims. After all we are all members of the community of the governed, and thereby obliged to show *mutual solidarity*. . . . It is a duty of this *international citizenship*."[38]

Postcolonial and feminist theological discourses help one to fundamentally acknowledge that no gender, no ethnicity, no

---

38. Michel Foucault, "Confronting Governments: Human Rights," in *The Essential Foucault: Selections from Essential Works of Foucault 1954–1984*, ed. Paul Rabinow and Nikolas Rose (New York: New Press, 2003 [1994]), 64 (italics mine).

religion, or "no race possesses the monopoly of beauty, of intelligence, of force, and there is a place for all at the rendezvous of victory."[39] Changes are possible only when one questions the colonial paradigm, discourses, and powers through which colonial power has laid its foundation. Colonial authority and powers today are often grounded on invisibility and absence. As Fanon articulates:

> Decolonization never takes place unnoticed, for it influences individuals and modifies them fundamentally. It transforms spectators crushed with their inessentiality into privileged actors. . . . It brings a natural rhythm into existence, introduced by new men [sic], and with it a new language and a new humanity. . . . In decolonization, there is therefore the need of a complete calling in question of the colonial situation.[40]

Postcolonial and feminist resistance and liberation begin therefore with the very questioning of the invisible, unspoken, but omnipresent colonial centers of male, heterosexual, white normativity. Only then can theological discourse function to promote the reinstitution of the fundamental religious values of dignity, equality of every individual human being, and the power to resist any colonizing power of domination and possession.

Radical Border-Traversing

We are living in a world in which the power disparity between and among people of different groups still exists. Engaging the context of power disparity for a transformative postcolonial feminist theological discourse, *border-traversing* can be a significant metaphor for postcolonial mission and has so many different implications. To determine the nature of border-traversing, therefore, one must raise

39. Said, *Culture and Imperialism*, 280.
40. Fanon, *Wretched of the Earth*, 36–37.

such questions as: Who is crossing the borders? What kind of borders? What ends do the border-traversing entail? What consequences will the border-traversing bring? Whose interest does the border-traversing serve? Derrida remarks: "The absolute victim is a victim who cannot even protest. One cannot even identify the victim as victim. He or she is totally excluded or covered over by language, annihilated by history, a victim one cannot identify."[41] In this sense, those who are able to cross the borders, whether the borders are physical, epistemological, geopolitical, political, cultural, religious, or metaphorical, are not, at least, absolute victims. Instead, they have a power and responsibility to persuade others to cross the borders to act for justice in an unjust world. Here, Christian theologians and practitioners should explore the ways in which they could actively produce, promote, and mobilize the passion for transformation and justice in the life of Christian churches and people within particular colonial-geopolitical contexts, beyond the borders of gender, race and ethnicity, religion, citizenship, or sexuality. I believe one of the most significant tasks of postcolonial feminist theology is moving beyond the various colonizing borders of discrimination, exclusion, dehumanization of people toward the world of decolonization, deimperialization, and justice. Here border-traversing can be a significant metaphor for doing postcolonial feminist theology.

One can rekindle the passion for postcolonial feminist theology through painful awareness of the reality of colonization, injustice, and our complicity with it, wittingly and unwittingly. The need for postcolonial passion and compassion grows out of an awareness of colonialist reality: "My first cup of coffee each day represents a decision to accept the benefits of unjust labor practices in the so-

---

41. Jacques Derrida, "Passages—from Traumatism to Promise," in *Points . . . Interviews, 1974–1994*, ed. Elisabeth Weber, trans. Peggy Kamuf, et al. (Stanford: Stanford University Press, 1995), 389.

called third world. . . . The cotton blouse that I wear is a constant reminder of the history of slavery in the United States that made cotton 'king' and put cash in the pockets of white people at the expense of black people's lives. . . . My every breath is a compromise with injustice."[42]

In this context, postcolonial feminist theology today is a discourse and practice of border-traversing, through which people acknowledge and experience multiple colonial locations and realities of the different part of the world. Border-traversing is not merely physical or geographical crossing but engaged, committed traversing through which people are able to get geopolitically, socioculturally, theoethically engaged in the reality of different religions, colonial contexts, identities of the world and the people in it. In this sense, border-traversing functions to promote compassion, hospitality, solidarity, equality, justice, and peace between and among people who experience multiple forms of colonialism and colonial mentality in a concrete reality. Postcolonial feminist theology can be a theopolitical discourse, practice, and movement of geopolitical alliances across the globe, transcending boundaries between different identities, nations, cultures, or religions: participating in God's *yes* to and radical affirmation of the entire world and of humans.

---

42. Karen Lebacqz, *Justice in an Unjust World: Foundations for a Christian Approach to Justice* (Minneapolis: Augsburg, 1987), 10.

5

From Epistemology to Hermeneutics

Theopolitical Implications of Postmodernism

Deconstruction ("there is nothing outside the text") means nothing else: there is nothing outside context.
—Jacques Derrida[1]

Deconstruction is the "hermeneutics" of the death of God.
—Mark C. Taylor[2]

I can endure death. . . . It is the *representation* of death that I cannot bear.
—Peter Ackroyd[3]

---

1. Jacques Derrida, "Afterword," in *Limited Inc.*, trans. Samuel Weber (Evanston: Northwestern University Press, 1988), 136.
2. Mark C. Taylor, *Erring: A Postmodern A/theology* (Chicago: University of Chicago Press, 1984), 6.
3. Peter Ackroyd, *Chatterton* (London: Hamish Hamilton, 1987), 2, 138 (italics mine).

Postmodernism:
Aesthetic, Epistemological, Theopolitical Criticism

It has almost become a commonplace to call our world "postmodern." In discussions about the contemporary world, the term *postmodernism* is one of those words that people use frequently and often abuse.[4] The range of interpretations, presentations, meanings, definitions, and descriptions of the term *postmodernism* is unbelievably broad, diverse, and complex, and often contradictory. It would be, therefore, appropriate for those who take one's *Dasein* ("being-in-the-world") seriously to engage this postmodern *Zeitgeist*, the ethos/spirit of our time. Federico De Onis (1882–1932) first conceived the term in his *Antologia de la poesia espanola e hispanoamericana*, published in 1934, and Arnold Toynbee also used the term in 1947 to designate a "new historical cycle in Western civilization, starting around 1875."[5] Irving Howe and Harry Levin first popularized the term *postmodernism* in 1959 and 1960 respectively.[6] Since the 1960s, the word *postmodernism* emerged first in artistic circles, mostly used too generally and vaguely. Since then, people have either uncritically glorified or blindly denounced postmodernism without carefully examining its multiple, complex layers of both its contextual background, strength, contribution, or potential, and its limitations and dilemma. Postmodernism is used to characterize modes of architecture,

4. Linda Hutcheon, *The Politics of Postmodernism* (New York: Routledge, 2002 [1989]).

5. Ihab Hassan, "The Question of Postmodernism," *Performing Arts Journal* 6, no. 1 (1981): 31. A slight revision of this article also appears in *Postmodernism: A Reader*, ed. Thomas Docherty (New York: Columbia University Press, 1993) with the title, "Toward a Concept of Postmodernism," 147. Also see idem, *The Postmodern Turn* (Columbus: Ohio State University Press, 1987).

6. Cf. Irving Howe, "Mass Society and Postmodern Fiction," *Partisan Review* 26 (Summer 1959): 420–36, reprinted in Irving Howe, *Decline of the New* (New York: Harcourt, 1970), 190–207; and Harry Levin, "What Was Modernism?" *Massachusetts Review* 1, no. 4 (August 1960): 609–630, also reprinted in Harry Levin, *Refractions: Essays in Comparative Literature* (New York: Oxford University Press, 1966), 271–95.

photography, the visual and performing arts, media, linguistics, literary criticism, philosophy, and theology as well as the social and political sciences. Since the word *postmodernism*, like the word *feminism*, has become too familiar, people tend to forget easily the fundamental complexities of postmodern discourses and need an in-depth analysis and context-specific interpretation in order to gain an understanding of what postmodernism is primarily about.

Needless to say, it is impossible for one to synthesize postmodernism as discourse and practice in a single chapter, when there is no agreement among postmodern theorists even about the use of a hyphen between *post* and *modernism*, for instance. Some would use *postmodernism* and *post-modernism* interchangeably, without necessarily indicating any negative or affirmative position about postmodernism.[7] But for some, the absence of a hyphen in *postmodernism* signals a certain affirmative position about postmodernism and recognition of its significant contribution, whereas the use of *post-modernism* indicates a critical position.[8] While there are a thousand different commentators on postmodernism, there is no single agreement as to the usage of the word. Needless to say, postmodernism is never a unified, homogeneous discourse, as is also true of modernism. Regardless, I discern postmodern discourse or theory to be a significant analytical tool that people can utilize in examining their complex contexts. I concur with Gilles Deleuze's illustration: "A theory is exactly like a box of tools. It has nothing to do with the signifier. It must be useful. It must function."[9]

---

7. For instance, Thomas Dumm prefers to use post-modernism with the hyphen because it reminds him of "aporias of modernity." Cf. Thomas Dumm, "The Politics of Post-modern Aesthetics: Habermas Contra Foucault," *Political Theory* 16, no. 2 (May 1988): 224. Pauline Marie Rosenau uses the hyphen out of the "grammatical conviction," not as an indication of negative judgment about postmodernism. Cf. Pauline Marie Rosenau, *Post-modernism and the Social Sciences: Insights, Inroads, and Intrusions* (Princeton: Princeton University Press, 1992), 19.

8. Cf. Ihab Hassan, "The Culture of Post-modernism," *Theory, Culture and Society* 2, no. 3 (1985): 125.

Postmodernism criticizes and challenges a number of modernist assumptions, especially modernism's notion of the subject, its belief in science, technology, and rationality, and its totalizing view that places the West at the center—"a unique and superior position from which to establish control and to determine hierarchies."[10] Modernist rhetoric in historical, political, economic, cultural, philosophical, and religious contexts has suppressed any difference and privileged the Euro/U.S.-centric culture, knowledge, and patriarchy with totalizing, homogenizing, and colonizing desire while repressing and marginalizing those whose race, ethnicity, class, or gender is outside the mainstream. With its diverse positions, postmodernism has tried to create new configurations of the self, language, power, knowledge, truth, time, and space while critically scrutinizing all forms of representation, knowledge, and meaning of modernism. With the postmodern celebration of differences, heterogeneity, and small narratives, instead of the sameness, homogeneity, and grand narratives of modernism, and deconstruction of the hierarchical binary of center–margin, the concept "return of the repressed"[11]—a return of the least, to use Jesus' term—has emerged in various discourses. As postmodernism makes the claim that there is no tradition, meaning, or knowledge that has a universal authority, it refuses to take the Euro/U.S. culture and tradition as the universal referent that constitutes *truth*—whether historical, cultural, political, or religious. The truth-claim should function to enlarge human liberation and possibilities, rather than to represent only the voice of those at the "legitimate" center. In this sense, postmodernism could

9. Michel Foucault, "Intellectuals and Power: A Conversation between Michel Foucault and Gilles Deleuze," in *Language, Counter-Memory, Practice*, ed. Donald F. Bouchard, trans. Donald F. Bouchard and Sherry Simon (Ithaca: Cornell University Press, 1977), 208.

10. Richard Nelly, "Postmodernism and Periphery," in Docherty, ed., *Postmodernism: A Reader*, 463.

11. For this concept, see Noel Carroll, "The Return of the Repressed: The Re-emergence of Expression in Contemporary American Dance," *Dance Theatre Journal* 2, no. 1 (1984): 16–19.

be a discourse of liberation and resistance that enlarges the circle of inclusion in terms of gender, culture, race and ethnicity, class, ability, or sexuality, as it could function to contest, deterritorialize, and dismantle any form of totalizing and colonizing power and knowledge.

Here, it is also important to note that the postmodern ethos or perspective is not unique in the West and that one always needs to diversify the genealogy of postmodern ethos. No one today can claim the ownership of virtue or truth and, therefore, "no race has a monopoly on beauty, on intelligence, on strength."[12] If one adopts the postmodern ethos as a transhistorical, though not ahistorical, point of view, which one does not necessarily need to connect to a specific historical moment such as modernism in the West, one can find the postmodern ethos in other philosophical traditions such as the Taoist philosophy. The *Tao Te Ching*, for instance, eloquently reveals the core of postmodern perspective:

> The Tao that can be told
> is not the eternal Tao;
>
> The name that can be named
> is not the eternal name.[13]

Postmodernism refuses to fix something that one cannot fix, such as the *Tao* [Way], the Divine, Truth, or God. This postmodern refusal of fixation, doxification, or essentialization is one of the cores of postmodernism and has theoethical and theopolitical significances. A postmodern reading of the Bible,[14] for instance, is a process of the destabilization of any fixation or doxification and of claim for

---

12. Edward Said, *Culture and Imperialism* (New York: Vintage, 1993), 231.
13. Lao Tsu, *Tao Te Ching*, trans. Gia-fu Feng and Jane English (New York: Vintage, 1972), ch. 1.
14. For various ways of doing a postmodern reading of the Bible, see George Aichele, et al., *The Postmodern Bible: The Bible and Culture Collective* (New Haven: Yale University Press, 1995).

mastery, and functions as an important theoethical and theopolitical response to other readings that often justify and sacralize multiple forms of oppression, discrimination, exclusion, and marginalization. In this sense, a postmodern reading of religious discourses and practices is a significant theopolitical activity that scrutinizes the epistemological and theological foundation and metanarratives.

Discursive Divide within Postmodernism

Postmodernism has never had a unified definition. As the word *postmodernism* is a compound derivative of *modernism*, postmodernism's relation to modernism gets entangled in an interesting way. In this sense, people often constitute postmodernism by its interplay between continuity and discontinuity with modernism. Consciously or unconsciously, and wittingly or unwittingly, the present moment is related ineluctably to the preceding time—the modern time. Postmodernism may improve upon modernism, abandon it, transform it, or castigate it, but it cannot simply repeat the preceding time. The so-called postmodern turn[15] comes from continental Europe, predominantly France and Germany. The irony is that, although the French get most of the credit for developing postmodernism, German philosophers, mainly Friedrich Nietzsche and Martin Heidegger, inspired it. Despite this intellectual debt, contemporary German philosophers, especially Jürgen Habermas, are among postmodernism's severest critics.[16] The appeal of postmodernism continues to grow outside of France. And

---

15. Cf. Jean-Francois Lyotard, *The Postmodern Condition: A Report on Knowledge* (Minneapolis: University of Minnesota Press, 1984).

16. Cf. Jürgen Habermas, "Modernity versus Post Modernity," *New German Critique* 22 (Winter 1981): 3–14; idem, "Modernity—An Incomplete Project," in *The Anti-Aesthetic: Essays on Postmodern Culture*, ed. Hal Foster (Townsend, WA: Bay Press, 1983).

now, postmodernism has become synonymous with inquiry itself in many areas of the humanities: literary criticism, social sciences, postpositivism, neostructuralism, postcontemporarism, poststructuralism, and post-Marxism. Postmodernism represents the coming together of elements from a number of different, often conflicting, orientations, such as French structuralism, romanticism, phenomenology, nihilism, popularism, existentialism, hermeneutics, or Marxism, and has significant conflict with every approach. In this sense, these multiple characters of postmodernism can be both its strength and weakness. Postmodern theorists, thinkers, and approaches are extremely heterogeneous and diverse, especially in terms of their primary concern, emphasis, or content. Thinkers such as Jacques Derrida, Jacques Lacan, Luce Irigary, Julia Kristeva, Richard Rorty, Jean-Francois Lyotard, or Michel Foucault, among others, are influences associated with postmodern discourses. Yet they utterly differ in terms of emphasis, focus, or position on certain issues. Interestingly, Lacan, Irigary, Kristeva, Derrida, and Foucault hardly use the term *postmodernism*.[17] By trying to map some central issues and types of postmodernism, I am fully aware that I run the risk of breaching some postmodern claims and values, such as the impossibility of mapping, heterogeneity and multiplicity, or *differance* and alterity. I assume, however, it is worthwhile to attempt to understand various types of postmodernism in order to seek its meaningful or useful aspects for mobilizing a discourse of reading our time.

There are at least two different forms of engagement with postmodernism, though there is not much consensus on how to name them. Hal Foster, for instance, distinguishes *neoconservative* postmodernism from *poststructuralist* postmodernism.[18]

---

17. Alessandra Tanesini, "Feminism and Postmodernism," in *An Introduction to Feminist Epistemologies* (Oxford: Blackwell, 1999), 237.

Neoconservative postmodernism, as a postmodernism of reaction, tries to "return to tradition (in art, family, and religion)," charging the modern culture "with the ills of society" and seeking "redress in a return to the verities."[19] On the other hand, *poststructuralist* postmodernism, as a postmodernism of resistance, addresses "'the death of man [sic]' not only as original creator of unique artifacts but also as the centered subject of representation and of history."[20] These two types of postmodernism therefore take different positions in their opposition to modernism: neoconservative postmodernist opposition is a matter of a *return to* representation, whereas poststructuralist postmodernist opposition is about a *critique of* representation. Here one can relate the postmodern critique of representation with poststructuralism. Andreas Huyssen identifies critical and affirmative varieties of postmodernism, especially in terms of its function as a discourse of resistance against totalizing, homogenizing, or imperializing attempts.[21]

David Griffin distinguishes between deconstructive or eliminative postmodernism and constructive or revisionary postmodernism. While *deconstructive* postmodernism overcomes the modern worldview through an anti-worldview that deconstructs or eliminates the ingredients necessary for a worldview, such as God, self, purpose, meaning, a real world, and truth as correspondence, *constructive* postmodernism seeks to overcome the modern worldview not by eliminating the possibility of a worldview as-such but by constructing a postmodern worldview through revision of modern premises and traditional concepts.[22] Within this diversity of

---

18. Hal Foster, "(Post) Modern Polemics," *New German Critique* 33 (Fall 1984): 67.
19. Ibid., 70.
20. Ibid., 67.
21. Andreas Huyssen, "Mapping the Postmodern," *Feminism/Postmodernism*, ed. Linda Nicholson (New York: Routledge, 1990), 234–77.

postmodern pronouncements, one can delineate two broad, general orientations: *skeptical* postmodernism and *affirmative* postmodernism.

Skeptical postmodernists argue that the postmodern age is one of fragmentation, disintegration, malaise, meaninglessness, or even absence of moral parameters, and "the end of the world [*Weltuntergang*] can no longer be a topic."[23] This skepticism can be the dark side of postmodernism, the postmodernism of despair that speaks of the immediacy of death, the demise of the subject, the end of author, the impossibility of truth, and the abrogation of the order of representation, which especially Heidegger and Nietzsche inspire. For skeptical postmodernists, the destructive character of modernity makes the postmodern age one of "radical, unsurpassable uncertainty,"[24] characterized by all that is grim, cruel, alienating, hopeless, tired, and ambiguous. Although affirmative postmodernists agree with skeptical postmodernism's critique of modernity, they have a more hopeful, optimistic view of the postmodern age, and are oriented toward process. *Affirmative* postmodernists are open to positive political action, struggle, and resistance, or content with the recognition of visionary, celebratory, personal, nondogmatic projects that range from New Age religion to New Wave lifestyles and include a whole spectrum of postmodern social movements. Most affirmatives seek philosophical and ontological intellectual practice that is tentative, nondogmatic, nonessentialist, nonfoundational, and nonideological.[25]

---

22. David Griffin, *God and Religion in the Postmodern World* (New York: State University of New York Press, 1989), x–xii.
23. Klaus Scherpe, "Dramatization and De-dramatization of "The End": The Apocalyptic Consciousness of Modernity and Post-modernity," *Cultural Critique* 5 (Winter 1986–87): 95.
24. Matei Calinescu, *Five Faces of Modernity* (Durham: Duke University Press, 1987), 305.
25. Charles Levin and Arthur Kroker, "Baudrillard's Challenge," *Canadian Journal of Political and Social Theory* 8, nos. 1-2 (1984): 15–16.

It is, however, important to note that although differentiating between the two poles within postmodern discourse could allow us to explain how postmodernism can have such diverse implications in religious discussion, there lies a danger of oversimplification and miscategorization of postmodernism's complex nature if one understands these two types of postmodernism as oppositional or binary, rather than as complementary. It is also significant to note that there is both continuity and discontinuity between modernism and postmodernism. As Ihab Hassan clearly states: "Modernism and postmodernism are not separated by an Iron Curtain or a Chinese Wall; for history is a palimpsest, and culture is permeable to time past, time present, and time future. We are all . . . a little Victorian, Modern, and Postmodern, at once."[26]

In this sense, understanding and interpreting postmodernism would depend on one's locationality and positionality in a specific context and discourse. It is not an exaggeration, therefore, to say that there are countless angles by which one can approach postmodernism. Brian McHale contends:

> There is John Barth's postmodernism, the literature of replenishment; Charles Newman's postmodernism, the literature of an inflationary economy; Jean-Francois Lyotard's postmodernism, a general condition of knowledge in the contemporary informational regime; Ihab Hassan's postmodernism, a stage on the road to the spiritual unification of humankind; and so on. There is even [Frank] Kermode's construction of postmodernism, which in effect constructs it right out of existence.[27]

Every discourse has its own specific context, and there is no discourse without its limitation or dilemma. In this context, we must ask whose or which postmodernism we are referring to, what function it plays, and whose interest it serves. What one needs to do is, therefore,

26. Hassan, "Question of Postmodernism," 32.
27. Brian McHale, *Postmodernist Fiction* (London: Methuen, 1987), 4.

neither total rejection nor total affirmation of a particular discourse. One must carefully examine what contribution a particular discourse or theory has made in a specific context and at the same time what limitation and dilemma it carries when one tries to implement such a discourse in reality. One needs to approach postmodernism in the context of modernism if one wants to understand the philosophical grounding of postmodernism because, as Edward Said eloquently points out, "a beginning immediately establishes relationships with works already existing, relationships of either continuity or antagonism or some mixture of both."[28] Instead of making a blanket judgment about postmodernism being *a*political, *a*historical, antiestablishment, antireligious, or anti-Christian, for instance, one needs to explore how postmodern thought can affect the religious tradition, discourse, and practice, and how the very religious discourse and tradition can meaningfully address such a postmodern world and its worldview.

Postmodern Challenges to Religion

The most fundamental challenge of postmodernism to religion is its rejection of absolute truth. Since every religion claims meta-truth, the rejection of truth itself seems to shake the very ground of religion. What postmodernists are suspicious of is, however, the modern versions of truth. Almost all postmodernists reject meta-truth even as a goal or ideal because it is the very epitome of modernity.[29] Truth makes reference to orders, rules, values, and foundations and

28. Edward W. Said, *Beginnings: Intention and Method* (New York: Columbia University Press, 1985), 3.
29. Michel Foucault, "Nietzsche, Genealogy, History," in *The Foucault Reader* (New York: Pantheon, 1984), 76–80.

depends on logic, rationality, and reason, all of which the postmodernists question.

From Epistemology to Hermeneutics:
Rejection of Meta-Truth and Foundationalism

There is a convergence between poststructuralism and postmodernism. The poststructuralist rejection of an epistemic foundationalism, which presupposes that there is a foundation on which all knowledge is built, is a significant point of departure for postmodernism. Modern epistemic foundationalism, what Jean-Francois Lyotard calls "metanarrative" or "grand narrative," assumes that there is a transcendent, unchanging realm, idea, or being. In this context, Lyotard describes "postmodern as incredulity towards meta-narrative."[30] Postmodernism challenges modernism on this and various grounds. Richard Rorty contends that "the intellectual tradition [of foundational epistemology] has not paid off, is more trouble than it is worth, has become an incubus," and that we need to displace philosophy-as-epistemology with philosophy-as-hermeneutics.[31] For deconstructionist or poststructuralist postmodernists, humans are incapable of grasping the comprehensive form of truth and therefore reject monopolistic claims to absolute meta-truth.

Derrida argues: "There is no such thing as *a truth* in itself. Even if it should be for me, about me, truth is plural."[32] Postmodernists perceive truth-claims to be merely the product of power, manipulated into position by those whose interests they serve. If this contention is so, if

30. Lyotard, *Postmodern Condition*, xxiv.
31. Richard Rorty, *Consequences of Pragmatism* (Minneapolis: University of Minnesota, 1982), xxxvii (italics mine).
32. Jacques Derrida, *Spurs: Nietzsche's Styles* (Chicago: University of Chicago Press, 1979), 103 (italics mine).

one's truth-claims are really arbitrary, then they do not merit special privileged status or superior authority. It is impossible to separate truth-claim from power, and humans are unable to comprehend any absolute, uncorrupted truth due to epistemological and ontological limitations. On the political economy of truth[33] and power, Foucault critically points out:

> Once knowledge can be analysed in terms of religion, domain, implantation, displacement, transposition, one is able to capture the process by which knowledge functions as a form of power and disseminates the effects of power. There is an administration of knowledge, a politics of knowledge, relations of power which pass via knowledge and which, if one tries to transcribe them, lead one to consider forms of domination designated by such notions as field, region and territory.[34]

In this sense, one cannot dissociate a truth-claim from the systems of hegemonic, discursive power. However, Foucault does not denounce power itself. Power is always already dangerous, and one must therefore resist oppressive systems of power to generate new power relations that are more just and less oppressive. In this context, "it's not a matter of emancipating truth from every system of power (which would be a chimera, for truth is already power) but of detaching the power of truth from the forms of hegemony, social, economic, and cultural, within which it operates at the present time," because "'truth' is to be understood as a system of ordered procedures for the production, regulation, distribution, circulation and operation of statements . . . [and] . . . is linked in a circular relation with systems of power which produce and sustain it."[35]

33. Michel Foucault, *Power/Knowledge: Selected Interviews & Other Writings 1972–1977*, ed. Colin Gordon (New York: Pantheon, 1980), 131.
34. Ibid., 69.
35. Ibid., 133.

In a similar vein with Foucault's critical position toward the entanglement of knowledge and power, deconstructionist postmodernists regard absolute truth-claims as a form of terrorism because they threaten and condemn those who disagree with them, operating a "'règime' of truth."[36] In this regard, absolute truth-claims come to justify the powerful and to make the powerless feel inadequate. Lyotard argues that truth eliminates the argument of the other, the point of view of someone else that upsets what we define as the truth even though it is only what we have come to take for granted.[37] Postmodern theory of language transforms truth into a largely linguistic convention. Jane Flax, for instance, argues that claims of truth can never be independent of language, that truth is an "effect of discourse" and "each discourse has its own distinctive set of rules or procedures that govern the production of what is to count as a meaningful or truthful statement."[38]

In this sense, the relationship between name and meaning, the signified and signifier, becomes problematic. If language produces and reproduces its own world without reference to reality, then it is impossible to say anything definite because language is purely an artificial sign system and cannot assure truth.[39] Linguistic meaning is, for instance, always personal and idiosyncratic and can therefore never be communicated from one person to another. Language has a will and a power of its own. There are no precise meanings for words, no definitive versions of a text, in short, no simple truth, according to deconstructive postmodernists. Nothing remains of truth, and it is only a product of our willing bewitchment by

---

36. Ibid.
37. Cf. Lyotard, *Postmodern Condition.*
38. Jane Flax, *Thinking Fragments: Psychoanalysis, Feminism, and Postmodernism in the Contemporary West* (Berkeley: University of California Press, 1990), 35–36.
39. John Murphy, "Computerization, Postmodern Epistemology and Reading in the Postmodern Era," *Educational Theory* 38, no. 2 (1988): 179.

language. Postmodern truth is, then, necessarily fragmentary, discontinuous, provisional, partial, and changing. The deconstructionists' postmodern understanding of truth is consistent with their postmodern view of author, subject, presence, history, time, space, representation, knowledge, and power.

Any truth-claim, for instance, implies an author. Thus, rejection of truth conforms closely with his or her view that no single person (such as the author) can tell us what a particular text really means. Here it is important to note that what postmodernists are rejecting is not truth itself but the way of representing truth in an absolute manner. It is also significant to distinguish between truth-itself and the representation of truth-as-such, because postmodernists deal with the representation of the truth. The only thing that may be possible is a relational truth or approximate truth, as sociologists of knowledge claim. Postmodernists almost universally accept the sociology of knowledge, especially in its analysis of the relationship between social factors and people's ideas and identities. Based on Marx's theory, Karl Mannheim developed the sociology of knowledge, and it shares at least two important claims with the postmodern understanding of reality. First, human beings are what their cultural environments make them: they are a social construction. Second, all human thinking is a social construct, which means that human patterns of thought, human cognitive approaches to the universe, are also a social construction. Therefore, the beginning truths we bring to the reasoning process are beliefs our society has conditioned us to accept, just as others have been conditioned to accept a completely different set of beliefs. Postmodernists assert that all such beginning beliefs are arbitrary.[40]

---

40. Cf. Karl Mannheim, *Ideology and Utopia: An Introduction to the Sociology of Knowledge* (New York: Harvest/HBJ Books, 1985 [1936]); and Paul Ricoeur, *Lectures on Ideology and Utopia*, ed. George H. Taylor (New York: Columbia University Press, 1986).

It is impossible, therefore, according to both the perspectives of sociology of knowledge and postmodernism, to conceive of absolute truth existing independently of the values and position of the subject and unrelated to the social context. Human beings may be able to obtain truth, but it is only partial truth, limited by their socially grounded perspectives. Therefore, as James Cone argues, "What people think about God, Jesus Christ, and the church cannot be separated from their own social and political status in a given society," and "theology is not a universal language; it is interested language and thus always a reflection of the goals and aspirations of a particular people in a definite social setting."[41] Truth assumes a belief in presence and the ability to distinguish between what is actually present and absent,[42] and postmodernists argue that presence is never absolute; the absent is always present to some degree, and the present is always absent. Skeptical postmodernists reject truth because "truth cannot be conceptualized in terms of completeness, adequation, transcendence, or self-identity" and therefore truth "cannot be the representation or mirror of an external or universal substance ('presence') or subject because none exists."[43]

Postmodernists question the value of truth because they consider it impossible to evaluate the adequacy of knowledge claims with any certitude. All criteria are for distinguishing between truth and falsehood and require that one choose between exclusive binary categories, or they expect one to establish a hierarchy of values that designates some values as good and others as bad. Postmodernists reject such binary distinctions and, rather, emphasize multiple realities and the view that one cannot claim a single, monolithic interpretation of any phenomenon to be absolutely superior to any

41. James Cone, *God of the Oppressed* (New York: Seabury, 1975), 45, 39.
42. Joel Schwartz, "Antihumanism in the Humanities," *The Public Interest* 99 (Spring 1990): 32.
43. Flax, *Thinking Fragments,* 200.

other. If there is no single best answer to every question, then there is no room for representation of absolute truth.

From Meta-Truth to Relational Truth: Reconfiguring Truth

Affirmative postmodernists are as likely as the skeptics to reject universal truth and dismiss the idea that truth is out there waiting to be discovered. However, many of them do accept the possibility of specific, local, personal, approximate, and relational forms of truth. The affirmatives are also less likely than the skeptics to say that all versions of truth are equal. They argue that truth varies according to place and historico-political context and that seemingly conflicting truths are not a problem because each one can be true in a different context and world.[44] Each person may have his or her own version of truth. Finally, they develop an antitheoretical form of truth as theory with a substantive focus on daily life and on local narrative.

The affirmative postmodernists, like the skeptics, understand truth's dependence on language to be a serious restriction, but they take a middle-of-the-road position rather than defend an extreme linguistic relativism. The affirmatives argue that there can be a certain consensus about words or concepts. Meaning is still erratic in the sense that it is always acquired, shaped, or invented by professional or social interaction: the community dictates the terms but not in an absolutely arbitrary fashion.[45] Affirmatives argue that a community of knowledge may establish a consensus of language and values, making it possible to communicate certain truths that, though not

44. Nelson Goodman, *Of Mind and Other Matters* (Cambridge: Harvard University Press, 1984), 30–35.
45. Barbara Herrnstein Smith, *Contingencies of Value* (Cambridge: Harvard University Press, 1988), 105.

universal, hold for that community at a specific place and time. Jane Flax contends: "A discourse as a whole cannot be true or false because truth is always contextual and rule dependent. Instead discourses are local, heterogeneous, and incommensurable. No non-discourse-dependent or transcendental rules exist that could govern all discourses or a choice between them. Truth claims are in principle 'undecidable.'"[46]

The affirmative postmodernists generally deny the truth-claims of theory and annul its privileged status. They diminish its role and reduce its stature, but in the end many of them retain it by transforming it into ordinary, pedestrian talk. They argue that although they aim to end the intellectual hegemony implicit in grand theory, this goal need not mean all truth-claims are equal. Postmodern truth is unsystemic, heterogical, decentered, ever-changing, and local. Nonrepresentational, postmodern truth is personal in character and community-specific in focus. It does not require the object–subject distinction of modernism, but is true only in terms of its own discourse.

Some affirmative postmodernists seek to substitute for modern truth an anti-theoretical focus on the events of daily life, on local knowledge, on detail, on the contingent, on personal testimony, on direct experience of individuals and communities. Because this ordinary life of ordinary people is so richly descriptive, it represents a revolt against grand theory, especially inductive theory that attempts to generalize. What goes on in the bedroom and bathroom takes on as much historical importance as what takes place on the battlefield and in government boardrooms, feminists also argue. Various paradigms of everyday life have emerged in other areas, and the concept "everyday life" is not the exclusive property of

46. Flax, *Thinking Fragments,* 36.

postmodernism. For example, neo-Marxists, such as Henri Lefebvre, abandon orthodox Marxism and integrate an everyday-life point of view into a general anticapitalist perspective.[47] As substitutes for truth, affirmative postmodernists also emphasize certain kinds of narratives: small/petit narratives, community-based narratives, rather than grand or meta-narratives. They praise traditional narratives that speak, for example, as folk wisdom, myth, popular stories, legends, fragmented creative snippets of wisdom, and little stories, because traditional narratives, according to affirmative postmodernists, focus on the local, assert neither truth nor totalizing theory, and propose no broad theoretical generalizations or ultimate truths. Traditional human narratives accept error, inconsistency, and relativism. These liberating narratives tell the collective story of the disempowered, placing their lives within the context of larger social and historical forces. They present a common story that unifies people and promotes a social bond among individuals in their everyday life. They explain the past to the present; they speak of fragments or heterogeneity rather than unity or homogeneity. Postmodernists reject modernism's meta-, master, or grand narratives, and narratives that claim to be scientific and objective, which often serve to legitimate modernity and assume justice, truth, theory, or hegemony. These modern meta-narratives are the same narratives the skeptical postmodernists reject as logocentric, linear, or totalizing. Postmodernists reject grand narratives because they all claim a beginning, an end, and a definitive theory, and this absolutized claim is impossible and pointless in a postmodern world.[48]

---

47. Cf. Henri Lefebvre, "Toward a Leftist Cultural Politics," in *Marxism and the Interpretation of Culture,* ed. Cary Nelson and Lawrence Grossberg (Chicago: University of Illinois Press, 1988), 77–87. Agnes Heller also emphasizes an everyday life approach to social phenomena, though she is not postmodernist. According to Heller, everyday life and everyday knowledge are pragmatic, concrete, factual, and cognitive as well as emotional. Cf. Agnes Heller, "The Sociology of Everyday Life," in *The Sociology of Structure and Action,* ed. Ulf Himmelstrand (Newbury Park, CA: Sage, 1986), 150–63.

Theopolitical Implications for Doing Feminist Theology

Decentering the Hegemonic Center of Knowledge

A central feature of postmodernism is its critique of totality, reason, and universality. Lyotard has most powerfully developed this critique. In his often-cited book *The Postmodern Condition*, Lyotard defines postmodernism as "incredulity toward metanarratives."[49] For Lyotard, meta-narratives do not problematize their own legitimacy; they deny the historical and social construction of their own first principles, and in doing so they wage war on difference, contingency, and particularity. Against Habermas and others, Lyotard argues that appeals to reason and consensus, when inserted within grand narratives that unify history, emancipation, and knowledge, deny their own implications in the production of knowledge and power. Against meta-narratives, which totalize historical experience by reducing its diversity to a one-dimensional, all-encompassing logic, Lyotard posits a discourse of multiple horizons and the terrain of micropolitics. Even the scientific meta-narratives do not capture the "totality of knowledge."[50] The legitimation of knowledge, according to Lyotard, therefore becomes plural and local. One of the limitations of his postmodern arguments is his ruling out "the sort of critical social theory which employs general categories like gender, race, and class,"[51] when any social movement like feminism requires adopting the grand categories and concepts such as sexism, patriarchy, justice, or liberation.

48. Taylor, *Erring*, 62–69, 153.
49. Lyotard, *Postmodern Condition*, xxiv.
50. Ibid., 7.
51. Nancy Fraser and Linda J. Nicholson, "Social Criticism without Philosophy: an Encounter between Feminism and Postmodernism," in Nicholson, ed., *Feminism/Postmodernism*, 24.

However, the postmodern challenge to the modernist notions of totality, meta-narrative, meta-truth, and universality provides a significant theological ground for the traditional construction of theological discourse with its decentering function of knowledge production and dissemination. It goes without saying that the construction and institutionalization of theological discourse and practice in Christianity has evolved in the West, the Euro/U.S. In this sense,

> It [the West] is a name for a subject which gathers itself in discourse but is also an object constituted discursively; it is, evidently, a name always associating itself with those regions, communities, and peoples that appear politically or economically superior to other regions, communities, and peoples. Basically, it is just like the name "Japan," which reputedly designates a geographic area, a tradition, a national identity, a culture, an ethos, a market, and so on, yet, unlike all the other names associated with geographic particularities, it also implies the refusal of its self-delimitation; it claims that it is capable of sustaining, if not actually transcending, an impulse to transcend all the particularizations.[52]

Here, postmodern discourse helps one to see the underlying assumption of the West-centrism within theological discourse and practice, in which the West has represented, produced, and archived the universal knowledge for all of humanity. Postmodernism provides a politics of representation and a basis for social struggle by asserting the primacy of the historical and contingent in the construction of reason, authority, truth, ethics, and identity. The postmodern attack on foundationalism can be a political act, since it expands the possibility for argumentation and dialogue. Moreover, by acknowledging questions of power and value in the construction of knowledge and subjectivities, postmodernism helps to make visible

---

52. Naoki Sakai, *Translation and Subjectivity: On "Japan" and Cultural Nationalism* (Minneapolis: University of Minnesota, 1997), 154.

important ideological and structural forces, such as race, gender, and class. For Ernst Laclau, the collapse of foundationalism does not suggest a banal relativism or a dangerous nihilism. On the contrary, the lack of ultimate meaning, he argues, radicalizes the possibilities for human agency and a democratic politics.[53]

Promoting Hypersensitivity to the Marginalized

Postmodernism offers a challenge to the sociocultural politics of modernism at a number of levels. Postmodernism not only provides a discourse for retheorizing culture as fundamental to the construction of sociopolitical subjects and collective struggle, but it also theorizes culture as a politics of representation and power. Modernist culture negates the possibility of identities created within the experience of multiple narratives and border crossings; instead, modernism frames culture within rigid boundaries that both privilege and exclude through the categories of race, ethnicity, class, gender, and sexuality.[54] Within the discourse of modernism, culture, in large part, becomes an organizing principle for constructing borders that reproduce relations of domination, subordination, and inequality. Within the cultural politics of modernism, people identify Euro/U.S. culture, for instance, with the center of human civilization and define high culture in essentialist terms against the popular culture of the everyday. In effect, postmodernism constitutes a general attempt to transgress the borders, such as the cultural borders between high and popular culture, sealed by modernism, to proclaim the arbitrariness

---

53. Ernst Laclau, "Politics and the Limits of Modernity," in *Universal Abandon? The Politics of Postmodernism*, ed. Andrew Ross (Minneapolis: University of Minnesota Press, 1989), 63–82.
54. Cf. Emily Hicks, "Deterritorialization and Border Writing," in *Ethics/Aesthetics: Post-modern Positions*, ed. Robert Merrill (Washington, DC: Maisonneuve Press, 1988).

of all boundaries, and to call attention to the sphere of culture as a shifting social, historical, and political construction.

In this sense, first, postmodernism has broadened the discussion regarding the relationship between culture and power by illuminating the changing conditions of knowledge embedded in the age of electronically mediated information systems, cybernetic technologies, and computer engineering. Second, postmodernism raises a new set of questions regarding how people inscribe culture in the production of center–margin hierarchies and the reproduction of postcolonial forms of domination–subjugation. At stake here is not only a reconsideration of the intersection of race, ethnicity, gender, class, ability, or sexuality but also a new way of reading history; that is, postmodernism provides forms of historical knowledge as a way of reclaiming power and identity for subordinate groups.[55] In this sense, postmodernism fosters an important theoretical service to enable mapping the relations of the center and periphery. It challenges the hegemonic notion that Euro/U.S.-centric culture is superior to other cultures and traditions.

Elisabeth Schüssler Fiorenza has coined the term *kyriarchy*, which means "the rule of the emperor/master/lord/father/husband over his subordinates."[56] By adopting the term *kyriarchy*, instead of patriarchy, I want to reveal the enormously complex structure of oppression-subordination, not only between genders but also between and across different races, ethnicities, classes, abilities, sexual orientations, religions, and so forth. One can define postmodernism's negation of totality as a critique and negation of kyriarchal culture and ethnocentricity. In this regard, postmodern criticism can be a critical

---

55. For a more detailed discussion, see Trinh Minh-ha, *Women, Native, Other: Writing Postcoloniality and Feminism* (Bloomington: Indiana University Press, 1989); and Gayatri Chakravorty Spivak, *In Other Worlds: Essays in Cultural Politics* (New York: Methuen, 1987).
56. Elisabeth Schüssler Fiorenza, *Jesus—Miriam's Child, Sophia's Prophet: Critical Issues in Feminist Christology* (New York: Continuum, 1995), 14.

toolbox that provides an important theoethical and theopolitical service in assisting those deemed as other, such as Asian in relation to the West and women in relation to the kyriarchal culture of Asia, to reclaim their own histories, voices, and subjecthood. By problematizing the dominant notion of tradition, postmodernism develops a power-sensitive discourse that helps subjugated, marginalized, and excluded groups through multiple forms of kyriarchal discourse and practice to make sense of their own social worlds and histories.

Here, it is important to note that the postmodern celebration of difference and its politics of inclusivity should avoid falling into a danger of tokenization or poeticization of the other such as women and racial or ethnic minorities by poetically and uncritically celebrating difference, diversity, or the other without ethically and politically challenging the structural absence of the very other. Doreen Massey critically points out: "If the problem of the postmodernists is that while celebrating the existence of the Other most of us are consigned to being means of constructing the identity of white, heterosexual men, the problem of the modernists is that they do not see us, really, at all. Or, if they do, it is as somehow deviations from the norm, troubling exceptions to the(ir) rule."[57] In this regard, one should be always cautious about the danger of tokenization and structural absence in some postmodern politics of inclusivity and diversity.

As long as postmodernism can avoid the danger of poeticization or tokenization of the other, postmodernism can offer, I contend, the possibility for developing a cultural politics that focuses on the margins, for reclaiming the right of formerly un- or misrepresented human groups to speak for and represent themselves. Postmodernism

---

57. Doreen Massey, "A Global Sense of Place," in *Space, Place, and Gender* (Minneapolis: University of Minneapolis Press, 1994), 228.

breaks down the distinction and rigid border between high and low culture, for instance, and makes the everydayness an object of serious study. As part of a broader politics of difference, postmodernism focuses on the ways in which modernity functions as an imperialist meta-narrative that links Western models of industrial progress with hegemonic forms of culture, identity, and consumption. By being suspicious of traditional authority, decentering the discursive center, and being attentive to the suppressed/repressed voices within the tradition and texts, a postmodern reading of the religious scriptures and engagement of the traditions promotes hypersensitivity to the marginalized, to the voice of the voiceless, and to the heterogeneous aspects in theological discourses, scriptural interpretations, institutional structures, and ministerial practices. In non-Western societies such as Asia, people tend to reject postmodernism, along with feminism, due to its foreign origin. Postmodernism is, however, discourses about culture, society, and histories and offers particular tools with which one can scrutinize the naturalization of oppressive structures, the institutionalization of asymmetry of religious power differential based on gender, or fixation and doxification through meta-narratives of the biological difference between different sexes.

Constructing Theology beyond Foundationalism

One of the significant claims that postmodern discourse makes is its negation of any sort of foundationalism. Foundationalism is a claim that there is an unchanging foundation of knowledge, truth, or belief and that one can stop the chain of justifications, as the justification process cannot be constantly circular or infinite. Foundationalism comes from human desire for epistemological certainty, whether philosophical or theological. As knowing subjects or believing subjects, humans want to avoid uncertainty and to attain certainty that would give them firm grounds for knowing and believing. People regard René Descartes as a forebear of modern foundationalism, who arrived at a belief that he could not doubt any further the fact that he was doubting/thinking.[58] As a result, he discovered a foundation as a knowing subject and declared: "I think, therefore I am." The modern preoccupation with epistemology further established the ground of foundationalism with two seemingly contradictory proposals: rationalism and empiricism. Whether people lay the epistemological foundation on universal human reason (rationalism) or on universal sense experience (empiricism), these two streams have one thing in common: the dire quest for certainty.

Some conservative foundationalist theologians retrieve their theological foundation from an "inerrant Bible," for instance, by arguing that the Bible is "free from all error, whether of doctrine, fact, or precept."[59] Perceiving the task of theology as finding the theological facts, foundationalist theologians do not acknowledge the aspect of a historical construction of the Bible, which contains not only the word of God as they claim but also culturally/historically situated knowledge and value systems. The major problems and dangers of foundationalism lie in its lack of concern about a system of power that pertains to the issue of the authority of the very foundation, of concern about the politics of inclusion and exclusion, and of affirmations of the significant values of alterity, hybridity, multiplicity, and plurality of truth-claims that are context-specific. The modern desire to seek the foundation of all authorities in Reason and Truth results in totalizing truth-claims and discourses of

---

58. Cf. John E. Thiel, *Nonfoundationalism*, Guides to Theological Inquiry(Minneapolis: Fortress Press, 1994), 4.

59. Charles Hodge, *Systematic Theology*, 3 vols. (New York: Scribner, Armstrong, & Co., 1872), 1:152. Cited in Stanley J. Grenz and John R. Franke, *Beyond Foundationalism: Shaping Theology in a Postmodern Context* (Louisville: Westminster John Knox Press, 2001), 34.

authority. Postmodern reconstruction and reformulation of theological discourse highlight heterogeneity, discontinuity, difference, and alterity in discourses of truth and authority. Postmodern construction of theology beyond foundationalism can be a "source of unsettledness that disrupts the at-homeness of all Judaisms, Christianities, mother-religions, mother-tongues, and mother-secularisms—which is not to say that it is something (tediously, predictably) 'disruptive,' or 'radical.'"[60] Postmodern efforts to reformulate the current configuration of theologies can produce strategies of resistance to and transformation of any totalizing oppressive religious discourses and practices, and revitalization of the suppressed histories and of the voices of the marginalized.

Seeking an Alternative Direction of Religion

The affirmative postmodernists encompass a more optimistic spirit than the skeptics, and they support a range of a new political movements organized around everything from peace, ecology/environment, feminism, green politics, queer politics, nationalism, and anarchism to New Age movements. They encompass a community of resistance and poor people's movements. They bring together the oppressed, the physically or mentally challenged, the homeless, and the generally disadvantaged. New Age postmodernists, for instance, share a preference for the emotional, the irrational, the mystical, and the magical over the analytical, scientific, and reasoned.[61] They focus on all that modern science cannot explain. Noninstitutional religion is a central focus and is regarded as an

---

60. Yvonne Sherwood, "Introduction: Derrida's Bible," in *Derrida's Bible (Reading a Page of Scripture with a Little Help from Derrida)*, ed. Yvonne Sherwood (New York: Palgrave Macmillan, 2004), 5.
61. Cf. Fritjof Capra, *The Turning Point: Science, Society, and the Rising Culture* (New York: Simon & Schuster, 1982).

alternative to modern, organized, mainstream Protestantism or the "one, universal, Catholic, or Jewish religion."[62]

These efforts at postmodern pluralism link up with special religious sentiments that differ from those of traditionally established religions and attempt to harmonize with the cosmos. In a broad sense, one can list postmodern challenges to Christianity as follows: anthropocentrism, ecclesiocentrism, denominationalism, clericalism, patriarchalism, androcentrism, dogmatism, and anthropomorphism in Christianity. Now options for the future seem to be three: first, we may embrace the totalizing discourse of proponents of the end of history, in which case we lock ourselves once again within modern models of progress and the good life; second, we may let our plurality become further fragmentation and even disintegration; and third, we may join one another in our pluralistic world in piecemeal collaborations in the name of a better world, of the *kindom* of God on earth, where freedom, equality, peace, and justice flow like a river. This third and final possibility may be the sole option for the kind of person and the kind of community shaped by Christian narratives.

Remaining theopolitical and theoethical questions that theologians and practitioners must ask are: What kind of God is compatible with the Christian narrative and yet makes us a faithful people, able to engage the postmodern world? What kind of community of believers must we be in order to shoulder Christian missions? Perhaps most difficult of all, what understanding of Christ and the universal, cosmic salvation Jesus brings can shape Christians and the community of believers for free and open discourse with those to whom traditional Christian truth-claims are quite irrelevant?

---

62. Matthew Fox, "A Mystical Cosmology: Toward a Postmodern Spirituality," in *Sacred Interconnections: Postmodern Spirituality, Political Economy, and Art*, ed. David Griffin (Albany: State University of New York Press, 1990), 37.

Rebirthing into a Religion of Life-Affirming:
Postmodernism and Its Theopolitical Implications

As a discourse of plurality, alterity, *differance*, and multinarratives, postmodernism resists being inscribed in any single, homogeneous, monolithic articulating principle in order to explain either the mechanics of domination or the dynamics of emancipation. The value of postmodernism lies in its role as a shifting signifier that both reflects and contributes to the unstable cultural, theopolitical, theoethical, and structural relationships that increasingly characterize the advanced industrial countries of the world. The important point here is not whether one can define postmodernism within the parameters of particular politics, but how one can appropriate its best insights with a progressive and emancipatory democratic politics in religious/theological discourses and practices. Although postmodernism does not provide a particular ordering principle for defining a particular political project, it presents significant problems and fundamental issues that "were not particularly problematic before but certainly are now."[63]

Some significant insights that postmodernism might offer us for doing feminist theology are: first, no standpoint is neutral, objective, value-free, or above suspicion. Second, meta-narratives erase otherness/alterity by including the other within my/our narratives, thereby removing its otherness. The postmodern rejection of meta-narratives leads to a discursive scrutiny of meta-narratives that have justified multiple forms of oppression, domination, colonization, and totalization. Third, we must carry out the task of understanding or interpreting society through piecemeal, tactical, pragmatic, and tentative means. And, fourth, we must conduct the task of

---

63. Linda Hutcheon, "Postmodern Problematic," in Merrill, ed., *Ethics/Aesthetics*, 5.

transforming religion, communities of believers, and society through grassroots, localized, tactical, and pragmatic means.

Since postmodernity belongs to our current context, it is important to address it theopolitically and theoethically. Beyond its contextual significance, it may have constitutive value as well. Although one can interpret postmodernism in many different ways, I believe we can draw theological insights and implications from it. Postmodern discourses are, in a way, all deconstructive in the sense that they seek to distance us from and make us skeptical about beliefs concerning absolutized truth-claims, naturalized knowledge, power, the self, and language, which people often take for granted. I contend that this deconstructive tendency of postmodernism is, in fact, a hyperaffirmative and constructive force for *re*-constructing and *pro*-constructing religion in its full sense. Here *re*-constructing is among the past-oriented categories while *pro*-constructing is among the future-oriented categories. Jürgen Moltmann advocates the term *pro*- because of its future-oriented connotation, maintaining that "in *Pro*volution, the human dream turned forward is combined with the new possibility of the future and begins consciously to direct the course of human history as well as the evolution of nature."[64] Although I concur with Moltmann, I am using both *re*- and *pro*-constructing because I think religion in a postmodern era has a paradoxical feature in the sense that it has to refer to the past in the midst of its fundamental clash with the past. Postmodernism appears in all its diversity to permit and encourage a selective attention to the past and an eclectic reconstruction of the present. So I attempt to reveal the paradoxical, self-contradicting tendency in postmodernism itself by juxtaposing *re*-constructing and *pro*-constructing. Postmodernism enables religion to be open, critical, and indeed

---

64. Jürgen Moltmann, *Religion, Revolution, and the Future* (New York: Scribners, 1969), 32.

prophetic by facilitating self-criticism about the tradition's inheritance from the past.

The emerging postmodern consciousness also has a vision of integrating wholeness and life-affirming. The medium of postmodern thinking itself draws theological explication in directions of greater comprehensiveness than were possible during the modern period. Postmodernism fundamentally challenges religion, especially institutionalized religion and community of faith, by rejecting any blind fixation or absolutization of one's truth-claims, which one cannot separate from realities of power and privilege. It also challenges established religion by harshly scrutinizing and criticizing a hierarchical and kyriarchal structure and dualistic mode of thinking. It may, furthermore, dismantle the asymmetrical power distribution among different strata of people by decentering the center of religious, discursive, and institutional power, and further provide a politics of representation for the marginalized and the powerless within religion by focusing on and celebrating small/local narratives, which people have often neglected and omitted in the religion of modernism.

We cannot simply deny the postmodern critique charging that most institutionalized religions have played the role of creating a totalizing ideology, in the sense that they have justified and perpetuated the existing order, negating the marginalized, the powerless, and the voiceless. We have little choice but to challenge the totalizing instincts of traditional theology and the theological hegemony of kyriarchal and Euro-/U.S.-centric ecclesiality. The alternative vision for religion today is grassroots-oriented, community-based, nonhierarchical, intersubjective, and small-scale. Religion, as a kenotic, deconstructive movement, would then be able both to mirror the best of postmodernism and to challenge the worst. Religion in the twenty-first-century world cannot be the same religion it was in the modern era. We need to redefine, reconceptualize, restructure, and retheologize religion today based on the "principle of holistic thinking."[65] Otherwise, religion will lose its vitality, its public accountability, and its sociocultural, theological, and ecclesiological relevance in the world.

---

65. Ted Peters, *God-the World's Future: Systematic Theology for a Postmodern Era* (Minneapolis: Fortress Press, 1992), 30. Here, Peters articulates two principles of postmodern thinking: the principle of holistic thinking and a version of the wager hypothetical reconstruction.

6

Out of Places

Feminist Theology of Dis/location in a Global Context

One is always on the run, and it seems I haven't really had a home base—and this may have been good for me. I think it's important for people not to feel rooted in one place.
—Gayatri Chakravorty Spivak[1]

Planting a Sign in a Deterritorialized Space

Questions of one's dis/location become more and more elusive today, geopolitically, historically, and discursively. Trying to find an answer to this question of dis/location is also a serious ontological endeavor of finding one's way of be-ing as an ever-moving verb, not a never-moving noun.[2] Dis/location is ever becoming and ever moving. My use of the term *dis/location*, compounded from the words *dislocation*

---

1. Gayatri Chakravorty Spivak, *The Post-colonial Critic: Interviews, Strategies, Dialogues*, ed. Sarah Harasym (New York: Routledge, 1990), 37.
2. Mary Daly talks about "Verbicide" as "killing of the living, transformative energy of words" in her proposing to change from God the Father, "Being," to God the Verb, "Be-ing." For more details, see Mary Daly, *Beyond God the Father: Toward a Philosophy of Women's Liberation* (Boston: Beacon, 1985 [1973]), xvii.

and *location*, is to reveal the entangled nature of those terms. A politics of location, first coined by Adrienne Rich, emerged in the early 1980s as a discourse of difference, especially in U.S. academic feminist discourse, as a method of scrutinizing and dismantling the fixed position, identity, and privilege of whiteness.[3] This discourse of political location is an outcome of more than a decade of struggles over how to define and position feminism as theory and practice. One can regard it as eruptions of difference after the painful splits, especially among women of different races.

Nowadays, one must also confront what one thinks, says, and writes from one's dis/location by positioning oneself along the axes of religion, race, ethnicity, class, gender, ability, sexuality, or nationality and citizenship. Furthermore, the pressure and internal demand to mark and locate oneself within the U.S. context is far greater on scholars of color than on those who are "noncolor," that is, white. Here I want to make clear that I am not content with using the term "women of color," in spite of the good intentions of some who view the terms "women of color" or "Third-World women" as representing "a viable oppositional alliance" that provides a "common context of struggle rather than color of racial identifications."[4] A very ambivalent meaning underlies the term "people of color," however. One can use it as one of the positive achievements of multiculturalism's celebration of diverse racial and ethnic people, and as a positive claim of self-identity and self-politicization by those of color. Yet, at the same time, it could continue to perpetuate a racial distinction made by those of noncolor, whites who were never a part of the people of color, as if white were not a color.

---

3. Cf. Adrienne Rich, *Blood, Bread and Poetry: Selected Prose, 1979–1985* (New York: Norton, 1986).

4. Chandra Talpade Mohanty, "Cartographies of Struggle: Third World Women and the Politics of Feminism," in *Third World Women and the Politics of Feminism*, ed. Changra Talpade Mohanty, Ann Russo, and Lourdes Torres (Bloomington: Indiana University Press, 1991), 7.

In doing so, whites, the people of noncolor, become normative of humanhood. In using the phrase "women of color," I would like to underscore the fact that "without adequately analyzing power differentials among groups positioned by racial categorizations and inequalities, the phrase 'people of color' still implies that white culture is the *hidden norm* against which all other racially subordinate groups' so-called 'differences' are measured."[5]

Positioning oneself along analytical axes such as race, class, gender, or sexuality should not be, however, static positions, because one's being is in itself fluid, complex, and multiple in many ways. Such a mode of strategic self-location can be, however, one way to make a connection between the private and the public, between the personal and the academic. This self-positioning is a political or historical choice and becomes one's site of enunciation and discursive space. When I identify myself as a woman or heterosexual, this self-positioning is not just a biological statement but denotes a political, cultural, societal, and historical standpoint. In the same vein, positioning myself as a feminist, postmodern, deconstructionist, or postcolonial border thinker, I am making a firm political statement, which clearly indicates to what I am committed. When I use an identity marker such as Asian feminist theologian, it is not a geographically or culturally essentialist statement, as is true for some theologians, but a political and historical statement. I am very critical of blind dichotomies between men and women, people of color and white people, heterosexual and homosexual, or West and East.

The separation of the personal and the academic has been a general practice in academia. However, feminist theorists have argued that such binarism between the personal and the academic is not just

---

5. Leslie G. Roman, "White Is a Color! White Defensiveness, Postmodernism, and Anti-racist Pedagogy," in *Race, Identity and Representation in Education*, ed. Cameron McCarthy and Warren Crichlow (New York: Routledge, 1993), 71.

insufficient or inappropriate but damaging because it seriously overlooks the very materiality and contextuality of knowledge that one produces. My initial realization of the strong need/urge to connect the personal and the academic began during the time when I left Korea for Germany in the mid-1980s to do my postgraduate work. I felt a huge discrepancy between the world in front of my desk and the world behind it. I did not know what language I should employ to analyze why I felt what I then felt. I didn't even know what to do with this discrepancy and the loss of academic passion that I once had. I grew very gloomy during my time in Germany. I felt that I lost not just external language but also my internal language that I used previously to organize both my internal and external life experience. In recent years, the cross-cultural movement has become the norm rather than the exception and leaving one's native country is simply not as dramatic as it once was. Yet, at that time, the detachment of my identity from a specific geographic place was very shocking for me. Through my first experience of geopolitical dis/location and relocation, I began to feel the deep-seated ontological dis/location in my reality as one positioned in the intersection of patriarchy, racism, sexism, and classism, as a married woman, a mother, a foreign student with no economic faculty in such an affluent Western country like Germany.

The great first lessons of my uprooting from my physical homeland, though by my choice, were in the tremendous importance of language and of culture. In other words, I realized that language and culture constitute us in a way that we perhaps remain unconscious of if we stay safely ensconced within one culture and the same geographic place. I felt departing from my homeland for Germany was somehow irrevocable, even when I would return to my homeland later. Even though the point of departure and arrival could be spatially the same, I knew that I could never be the same inside, in my interior world. Those academic books that I used to read on my desk did not deal with such pressing issues that I had to wrestle with in my physical reality behind the desk.

The feminist-theology seminar I took as a doctoral student in the United States, after I left Germany, became the epistemological space where I began to learn the internal languages with which I can organize my experience, analyze why I feel what I feel, negotiate with the gap between the two contradicting worlds—in front of and behind the desk—and affirm the fact that it is possible and even necessary to connect the personal to the academic. This exposure to feminist discourse became my epistemological/ontological conversion experience which made me realize that reality was not as it appeared and that we should materialize theology by interlinking the academic/theological and the personal in a specific time and space. Otherwise, theology can be just an instrument for certain groups of people to create a discursive hegemony by falsely universalizing their abstract speculation on the world, in the name of objectivity, universality, and value-neutrality of academism, both wittingly and unwittingly. In this regard, the personal is not just political, as feminists have argued; the personal is cultural, sociological, and theological as well.

Since feminism touched my life, I have begun to have mixed feelings: feeling myself standing on the wrong corner wherever I am in my reality but, at the same time, feeling that I have found a new space in which I can finally be who I really am. I realized, however, that the more feminist discourses intrigued me, the more I felt out of place in my materialized reality. Living simultaneously in two spaces—the actual space of patriarchy and the discursive space of feminism—means living in an in-between space. So I have become an ongoing traveler, traveling back and forth between these two worlds. At the same time, entering this feminist space means I experience a constant ontological displacement in my physical reality where patriarchy permeates every sector of society. I begin to feel out of place, as if there were no places to which I belong. This is a feeling of being uprooted from every sector of reality and not "at home" in any. Since then, the question of "home" has been lingering deep in my mind. What would one mean by being out of place, of being dislocated from the point of departure?

Ever since I left my home in Asia, where the physical address of my personal place used to be, the most frequent question that I receive from people is, "Where are you from?" It did not take a long time for me to realize the harsh reality of deep-seated racism, even in people with good intention. And it becomes clearer that *who* is asking this question *to whom* has a totally different political connotation. When an Asian asks this question to a Caucasian, it would be an innocent question in terms of a sense of ownership. But if a Caucasian asks it to an Asian in a white-dominant context, for instance, it carries a different political connotation because it often presupposes an unwitting claiming of an ownership of the space. This question often entails the underlying presuppositions that (1) "You do not belong here," and (2) that "You have a 'home' to which to return." It does not matter whether one is a student, full-time pastor, or a full-time professor. Neither does it matter whether one has lived in a space for a month or for seven years, or if one has a permanent resident card or student visa. This Where-are-you-from? question is also a question of one's identity, and tends to force one to formulate one's identity grounded on where one belongs, binding one to the past. So how I interpret this question, seemingly simple but politically complicated, depends on who is asking this question and what kind of discursive consequences it would bring.

I often answer this question with, "I am from where I am," especially to those people who would eventually understand the political and discursive implication of the question. This periodic question has made me aware how one comes to locate one's life in the intersection of sexism, racism, classism, and linguicism, which Robert Phillipson defines as "ideologies, structures, and practices which are used to legitimate, effectuate, and reproduce an unequal division of power and resources (both material and immaterial) between groups which are defined on the basis of language."[6] Certainly, this home question does not just convey a simple geographical concern. The question often carries, wittingly or unwittingly, a racist implication, especially when asked by racially privileged people whom society regards as normative. It is clear to me that how one understands home is not just a question of geographical, historical, or any sort of physical space. Instead, the home question, the Where-are-you-from? question is indeed an utterly complex political question that reveals one's geopolitical, epistemological, and ontological location.

What interests me is the fact that the question of home is tied to the multiple questions of one's ontological, geopolitical, and theological awareness. How and who defines home is not just a personal matter but also a sociopolitical issue, in that one can always relate it to the "glocal" (see chapter 7, below) reality today. Furthermore, one's being out of place reveals the discrepancy between home and unhome, as well as the disparity of power between those who have home by being rooted in a certain territory and those who have not by being deterritorialized, either by internal choice or by external force. Thus, I have come to believe that theology cannot acquiesce to the status quo. A theology of dis/location that I propose here starts with straddling home and unhome to state and elaborate the conditions of the imaginary geography of Home, with one foot in and one foot out, being both in a world of already and of not-yet.

6. Robert Phillipson, *Linguistic Imperialism* (New York: Oxford University Press, 1992), 47.

Out-of-Places:
A Transformative Relocation

The discourse of dis/location in Christianity begins with the dis/location of Adam and Eve from the Garden of Eden, after eating the fruit of the Tree of Knowledge, and continues in God's command to Abraham to leave home. It is interesting to see how Eve's epistemological awakening to good and evil, after tasting the forbidden fruit of the Tree of Knowledge, has the consequence of her "ontological" dis/location from the Garden of Eden—*Home*. The Israelites' forty-year exodus experience in the wilderness is also a collective experience of dis/location. In this sense, it is not wrong to say that Judeo-Christianity starts with a theology of dis/location from the outset and that the discourse of dis/location is in fact not new. What *is* new stems from the awareness that "our contemporary world has seen migrations of people on a scale as never before in human history" and that "for colonized peoples, migrations by 'choice' and/or by economic necessity are rooted within a colonial and postcolonial history and within continuing imperialist dominations today."[7] Therefore, the politics of home and of de/territorialization of the empire continue to influence current ideas of identity—both individual and national. A displaced person draws attention to the precariousness of home as materialized location and to the experience of "the unhomely" in a contemporary geopolitical reality. Homi Bhabha eloquently remarks that the word *unhomely* "captures something of the estranging sense of the relocation of the home and the world in an unhallowed place" and that "to be unhomed is not to be homeless, nor can the 'unhomely' be easily accommodated in that

---

7. Ketu H. Katrak, "Colonialism, Imperialism, and Imagined Homes," in *The Columbia History of the American Novel*, ed. Emory Elliott (New York: Columbia University Press, 1991), 649.

familiar division of social life into private and the public spheres."[8] In this sense, "the unhomely is the shock of recognition of the world-in-the-home, the home-in-the-world."[9] The contemporary experience of transnational migration and exile have accompanied the discourse of dis/location. Considering the current situation in global context, articulating how one understands the experience of uprootedness, of dis/location, of deterritorialization, of homelessness, or the unhomeliness[10] is an urgent and significant theological task today.

Dis/location, whether geopolitical or ontological, entails in a way the loss of all familiar external and internal parameters, and therefore could be very painful. There is also gain, however, not just all pain. Such dis/location can make a different understanding possible and provides a perspective, a vantage point. This experience of dis/location as an experience of not being at home can also be a crucial liberating step in self-discovery. Becoming out of place makes one distant from who one used to be and makes one rewrite oneself from a totally new point of view. Furthermore, being a feminist, for instance, also means being in exile even in one's own homeland. Although being in exile is "compelling to think about but terrible to experience,"[11] this experience of being out of place can develop into a way of thinking about Home. Here Edward Said says that the "only home truly available now, though fragile and vulnerable, is in writing."[12] This situation creates a kind of paradox between loss and recovery. An experience of dis/location can be an experience of radical, transformative relocation. And the displaced person becomes

---

8. Homi Bhabha, "The World and the Home," *Social Text* (Third World and Post-Colonial Issues) 31/32 (1992): 141.
9. Ibid.
10. Ibid.
11. Edward Said, "Reflection on Exile," in *Out There: Marginalization and Contemporary Cultures*, ed. Russell Ferguson, et al. (Cambridge: MIT Press, 1990), 357.
12. Ibid., 365.

a permanent homeless traveler who is looking for Home by being displaced from home.

One of the few benefits of the condition of exile is an "originality of vision," which is the product of seeing "the entire world as a foreign land."[13] Being unattached to or detached from an existing world, those who are discursively or geopolitically dislocated can be in the best position to demystify the transparence of social relations and the self-evidence of religious or sociopolitical ideologies. It also seems that dis/location can be the instigator of new vision. But I wish neither to romanticize being out of place nor to underestimate the sheer human cost of actual exile or dis/location as well as of its psychic implications. I am also fully aware of the different kinds of status of being out of place, of not being at home, some chosen, some not. I am also interested less in the epistemological/cognitive advantages of being dislocated and more in its other productive consequences, especially in terms of transformative theological construction. I believe, however, in *being* out of place—whether that be geopolitical, ontological, or epistemological—and believe in its capacity for deterritorialization, transgression, and radical openness to the new that one can channel into the fight against sexism, classism, racism, ageism, linguicism, xenophobia, or homophobia, all of which draw a rigid boundary between people on various grounds. The experience of marginality by those who have escaped from home or are forced to leave home can be an experience of developing who they are and what they are capable of. They become sensitive to the issue of who is in and who is out of the mainstream of a given society and develop concern for those who are out of the dominant circle—those dislocated and deterritorialized.

---

13. Ibid., 366.

Nomadism or pilgrimage entails a constant state of being in processor becoming, which Rosi Braidotti refers to as the philosophy of "as-if." Her figuration of the nomad is a political definition as well as a critical consciousness, an attempt to "explore and legitimate political agency, while taking as historical evidence the decline of metaphysically fixed, steady identities."[14] The practice of "as-if," is a "technique of strategic re-location in order to rescue what we need of the past in order to trace paths of transformation of our lives here and now."[15] She also understands "as-if" as the "affirmation of fluid boundaries, a practice of the intervals, of the interfaces, and the interstices." While grounded in postmodernist theory of repetition, parody, pastiche, and the like, she insists that for "as-if" to be useful, it must be grounded in deliberate agency and lived experience. Postmodern subversions and parody in the "as-if" mode "can be politically empowering on the condition of being sustained by a critical consciousness that aims at engendering transformations and changes," and opens up "in-between spaces where new forms of political subjectivity can be explored."[16]

Although I do find empowerment in the discourse of nomadic subjects, I would like to employ the term "the dislocated," rather than "nomad," as a metaphor for my theologizing. Nomadism seems to me to have a danger of being *a*geopolitical and *a*historical by tending to celebrate a constant traveling, even without having to move physically from one's habitat to another. The points of departure and of arrival for a nomad do not have to be different, while for a dislocated person the difference between the two places is crucial. Unlike a nomad, when the dislocated person travels, she or he looks for a Home. Here, travel, as a metaphor, provides a possibility

14. Rosi Braidotti, *Nomadic Subjects: Embodiment and Sexual Difference in Contemporary Feminist Theory* (New York: Columbia University Press, 1994), 5.
15. Ibid., 6.
16. Ibid., 7.

for an intellectual/cognitive uprooting and contains the potential for transformation. For me, identifying oneself as a dislocated traveler makes a political statement which reveals what is lacking in the existing reality that makes oneself uprooted and dislocated, and therefore creates a need for establishing an authentic Home where one is able to feel truly homely, and to be truly the whole self, not a fragmented self. Looking for Home from homes requires a radical transformation of one's relationship with self, community, and the divine. It also requires a radical openness to those who are dislocated on various grounds because they are the ones with whom the "homeless, dislocated traveler" could share what they are yearning for and what they need to do to actualize Home in a geopolitical reality. Here there is a possibility of passionate solidarity among/for those who are out of place.

I also believe in being detached from everything familiar, either by choice or force, because it can make for a certain creative defamiliarization, which often gives one new ways of observing and seeing the world. In this context, leaving home for Home or being displaced can be a liberating step in self-discovery. By being defamiliarized, one can see in reality what one has not seen due to the sociopolitical or religious convention and practice that constrain one's view of the world. In this regard, one can join in the "gatherings of exiles and émigrés and refugees; gatherings on the edge of 'foreign' cultures . . . gathering in the half-life, half-light of foreign tongues . . . gathering the signs of approval and acceptance . . . gathering the past in a ritual of revival; gathering the present," as Homi Bhabha poetically illustrates.[17] When God commands Abraham, "Go from your country and your kindred and your father's house" (Gen. 12:1), Abraham's leaving home is a journey of

---

17. Homi K. Bhabha, "DissemiNation: Time, Narrative and the Margins of the Modern Nation," in *Location of Culture* (New York: Routledge, 2004), 199.

defamiliarization that gives him new eyes through which he is able to see the self, the world, and the divine from a totally different perspective, seeing everything afresh. The Bible does not give clear reasons why God commands Abraham to leave his home. It seems to me, however, very clear that Abraham must have experienced total dis/location—a loss of familiar space and life, the fear and frustration for the unknown future, yearning and longing for Home away home, ongoing daily survival, and hope and vision for the future Home. Through this experience of being out of place, Abraham becomes who he is. In this case, dis/location turns out to be a transformative relocation, which offers a powerful mode of interpretation of in-between space as a form of accountability to more than one location.

Feminist Theology as Deep Minority Discourse

Gilles Deleuze and Felix Guattari distinguish minority discourse from great literature by citing three characteristics: deterritorialization, an emphasis on politics, and collective value. In discussing the deterritorialization of a major language through a minor literature written in the major language from a marginalized or minoritarian position, Deleuze and Guattari explain that it does not arise from a literature written in a minor language, or in a formerly colonized language. Rather, it is written in a major language, which is "affected with a high coefficient of deterritorialization."[18] The second feature of minor literature is its emphasis on politics. Everything in the minor literature is political, in that the individual subject is linked to the political. Therefore, "its cramped space forces each individual intrigue

18. Gilles Deleuze and Felix Guattari, "What is a Minor Literature," *Kafka: Towards a Minor Literature* (Minneapolis: University of Minnesota Press, 1986), 16.

to connect immediately to politics" and the "individual concern thus becomes all the more necessary, indispensable, magnified, because a whole other story is vibrating in it."[19]

The third characteristic of minor literature is its collective value. Collective value refers to the writer's terrain, where utterances reflect a community's usage, which is inseparable from the political nature of a minor literature. Deleuze and Guattari argue the inextricability of the political and the collective, which seems to me to coincide with the feminist argument that the personal is political. Deleuze and Guattari rightly point out that what each author says individually already constitutes a common action, and what he or she says or does is necessarily political, even if others aren't in agreement. The political domain has contaminated every statement. But above all else, because collective or national consciousness is "often inactive in external life and always in the process of break-down," minor literature finds itself positively charged with the role and function of the collective and even revolutionary enunciation. Its enunciative value is both political and collective, and therefore even what an author says individually is necessarily political and revolutionary. The revolutionary potential of a minor literature is written from the margins, deterritorializing the "fragile community" from the border from where it is possible "to express another possible community and to forge the means for another consciousness and another sensibility." In this sense, a minor literature is political and subversive because it creates "the opposite dream."[20]

It is clear, according to the criteria Deleuze and Guattari outline, that feminist theological discourse is certainly a minority discourse. But are all feminist theological discourses minor to the same degree? The answer, for me, is definitely *no*. I would argue that Asian feminist

19. Ibid., 17.
20. Ibid., 27.

theological discourse is on the margin of the margin in a global discursive world. Asian feminist theologians are the ones doing theology in the intersection not only of racism, sexism, and classism, but also of linguicism. I would argue that in an era of so-called globalization, we have to add language to those discursive axes of race, gender, class, and sexuality, because of the influential power of linguicism in every sector of our reality today, especially in a form of English linguistic imperialism, which Robert Phillipson defines as "the dominance of English asserted and maintained by the establishment and continuous reconstitution of structural and cultural inequalities between English and other languages."[21] When people consider English as a normative language, they consider those whose first language is not English as subsocial, especially in the English-speaking countries of the global North. That all knowledge production and reproduction in the world today is bound up with the hegemony of English means that the politics of hegemonic language is strongly tied to linguistic terrorism. It also becomes so problematic in an era of globalization that those who speak English as their first language always tend to dominate all international meetings. In this case, an international meeting often ends up being *English*-national, instead of *inter*-national. In this sense, English-holder becomes power-holder. Needless to say, language has been a powerful means of imperialistic domination. Gloria Anzaldua shows how the hegemony of English terrifies people of languages other than English, which she calls "linguistic terrorism": "Because we speak with tongues of fire we are culturally *crucified*. Racially, culturally and linguistically. . . . we speak an *orphan tongue*. . . . as long as I have to accommodate the English speakers rather than having them accommodate me, my tongue will be illegitimate."[22]

---

21. According to Phillipson, "English linguistic imperialism" is a subtype of "linguicism." Cf. Phillipson, *Linguistic Imperialism*, 47.

In this regard, most Asians, as non-English-nationals, are doomed to be considered subsocial in the global context because they are the ones who permanently speak in orphan tongues in today's world where English has become an exclusively global language, and where only former colonial languages are officially translated and considered normative languages. English-centrism justifies an ideology of superiority among English-speaking people and in their culture; English has become also a determinant of whether one is sufficiently intelligent and accountable. It would be interesting to see the difference between feminist theologians from the West and those from the non-West in terms of their global status, along the line of an analysis of the difference between antisemitism and racism against African Americans. Thus, Oliver Cox points out (using the common racial parlance of the time of "Negroes"):

> The dominant group is intolerant of those whom it can define as *antisocial*, while it holds race prejudice against those whom it can define as *subsocial*. . . . Thus we are ordinarily intolerant of Jews but prejudiced against Negroes. In other words, the dominant group or ruling class does not like the Jew at all, but likes the Negro in his place. To put it still another way, the condition of its liking the Jew is that he cease being a Jew and voluntarily become like the generality of society, while the condition of liking the Negro is that he cease trying to become like the generality of society and remain contentedly a Negro. . . . We want to assimilate the Jews, but they, on the whole, refuse with probable justification to be assimilated; the Negroes want to be assimilated, but we refuse to let them assimilate.[23]

Although this analysis does not show the sophisticated nature of the power disparity between feminists from the global South and those from the global North, it shows how racism or racial prejudice works

22. Gloria Anzaldua, *Borderlands/La Frontera: The New Mestiza* (San Francisco: Spinsters/Aunt Lute, 1987), 58, 59 (italics mine).
23. Oliver C. Cox, *Caste, Class and Race* (New York: Monthly Review, 1959 [1948]), 400–40 (italics mine).

in the intersection of sexism and other forms of discrimination. While people would consider feminist theologians of the global North as antisocial due to their violation and transgression of the sociocultural code, they would regard feminist theologians from the global South as subsocial due to their second-class status in a global context. It is misleading, therefore, if we reduce racism/ethnocentrism and classism to sexism and search for a general theory of oppression incorporating race, gender, class, and ethnicity with various linguistic dis/ability. In this regard, Asian feminist theological discourse is not just minority discourse, but *deep* minority discourse, which is more repressed or marginalized than those feminists whose heart language is a dominant language, due to the hegemony of English, which entails the neoimperialistic reality that the women from the global South experience. Linguicism in the construction of theological discourse on a global level is not just the struggle between hegemonic culture and minorities. It is also a struggle with the homogenizing power that exoticizes or stereotypes Asian as Orientals, as in Edward Said's notion of orientalism. Considering the complexity and diversity of minority discourse, the political concerns of Asian feminist theological discourse, as deep minority discourse, have their unique tasks in a global context.

A Feminist Theology of Dis/location in a Global Context

I have often met Asian theologians, both women and men, who reject feminist discourse as a Western construct and instead claim that Asian theology defends the uniqueness and rights of Asians. For them, the constitution of "Asian" and the nature of the adjective *Asian* seem self-evident and therefore natural. Such a naïvely nativist stance is "a real denial of history" because the concept of human

rights, including women's rights and the rights of the ethnically/
racially marginalized, has "a deep complicity with the culture of
imperialism."[24] I am aware of the problems of feminists in the global
North who often deny the otherness of women in the global South
and judge them according to the high feminist norm of the global
North or patronize them by participating in an "information
retrieval" approach, grounded in a "What I can do *for* them"
attitude.[25] However, overlooking the ideological intersection of
sexism and ethnocentrism in such nativist claims for Asian culture and
tradition by Asians is as dangerous as the uncritical absorption of the
Western feminist claims.

Theologizing in an Acquired Language in Global Context

Articulating feminist theology in an internationally accepted
vehicular language, such as English, is doing theology with an
acquired language, not with a heart language. *Vernacular* language is,
according to Deleuze and Guattari in their adoption of the linguistic
theories of the tetralinguistic model, a language of territorialization,
while the *vehicular* language is "a language of the first sort of
deterritorialization." They go on to explain that the four languages in
the tetralinguistic model differ according to spatiotemporal location:
"*vernacular* is here; *vehicular* language is everywhere; *referential*
language is over there; *mythic* language is beyond."[26] The distribution
of these language functions is also determined by historical, cultural,
and national location, as Deleuze and Guattari illustrate through the

24. Gayatri Chakravorty Spivak, "Neocolonialism and the Secret Agent of Knowledge: An
Interview with Robert J. C. Young," *Oxford Literary Review* ("Neocolonialism" issue) 13, no. 1
(July 1991): 232.
25. Gayatri Chakravorty Spivak, "French Feminism in an International Frame," in *In Other Worlds:
Essays in Cultural Politics* (New York: Routledge, 1988), 135.
26. Deleuze and Guattari, *Kafka*, 23 (italics mine).

shifting functions of Latin: "vehicular" in the classical Roman era; "referential" in the medieval period; "mythic" during the Renaissance and after. According to Deleuze and Guattari, these language functions "can have ambiguous edges, changing borders that differ from this or that material. . . . Each function of language divides up in turn and carries with it multiple centers of power. A blur of languages, and not at all a system of languages."[27]

I have experienced that articulating theology in this global vehicular language, English, is a process of "becoming minor" and that I feel "a sort of stranger within"[28] the allegedly vehicular language I am using: the language of *everywhere*. But will there be any time in human history when the hegemony of English will give away its power of being a global vehicular language to another language, as in the case of Latin, especially in this era of neoimperialism? My observation does not yet allow me to give a positive answer to this question. In the current geopolitical context, as long as my first language, Korean, remains only a referential or vernacular language, constructing theological discourse in a global context will remain a deep minority discourse. This fate of the dislocated Asian feminist theologians in a global context, who become the writers of theology in an acquired language, shall have to offer a vision of a transformative theologizing with their persistent attention to the complicated intersection of sexism, racism, classism, ethnocentrism, homophobism, linguicism, and neoimperialism in our geopolitical reality. In this sense, the space of their theologizing should be a space of deterritorialization that resists microfascisms which homogenize, exoticize, stereotype, totalize, and subjugate people on any ground. For we need to make a "qualitative shift away from hegemony, whatever its size and however 'local' it may be."[29]

27. Ibid., 24.
28. Ibid., *Kafka*, 26.

Dismantling Naturalization of Asian Women

Ecofeminism analyzes the Western tradition's naturalization of women and feminization of nature, drawing the conclusion that the domination of women and the domination of nature are inextricably connected and mutually reinforcing. This connection of the oppression of women and of nature as twin oppressions gives rise to a common formative structure of othering. This epistemological framework of the naturalization of women and nature in the Western tradition can also apply to the naturalization and feminization of the Orient. As Edward Said relevantly points out, the invention of the Orient is an outgrowth of a will to power of the West, and therefore orientalism "is a Western style for dominating, restructuring, and having authority over the Orient."[30] In this construction of the Orient, Asia is very often feminized and Asian women are more naturalized, ethnicized, mystified, and exoticized by both the West and Asia. Albert Memmi articulates this process of naturalization of the colonized as follows:

> The colonialist removes the factor from history, time and therefore possible evolution. What is actually a sociological point becomes labeled as being biological, or preferably, metaphysical. It is attached to the colonized's basic nature. Immediately the colonial relationship between colonized and colonizer, founded on the essential outlook of the two protagonists, becomes a definitive category. It is what it is because they are what they are, and neither one nor the other will ever change.[31]

The danger of any naturalization of analytic categories such as "woman" or "the Orient" is the fact that it ends in a dehistoricization, depoliticization, and mystification of difference between women and men, between the West and Asia, between Asian women and

29. Braidotti, *Nomadic Subjects*, 5.
30. Edward Said, *Orientalism* (New York: Vintage, 1978), 3.
31. Albert Memmi, *The Colonizer and the Colonized* (Boston: Beacon, 1967), 85.

Western women. In the name of formulating cultural difference between Asia and the West, ethnic markers such as "Asian" easily become a method of differentiation and naturalization that blocks criticism from the critical task of theology, and Asian theological discourses tend to be easily geographically deterministic and hence culturally essentialist. Choan-Seng Song's book title, *Theology from the Womb of Asia*, for instance, is a good example of typical naturalization and feminization of Asia, in its adoption of the metaphor *womb* from feminine biology as a ground of Asian theologizing.[32] Some may say that Edward Said's theory does not apply to East Asia because many East Asian countries such as Korea, Japan, Singapore, or China were not, territorially speaking, Western colonial possessions. However, this kind of positivistic approach overlooks the colonial situation today, where the fate of Asia is entirely interlinked with the foreign policy of the United States, the neoempire, with its major military bases in Asian countries such as Japan, Korea, Taiwan, the Philippines, and Vietnam. I often find myself, as an Asian woman faculty of color teaching in First-World academia, being located in the scene between orientalism and nativism. When I do not play the role of a native informant, both Asians and non-Asians suspect my authentic Asianness. Asian feminist theology in the global context has to dismantle thoroughly the naturalization of Asian women by moving beyond Asian women's identity politics that privileges their narrowly defined authenticity. People too easily regard Asian women as "pieces of exotica" and "manageable others."[33] This scene of postcoloniality is a site of Asian feminist theology of dislocation, which is to be a persistent critique of totalization.

---

32. Choan-Seng Song, *Theology from the Womb of Asia* (Maryknoll, NY: Orbis, 1986).
33. Spivak, *The Post-Colonial Critic*, 94, 114.

Asian as Transethnic

What does make Asian theology *Asian?* This question is not as easy to answer as it sounds. It is obvious that what we call Asian theology does not simply mean theology done by the ethnically Asian. I do not agree with the idea that Asian theology is theology that primarily deals with unique Asian resources that the West does not have. "Asian" as uniqueness or specialness has both positive and negative connotations: positive when interpreted geopolitically as subversive of the West-centeredness of theological discourse, and negative when understood in an essentialist way, which is misleading and confining. I do not have any problems with starting from the position that "Asians are suffered from poverty and their context is religiously very plural,"[34] because, in order to start one's theological construction and practice, one has to have some kind of provisional point of departure. However, when such a claim becomes monolithic and essentialist and tends to define what constitutes Asian theology as such, that is when I begin to have trouble. It is true, simplistically speaking, that Asia, as the global South, is poorer than those countries in the global North. Yet, it is also true that one cannot shift economic conditions at will, so that Western people of a poorer class are not immediate oppressors of Asians of a much richer class. If one is aware of the tremendous complexity and diversity of the context of people in every continent of the globe, such awareness cleanses that kind of monolithic and essentialist claim that one is speaking for all Asians' suffering and oppression.

When academics or religious leaders in Asia involved in power struggles in a regional context—which is quite often the only really political activity in which they are fully engaged—use the excuse

---

34. Cf. Aloysius Pieris, "Towards an Asian Theology of Liberation: Some Religio-Cultural Guidelines," in *Asia's Struggle for Full Humanity*, ed. Virginia Fabella (Maryknoll, NY: Orbis, 1980).

of Asians' universal suffering and oppression, they are certainly not thinking about their institutional hegemonic power that oppresses other people in their own academies and denominations, or of the urban subproletariat in New York, or about women's issues in Uganda or India. Using "Asian" in an essentialist way oversimplifies differences between and among Asian countries and overlooks the ironical contrast between the rich in poor Asia and the poor in the rich West. I use the word *Asian* with full awareness of its problems, when interpreted in a geoculturally essentialist way. It is a general principle of feminist inquiry to be skeptical about any account of human relations that fails to mention gender or consider the possible effects of gender differences: for in a world in which there is sexism, obscuring the workings of gender is likely to involve—whether wittingly or unwittingly—also obscuring the workings of sexism. We thus ought to be skeptical about any account of race/ethnicity relations that fails to mention gender and vice versa. Asian theologies often fall into a trap of genderlessness.

One's identity is defined in terms of gender, race, class, sexuality, religion, educational background, or family background, and so forth. It is thus evident that thinking about a person's identity as made up of only neatly distinguishable parts may be very misleading. It can mistakenly lead to taking "Asian" as a generic working category, as if race or ethnicity exists in isolation from other variables of human identity such as gender, class, ability, sexuality, or religion. In this sense, we need to go beyond the cultural essentialist perception of "Asian," and perceive it as transethnic or postethnic, which denotes "a radical and necessary extension of the 'ethnic.'"[35] The situation of the sociopolitical and historico-economic specificity of Asia cannot be a ground of essentializing Asia. Asian feminist theology of dis/

---

35. R. Radhakrishnan, *Diasporic Mediations: Between Home and Location* (Minneapolis: University of Minnesota Press, 1996), 65.

location requires, I would argue, a discursive move from politics of homogeneity to politics of heterogeneity, not as a political indifference but a political affirmation of the diversity among, between, and in us, Asian women.

Theology from Spaces of Dis/location and Liminality

Technique of survival is a very serious issue for feminist theologians in Asia. After several decades of the feminist movement in Christianity and society, many feminist theologians realize that little fundamental change has occurred in the "malestream" of Christianity. Thus, the question, How to survive in an extremely patriarchal society and religion?, becomes increasingly difficult to answer. Without survival, challenging and transforming Christianity and society is very hard to achieve. I strongly feel that the early intellectual/theological excitement about feminist theology has become routinized and, in a way, institutionalized. It becomes just a theoretical production without having a sense of passion for transformation. The absence of passion for change is, I believe, a consequence of internalized defeatism of those women who have hardly been in charge in the malestream religion, and whose radical discourse and practice the malestream ongoingly threaten. I have seen how feminist theologians both in academia and in the church, and especially those in theological schools and seminaries, are vulnerable to tenure and to ordination problems, and even to dismissal at any time.

Doing feminist theology means to imagine a religion and world from a totally different perspective and to envision an alternative way of practicing religion without any kind of hierarchy or exclusion of the poor, women, or sexual minorities. The criterion for measuring whether a religion is egalitarian and liberating consists in the practical test of whether it allows for the full participation and leadership of women. Since the control of public discourse is a principal element of maintaining authority and power, the absence of central feminist questions from public theological discourse is an important form of women's ecclesial exclusion. Broadly speaking, a primary goal of the construction of feminist theological discourse is to promote humanization by transforming self, community, and the world with the spirit of radical equality and inclusivity. Here, we need to wrestle with the following issues: What is the goal of Asian feminist theology? How far is it possible for feminist theologians to make exodus from the existing traditional religion and institution as their survival itself is ongoingly threatened even by their act of raising voices against the patriarchalism in religion? If we understand exodus not just as a metaphoric meaning but as a physical and materialized act, how far can we expect feminist theologians to take action for exodus making? What has to be done to broaden and radicalize feminist theology?

Doing Asian feminist theology requires creating ways of thinking without home, and carrying a perspective of interstice that goes beyond the trap of fixed identity as-(ethnic)-women. Taking dis/location as a metaphor becomes an element in the very staging of the feminist in an extreme patriarchal culture, and being a Christian theologian in a multireligious society, in which people still regard Christianity as a foreign religion and disregard feminism due to its foreign origin, means to be constantly out of place. These three components of hyphenated identity—Asian, feminist, Christian theologian—lead Asian feminist theologians to a peculiar space of an uprootedness and dislocatedness: they are constantly in exile even in their own home country. Due to gender illiteracy in the homeland, Asian feminists leave home for Home either by choice or by institutional force. This being dislocated, however, gives rise to a new consciousness—a consciousness of dis/location.

The feminist consciousness of dis/location here refers to a kind of critical consciousness that resists settling into socially coded modes of thought and behavior, and to the subversion of conventions that define Asian women as exoticized, ethnicized, and idealized, both by Asia and the West. Asian feminist identity of dis/location is the starting point through which they connect with the rest of humanity, not the end point used to distance oneself from it. They would feel a true homecoming in a space of resistance, solidarity, and compassion. Being Asian feminist theologians often requires residing simultaneously in more than two worlds. Feminists are those who are homesick. Being homesick is a desire of becoming other than what one is. Becoming other than what one is involves not only philosophical work but also work on the self. The strategic work of self-transformation requires not only the genealogical practice of defamiliarizing the present, the current configuration of the world, but also the invention of new forms of discipline. Many feminist theologians get constantly exposed to condemnation as heretics and are excluded from patriarchal religion and society. Such exposure to condemnation creates the need and the capacity for spiritual exercises, for self-mastery and transformation. Feminist theologians are those who counter common sense, who swim against the tide, who shake the fundamental epistemological framework of theological institutions, church, and society, and who have in-between consciousness standing in in-between-spaces of the world of already and of not-yet.

Those who have a history of being marginalized on the basis of their skin color, gender, class, sexuality, ability, or any other axis of categorization, read, write, imagine, theorize, and theologize in the interstices of dominant cultures, moving between the language of the center and that of marginality, which Argentinean philosopher Maria Lugones rightly depicts this way: "I wrote this paper from a dark place: a place where I see white/anglo women as 'on the other side,' on 'the light side.' From a dark place where I see myself dark but do not focus on or dwell inside the darkness but rather focus on 'the other side.' To me it makes a deep difference where I am writing from."[36] Similarly, those who have an experience of crossing the borderline between the cultures, languages, and the various configurations of power and meaning in complex hegemonic situations possess what I would call "liminal consciousness." This consciousness is an in-between consciousness or consciousness of interstice. And liminal consciousness gives one the ability to see things from multiple perspectives. Being and living the multiple interstices, one potentially may lock oneself away in isolation and hopelessness, or may gain critical consciousness and particular creativity in thinking, observing, and being engaged with the reality. Rather than being trapped in anger, pain, or isolation, developing this liminal consciousness in a creative way in the experience of dis/location has a potential of resistance against hegemonization and homogenization of the marginalized and a possibility of forming solidarity with the racialized, genderized, or sexualized other. Radhakrishnan rightly argues: "The diaspora is an excellent opportunity to think through some of these vexed questions: solidarity and criticism, belonging and distance, insider spaces and outsider spaces, identity as invention and identity as natural, location-subject positionality and the politics of representation, rootedness and rootlessness."[37]

---

36. Maria Lugones, "On the Logic of Pluralist Feminism," in *Feminist Ethics*, ed. Claudia Card (Lawrence: University Press of Kansas, 1991), 35.
37. R. Radhakrishnan, "Is the Ethnic 'Authentic' in the Diaspora?" in *The State of Asian America: Activism and Resistance in the 1990s*, ed. Karin Aguilar-San Juan (Boston: South End, 1994), 232.

Asian feminist theology today in a global context is relevant only when Asian feminist theologians utilize our being dislocated from multiple places to destabilize unexamined or stereotypical images of certain groups of people that are vestiges of colonial discourse and other manifestations of neoimperialist structural inequalities among people of different race, gender, class, ethnicity, or sexual orientation. I believe that feminist theologians today need to consciously develop a geopolitical sensitivity in our theologizing by embarking on "world-traveling," a process of simultaneous displacement and placement that acknowledges multiple locations. This world-traveling, as a theological/discursive travel, would offer us alternatives to theological/cultural/geopolitical imperialism and appropriation because "through travelling to other people's 'worlds' we discover that there are 'worlds' in which those who are the victims of arrogant perception are really subjects, lively beings, resistors, constructors of vision even though in the mainstream construction they are animated only by the arrogant perceiver and are pliable, foldable, file-awayable, classifiable."[38]

The rhetoric of Asian feminist theology of dis/location indicates a kind of theological progression that is constantly marking out new thresholds, and keeps crossing and transcending these thresholds in this very marking. It also represents a discovery of a temporality that relativizes and dismantles the absolutized authority and discourse that have justified domination of one group of people over the other. This experience and its theological construction of dis/location would offer a critical and passionate energy to work for justice, peace, and equality of all living beings. Asian feminist theology of dis/location is, in its true sense, an ongoing theological world-traveling

---

38. Maria Lugones, "Playfulness, 'World'-Traveling, and Loving Perception," in *Haciendo Caras/ Making Face, Making Soul*, ed. Gloria Anzaldua (San Francisco: Aunt Lute, 1990), 402.

for discovering the others as really, lively subject-beings who cannot be classifiable.

7

Glocal Feminist Theology in an Era of Neoempires

To make the liberated voice, one must confront the issue of audience—we must know to whom we speak.

—bell hooks[1]

"Nativization" of third world women . . . forms a significant context for understanding production of knowledge "about" third world women.

—Chandra Talpade Mohanty[2]

1. bell hooks, *Talking Back: Thinking Feminist, Thinking Black* (Boston: South End Press, 1989), 15.
2. Chandra Talpade Mohanty, "Cartographies of Struggle: Third World Women and the Politics of Feminism," in *Third World Women and the Politics of Feminism*, ed. Chandra Talpade Mohanty, Ann Russo, and Lourdes Torres (Bloomington: Indiana University Press, 1991), 32.

Problematizing *Asian Women*: The Question of Authenticity

Asian feminist theology, like any other theology, is always in the making. I use the word *Asian* in italics in *Asian* feminist theology to denote its contestable and stereotypical nature when people use the term in different types of Asian theological discourses. As *Asia* can never be regarded as a monolithic entity, it is misleading and even distorting to define in a monolithic way what constitutes Asia primarily as overwhelming poverty and multifaceted religiosity. The history of Asian theological engagement with feminism has not been explored in great detail in the various disciplines of theology over the last few decades. *Asian* feminist theology has emerged in the context of an ecumenical movement. Theologically trained women raised the issue of the invisibility of women in the Asian ecumenical movement and its institutions. While Western feminist theological discourse was developed by individuals with a theological and biblical critique of the sexist and patriarchal system both in theology and the church,[3] *Asian* feminist theology did not raise a theological agenda per se at the beginning of its development. The main issues were bringing out women from invisibility to visibility in ecumenical organizations such as the CCA (Christian Conference of Asia). The women question in Christianity in Asia was first raised in 1977 at the Sixth CCA General Assembly in Penang with the following statement: "Even though Christ restored the image of women, the church consciously and unconsciously still refuses to accept the real

---

3. For more details on the historical development of the women's movement and feminist theology in the West, see chs. 5, 6, and 7 in Rosemary Ruether, *Women and Redemption: A Theological History* (Minneapolis: Fortress Press, 1998); and in Asia, see Wong Wai Ching Angela, "Women Doing Theology with the Asian Ecumenical Movement," in *A History of the Ecumenical Movement in Asia*, vol. 2, ed. Ninan Koshy (Hong Kong: CCA, 2004), and Kwok Pui Lan, *Introducing Asian Feminist Theology* (Sheffield, UK: Sheffield Academic Press, 2000).

status of women. It has almost completely disregarded the wholeness which Christ has brought about."[4]

An official request followed this statement at the Seventh CCA General Assembly in Bangalore, India, in 1981: "Asian women have remained backward and marginalized in all sectors of society. Thus, women's concerns pose an enormous task for responsible Christians in Asia. The Christian Conference of Asia can best respond to this challenge by creating a specific program for women's concerns and appointing a full-time executive staff."[5] For the first time in its history, the CCA set up an official Desk for Women's Concerns in 1981. Virginia Fabella and Sun Ai Lee Park published the first anthology of Asian feminist theology, *We Dare to Dream: Doing Feminist Theology As Asian Women*, in 1990.[6] One should note, however, that *Asian* feminist theological discourse written in English shows only a very small part of what has been done in Asia simply because the majority of Asians do not use English as their first language.

I am increasingly convinced that the use of English as an international language carries more and more discursive imperialistic implications, especially in an era of globalization. The discursive hierarchy of English-speaking scholars and nations over against non-English-speaking scholars and nations becomes a form of discursive hegemony. Moreover, the strong tendency of the standardization of academic language only in the four former colonial languages, English, French, German and Spanish, in U.S. academia makes "Asian" seem inadequate for the production and reproduction of

---

4. Christian Conference of Asia, *Christian Conference of Asia Sixth Assembly, Penang* (Singapore: CCA, 1977), 103.
5. Christian Conference of Asia, *Christian Conference of Asia Seventh Assembly, Bangalore* (Singapore: CCA, 1981), 116.
6. Virginia Fabella and Sun Ai Lee Park, eds., *We Dare to Dream: Doing Theology as Asian Women* (Maryknoll, NY: Orbis, 1990).

academic discourse. In this era of globalization and neoimperialism, non-Western academics do not have the luxury of ignoring what is happening in the U.S. academy because of its powerful influence on the global and local context of academic discourse and disciplinary structure. One can hardly deny that English linguistic imperialism, as explained in previous chapter, has been at work not only in the academy but also in various sectors of societies in the world. English, as an international language, privileges and benefits feminist theologians and scholars in the West and identifies them as universal, global, and international, while those from the non-West are labeled as particular, indigenous, local, or vernacular.

The major methodologies that Asian woman theologians have adopted for their theological articulation, especially when writing in English as a second language, are case studies and the storytelling of grassroots people. One can use the narrative methodology of storytelling constructively to enable women to talk about personal experience. However, it is meaningful only when one is able to locate such experience in a wider theoretical, sociocultural, and theopolitical context. One should connect one's individual and particular experience to a collective reality so that the storytelling and case studies can be a process of conscientization, historicization, politicization, and theorization. What has been lacking in *Asian* feminist theological discourse thus far is the theorization or theologization of such stories of Asian women. A possible danger in this narrative methodology is that it can promote the construction of stories of Asian women's experience that becomes so normativized and authenticized that people tend to regard all experience that does not fit the model of normative Asian women's stories as inauthentic.

In Asian feminist theological discourse, Asian feminist theologians have often presented Asian women as a unitary group. Although this tendency of homogenization can be politically unavoidable, especially at the initial phase of forming a coalition among them, there are underlying problems. Under- or misrepresentation of the tremendously diverse reality of Asian women has hampered our capacity to transform the concrete representations of women in theology and their condition in ministry. Nevertheless, in its initial stage of liberation from the Western discursive imperialism and in the process of its own theological construction, it is understandable that Asian feminist scholars characterized Asian women as a unified entity in terms of "discriminated against, exploited, harassed, sexually used, abused,"[7] as those who are pure victims of extreme poverty. One can also find Asian women described as pure victims in many early works by Asian feminist theologians. Here is a typical example of this stereotyping of Asian women as pure victims and Asian men as pure victimizers: "Asian women are beaten by their fathers or sold into child marriage or prostitution. Asian women's husbands . . . batter their wives. . . . Asian women's brothers . . . often further their own higher educations by tacitly using their Asian sisters, ignoring the reality that their sisters are selling their bodies to pay for tuition."[8]

Ironically, these oversimplifying, overstating, dramatizing, and homogenizing stories about Asian women, disseminated in English, seemed to enjoy a wider welcome in the West than in Asian countries. For Western readers, the satisfaction of these stories seems to derive from their depiction of the images of Asian women as totally different from the images of Western women, but entirely the same among Asian women themselves. Some Asian feminist theologians in the West cling, in their feminist theological discourse, to the stories and case studies of Asian grassroots women and

---

7. Virginia Fabella and Mercy Amba Oduyoye, eds., "Final Statement: Asian Church Women Speak (Manila, Philippines, Nov. 21-30, 1985)," in *With Passion and Compassion: Third World Women Doing Theology* (Maryknoll, NY: Orbis, 1988), 119.
8. Chung Hyun Kyung, *Struggle to Be the Sun Again: Introducing Asian Women's Theology* (Maryknoll, NY: Orbis, 1990), 54.

moralistically criticize the West in the name of real "Asian women's experience." Those Asian feminist scholars often become native-informants, primary providers of knowledge about Asian women's authentic experience and Asian culture, which are purported to be entirely different from those of Western women. In the process of discursive authenticization of Asian women's experience, they contribute to the stereotyping of Asian women themselves. I seek to problematize the very notion of Asian women and their stereotyped image as the point of ongoing struggle of liberation because one's act of stereotyping a specific group of people is a primary form of oppression regardless of whether it is done by outsiders or insiders. Scholars have often portrayed Asian women in Asian discourses in a culturally essentialized manner, more in works in English than in vernacular languages.

Here one should note that the gendered subject is "simultaneously a racial, ethnic, and class-determined subject,"[9] and that this subject occupies different subject positions at different historical and cultural locations. Even among the same ethnic/gender/class group, diversity and difference within a group are hardly avoidable. When the notion of Asian women becomes a fixed image, Asian women's unified subjecthood can become more and more constraining rather than truly liberating.

Asian Womenness:
Deconstructing the Myth

When women began to realize that they have been silenced throughout human history, their first question was, Who are *WE* as

---

9. Teresa de Lauretis, *Technologies of Gender: Essays on Theory, Film, and Fiction* (Bloomington: Indiana University Press, 1987), 137.

women? In the early feminist movement in the West, women based this we-question on the binary nature of men as the victimizer and women as the victimized. It did not take long, however, for women to realize that they needed to connect this we-question to the I-question. Feminist women in the West soon realized that the *we*—as with the multiple *I*'s—is not one but is divided by social class, race, sexuality, ethnicity, age, ability, or religious affiliation, and that the we-ness and I-ness are inseparable. Asian feminist theologians easily adopted the articulation of we-ness of women because most Asian cultures have emphasized the significance of collectivity, the we-ness, rather than individuality, the I-ness. While feminist theologians in the West shifted their emphasis from the unified we-ness to the differentiated I-ness in the very we-ness, Asian feminist theologians have not made such a discursive shift.

In most Asian culture, the individual is not central and there is hardly any conception of individuality in the sense that feminists in the West know. Confucian culture, for instance, focuses not on individual liberty or equality but on order and harmony; not on individual independence but communal harmony, which is often extremely patriarchal in its nature. In this context, a woman's claim for individual rights and freedom is against the purpose of society, which is not to preserve and promote individual liberty but to maintain the so-called harmony of the hierarchical and patriarchal order. This culture of patriarchal hierarchy, in the guise of harmony and communitarian virtue, makes it very hard for Asian women to make a shift from the unified *we* into the multiple "*I*"s.[10]

Here I am not trying to perpetuate the stereotyped dichotomy of the individualist West versus communitarian Asia, especially as the very notion of individualism and communitarianism is contested. However, it is undeniable, from my feminist perspective, that the individuality of Asian woman has been unthinkable, especially under the Confucian culture. It is also significant to note that in Confucian practice, the notion of harmony and relationality between the members of community is itself very hierarchical in terms of gender, age, social status, and familial rank, and is overtly androcentric.

A less visible but more critical problem in the positioning of Asian women in a fixed image is related to the issue of representation, which deals with the question of whether Asian feminist theologians can truly represent less privileged Asian women by selecting particular stories of other oppressed Asian women and telling their stories on their behalf. I agree with Gayatri Spivak's argument: the authentic feelings of the subaltern once named will be misrepresented,[11] because of the multiple mediations of more powerful groups and institutions, both local and global.

If feminist theologians, both outsiders from the West and insiders from Asia, portray Asian women as a unitary entity, feminist theologians are then repeating the misrepresentation of women that they have criticized in patriarchal discourse, in which women have been named and portrayed as a unified subjecthood, and spoken on behalf of, and thus misrepresented in their true situation as multiple and hybrid subjects. Women's life stories can be a powerful mechanism to convey authentic experiences and the relationship

---

10. Cf. Louis Henkin, "The Human Rights Idea in Contemporary China: A Comparative Perspective," in *Human Rights in Contemporary China*, ed. R. Randle Edwards, Louis Henkin, and Andrew J. Nathan (New York: Columbia University Press, 1986).

11. Gayatry Chakravorty Spivak, "Can the Subaltern Speak?," in *Marxism and the Interpretation of Culture*, ed. Cary Nelson and Lawrence Grossberg (Urbana: University of Illinois Press, 1988), 271–316.

between the self and others, but only as long as the stories represent a "process of struggling towards a particular consciousness"[12] that both reinterprets and remakes the world. Asian feminist theology in the past did not succeed in offering critical theories of language, social location, and gender capable of displaying the multiplicities of Asian women's being. Images of Asian women, the characterization of their authentic experiences, and the problematization of Asian women's reality as presented in Asian feminist theological discourses in the past have tended to be geographically deterministic and hence culturally essentialist.

Hence, theologians did not illustrate the tremendously diverse range of Asian women's experiences and their theological quests. Two identities, *Asian* and *woman*, dominated in the following monolithic manner: "Asian women have also been raped, tortured, imprisoned, and killed for their political beliefs. . . . in the process of the struggle they are giving birth to a spirituality that is particularly *woman's* and specifically *Asian*."[13] Some Asian feminist theologians often ground their portrayal of Asian womenness in ethnicized and gendered essentialism: "Asian women's theology is also '*very women.*' . . . Asian women share all the blessings and the problems of being Asian and Third World people with Asian men. What distinguishes Asian women's struggle from the men of the continent is their *women-ness*. Asian women are oppressed economically, socially, politically, religiously, and culturally in specific ways just because they are women."[14]

This simplistic portrayal can be an example of typical stereotyping of Asian women by Asian feminist theologians: either pure victims

---

12. Susan Geiger, "Women's Life Histories: Method and Content," *Signs* 11 (1986): 348.
13. Mary John Mananzan and Sun Ai Park, "Emerging Spirituality of Asian Women," in Fabella and Oduyoye, eds., *With Passion and Compassion*, 79.
14. Chung, *Struggle to Be the Sun Again*, 24 (italics mine).

or heroic figures. Like all other forms of stereotypical images, the image of Asian women here has both an upgrading connotation and a degrading one. To imply that all Asian women suffer the same oppression simply because they are Asian women is to lose sight of the many varied tools of patriarchy and to serve, often unwittingly, the patriarchal interest by failing to present a positive, alternative image of women except that of victim. Making culturally essentialist generalizations about Asian women's authentic experience has been the central limit of Asian feminist theological discourse in the past. Asian feminist theological discourses that generalize authentic Asian womenness tend to create a "theoretical diaspora"[15] among Asian women whose subjecthood they fundamentally overlook and who do not fit this authentic image of Asian women. In this context, the huge discrepancy between the discursive Asian women and the real Asian women is hard to avoid.

As-Discourses:
Grounds for Feminist Theology Reconsidered

Universality and particularity have been primary issues with which feminist theories and practices have wrestled from their inception. Feminists have emphasized the universality of women's victimization by patriarchy on the one hand, and the particularity of women, who are essentially distinctive from men, on the other. Common ground among women and a universal sisterhood erupted in the late 1960s. In order to speak of women as victims of patriarchy, as being discriminated against on account of their biology, a woman has to be socially identifiable as-woman. The underlying presupposition of

---

15. Laura E. Donaldson, *Decolonizing Feminisms: Race, Gender, and Empire-Building* (Chapel Hill: University of North Carolina Press, 1992), 15.

this as-discourse is that underneath the possible differences among women there must be some shared experience and identity as-women in a patriarchal world. The as-discourse appeared especially to be a political prerequisite for a coalition of the marginalized such as women. This as-discourse made women collective entity as-victims of patriarchy and as-sisters in a universally patriarchal world. Feminists in the 1970s, therefore, based their search for a universal sisterhood either on a biological essentialism or on the universal victimization of women under patriarchy.

However, criticism emerged within the feminist circle, mostly on the part of black feminists who claimed that feminists grounded their searching for a universal sisterhood in fact on the experience of white women and excluded the experience of nonwhite women who suffer not only from sexism but from racism and classism as well. In this regard, "Black women are not white women with color,"[16] they argued. In this context, it is hard to deny that the search for the universal sisterhood in the 1970s tended to be raceless and classless, as if the differences among women were threatening to the irrefutable fact that all women are somehow women, whereas racism and classism were still overshadowed the everyday lives of the majority women in the USA in particular and around the globe in general. Many began to call into question those feminisms that reduce domination and oppression to a single cause, focus exclusively on sexual difference, and ignore women's differences as they intersect across other vectors of power, particularly with regards to race, class, and sexuality.[17] Nonwhite women began to raise their racial and ethnic voice using the same set of as-discourses but with a different focus—discourses of as-Asian, as-black, or as-Mujerista.

---

16. Barbara Omolade, "Black Women and Feminism," in *The Future of Difference,* ed. Hester Eisenstein and Alice Jardine (New Brunswick, NJ: Rutgers University Press, 1985), 248.
17. hooks, *Talking Back,* 23.

The question of how to redefine difference for all women, which Audre Lorde raised in 1980, came to the fore in feminist theological discourse. Lorde declares that "it is not our differences which separate women, but our reluctance to recognize those differences."[18] Feminist difference discourse, emerging in the 1980s, was twofold: women's difference from men, primarily based on biological essentialism; and the difference among women, primarily based on race and class. Multiple voices within the feminist theological discourse have been raised: feminist, womanist or black feminist, Mujerista, or Asian feminist theology and so forth.

The question of why racially white people, both men and women, do not use the discourse of *as-white*, even when white women express their victimization by sexism *as-women*, is easy to answer: it is due to the mainstreamness of their race on national, regional, and global levels, even in the midst of the marginality of their sex. It is like men not adopting the discourse of as-men. What is it, then, to think of woman as-woman? Is it really possible for us to think of woman's woman-ness without taking her living in the USA, France, Bangladesh, Korea, Kenya, Fiji, Britain, or Palestine into consideration? Or her being upper-middle class in Uganda or lower class in Germany? One can identify any and all women as-women but can also identify them *as* yellow, brown, white, black, professor, politician, housewife, actress, married, single, first lady, factory worker, queen, Eastern, Western, straight, lesbian, and so forth.

In this complexity around the discourse of *as-women*, justifying the claim in any particular case that it is sexism that has harmed a woman the most requires proving that the harm comes to her because she is a woman and not because of some other fact about her—her race or class, marital status, religious affiliation, cultural heritage, sexual

18. Audre Lorde, *Sister Outsider: Essays and Speeches* (Trumansburg, NY: Crossing, 1984), 122.

orientation, or physical disability. Moreover, even if a woman is oppressed by sexism, and even if we say that all women are victimized by sexism, we cannot automatically conclude that discrimination and oppression by sexism are the same. One needs to elaborate in detail what one's oppression *as-woman* means in each case. In this context, producing an accurate picture of Asian women's lives and experiences requires not only reference to their identity *as-women* but also to other multiple factors which are deeply interlinked to one another.

Asian feminist theology has also started with as-discourse, like feminist theology in the West, but the as-discourse has multiple dimensions, unlike feminist theology in the West: "We belong to different Christian denominations; we come from diverse and complex cultures and backgrounds, but we experience a common bond and a common bondage—*as Asians* and *as women*."[19] Asian feminist theology has dealt with the as-discourse as a form of difference-discourse in four ways: (1) difference from men *as-women*; (2) difference from Western feminists *as-Asian-feminists*; (3) difference from the Western *as-Asian*; and (4) difference from the other religions *as-Christians* in a religiously pluralistic world. The question as to how feminists, in Asia and other part of the world, can then relate to one another across difference, or despite difference, becomes one of the urgent issues with which feminist theologians wrestle.

Feminists can, of course, have political reasons for speaking about the shared experience *as-women* of being oppressed by sexism, which can be the solid ground for a women's movement. However, constantly speaking from and holding on to the perspective of as-discourse of Asian women is politically dangerous and confining because it can only lead to an ongoing "balkanization"[20] of feminist

---

19. Fabella and Oduyoye, eds., "Final Statement," 118 (italics mine).

theological discourse. If the coherency required for any political movement to get heard and to make change requires a group to speak in a single voice of as-discourse, how will one shape a single voice from the multiplicity of voices, and whose voice will predominate? Who has the rights, authority, or ability to find a single voice among many *as-women*, *as-Asians*, or *as-Asian-women*? Although Asian or other nonwhite feminists criticize the homogenized version of white women's experience as universal women's experience propagated by Western feminists, Asian feminists tend to homogenize their own version of Asian women based on the same logic of *as-discourse*. There is, of course, a danger in overemphasizing the difference:

> The very theme of difference, whatever the differences are represented to be, is useful to the oppressing group. . . . any allegedly natural feature attributed to an oppressed group is used to imprison this group within the boundaries of a Nature which, since the group is oppressed, ideological confusion labels "nature of oppressed person". . . to demand the right to Difference without analyzing its social character is to give back the enemy an effective weapon.[21]

As-discourse in *Asian* feminist theological discourse has tended to claim essential female and ethnic difference and to produce a standardization of the authentic Asian women, wittingly or unwittingly. I would argue that the *as*-discourse should be shifted to a *with*-discourse, the firm ground of which is the radical realization of the interconnectedness of our lives across gender, race, class, sexuality, and region; and of the need for solidarity for the common good. I would also argue that Asian feminist theological discourses need to make a shift from a politics of identity to a politics of

20. Elisabeth Schüssler Fiorenza, "Introduction: Transforming the Legacy of the Woman's Bible," in *Searching the Scriptures: A Feminist Introduction*, ed. Elisabeth Schüssler Fiorenza (New York: Crossroad, 1995), 17.

21. Elaine Marks and Isabelle de Courtivon, eds., *New French Feminisms: An Anthology* (Amherst: University of Massachusetts Press, 1980), 219.

solidarity. Exclusive focus on difference between identities based on culture, geopolitics, or other factors of women's lives tends to overlook the interactive mediations between differences, and obscure the overlapping and hybridizing that takes place in the contact space in between differences. As a starting point, many understand difference to mean essentially *division*, and difference can be no more than a tool of either self-defense or conquest. Trinh Minh-ha relevantly points out the problem of as-discourse of difference:

> We (with capital W) sometimes include(s), other times exclude(s) me. You and I are close, we intertwine; you may stand on the other side of the hill once in a while, but you may also be me, while remaining what you are and what I am not. . . . . "I" is, therefore, not a unified subject, a fixed identity, or that solid mass covered with layers of superficialities one has gradually to peel off before one can see its true face. "I" is, itself, *infinite layers.*[22]

The fixed identity *as-Asian-women*, which both Asian and Western feminism have portrayed in Asian feminist theological discourse, is both limiting and in a way deceiving. If my identity as Asian woman, for instance, refers to the whole pattern of sameness within my life as Asian woman, how am I to lose, maintain, or gain my identity as Asian woman? One can never define Asian women as such. Not every Asian woman can be a *real* and *authentic* Asian woman. Feminist theologians should use as-discourse only when understood sociopolitically as a subversive force, not as a portrayal only as pure victims. Otherwise, Asian feminist theologians are contributing to their own homogenizing, romanticizing, or stereotyping. In order to avoid this false representation, feminist theologians should persistently wrestle with the following questions: How can we articulate Asian women's difference without having that

---

22. Trinh T. Minh-ha, *Woman, Native, Other: Writing Postcoloniality and Feminism* (Bloomington: Indiana University Press, 1989), 90, 94.

difference turned into a cultural ghettoization of Asian women? How can Asian women *speak*?

One should also note that Asian women are not inherently more life affirming, nurturing, caring, or nonviolent as theologians than are men, as often portrayed in *Asian* feminist theological discourse. This kind of exaltation of women is a dangerous perspective because it leads to a focus on women's biology and tends to reinforce the patriarchal notion that to be a woman means to be a mother as nurturer and caregiver. Asian women have not initiated wars simply because of their material and sociopolitical circumstances and not because they are innately more moral and life affirming than men. It is very clear that women's works, in either private or public sectors, supports both war and peace activities. The socialization of Asian women and Asian men complements the needs of the culture in which they live, which is still very much patriarchal. As Gerda Lerner rightly points out, "the system of patriarchy can function only with the cooperation of women."[23] A perpetuation of *as-discourse* in *Asian* feminist theology is more constraining than empowering and weakens solidarity among feminists in the world. One would need as-discourse only as a means of resistance but not as an end. If someone attacks one *as-woman* or *as-Asian*, for instance, one needs to defend herself *as-woman* or *as-Asian*. Asian feminist theologians will have to create the identity of *as-Asian-women* through actions of resistance to any form of power that limits, exploits, distorts, and degrades the lives of women and the marginalized.

23. Gerda Lerner, *The Creation of Patriarchy* (New York: Oxford University Press, 1986), 217.

Emergence of Neo-Empires:
New Contexts for *Asian* Feminist Theology

Over the last decade, especially after the end of the Cold War, the so-called empire discourse has emerged in the context of neoimperialism and globalization. Many works depict the U.S. victory over communism and the matter of U.S. hegemony in world geopolitics, economics, and mass culture. In their thought-provoking work, Michael Hardt and Antonio Negri interpret empire as "a *decentered* and *deterritorializing* apparatus of rule that progressively incorporates the entire global realm within its open, expanding frontiers."[24] This interpretation is, in a way, a radicalized version of the globalization that we experience today. The empire discourse tries to set the economic, cultural, and political world today within a political framework, and it further shows us how neocolonialism and neoimperialism take new forms of political, cultural, and economic dependency on particular Western nations such as the United States. Here, one can define colonialism as the organized deployment of racialized and gendered constructs for practices of political rule over other racial ethnic groups, which requires a territorial invasion. Imperialism shares with colonialism a tendency of domination over other peoples. However, imperialism can refer to an organized power's intention to institutionalize and expand its dominating, ruling power. So, even though one can use the terms *colonialism* and *imperialism* interchangeably, it is important to note that imperialism refers to the specific actions of colonizers to constitute their power as a political machine that rules from the center and extends its control to the peripheries.[25]

24. Michael Hardt and Antonio Negri, *Empire* (Cambridge: Harvard University Press, 2000), xii.
25. Cf. Robert J. C. Young, *Postcolonialism: An Historical Introduction* (Oxford: Blackwell, 2001), 27; see also Mark Lewis Taylor, "Spirit and Liberation: Achieving Postcolonial Theology in the

Generally speaking, colonialism or imperialism is about power and ruling, and thereby about domination and subjugation. Therefore, efforts to change the subordinate status of a certain group of people, like women, require one to consider the nature of power. One must note at the outset that power is an elusive concept that one must characterize as essentially contested. Different theories of power rest on different assumptions about both the content of existence and the ways one comes to know it. That is, different theories of power rest on differing ontologies and epistemologies, and a feminist rethinking of power requires attention to its epistemological groundings. Epistemologies, or theories of knowing, grow out of differing material contexts.

Feminism has often depicted women's oppression with the metaphor of the colonizer and the colonized. There exist certain similarities between the colonization of undeveloped countries and women's oppression within patriarchy: economic dependence, the cultural takeover, the identification of dignity with resemblance to the oppressor.[26] Like the relationship of colonizer to colonized, patriarchal culture has defined women as different in kind from men, denied women's right to own property, and prevented their sharing in the economic means of production. Therefore, "if we transpose the descriptions of colonized and colonizer to women to men, they fit at almost every point," and "like slave-masters and colonizers they have expected women to identity their interests with their oppressors."[27] Just as colonization denies the colonized voices in their own culture, feminists argue, men in patriarchal cultures have

United States," in Catherine Keller, Michael Nausner, and Mayra Rivera, *Postcolonial Theologies: Divinity and Empire* (St. Louis: Chalice, 2004), 42.

26. Sheila Rowbotham, *Women, Resistance, and Revolution: A History of Women and Revolution in the Modern World* (New York: Vintage, 1971), 201.

27. Marilyn French, *Beyond Power: On Men, Women, and Morals* (New York: Ballantine, 1985), 130–31.

deprived women of their own voices. However, adopting the men as colonizer and women as colonized homology in our theorizing runs the risk of oversimplifying the complexity of empire experience of neocolonization or neoimperialization today. One cannot, however, deny the fact that this metaphor possesses power, particularly in articulating the oppression of Asian women today.

Women in patriarchy, as the colonized in colonization, are othered in many different ways. The creation of an "other" is the necessary precondition for justification and legitimation of both imperialism and patriarchy. The colonized are portrayed as opposite to the colonizer, who purports that the colonized carry all the negative quality.[28] In this act of othering, the desire to dominate gains its end. Empire building is, therefore, all about power building by creating a devalued other. The empire then dominates the othered subject. Interestingly, in the construction of the empire, the colonizer often feminizes the colonized. The colonizer creates itself as a ruling being that sees it as located at the center and possessed of all good qualities. As Albert Memmi rightly elaborates: "The colonized is always degraded and the colonialist finds justification for rejecting his [sic] subjectivity. . . . The colonialist removes the factor from history, time, and therefore possible evolution. What is actually a sociological point becomes labeled as being biological, or preferably, metaphysical. It is attached to the colonized's basic nature."[29]

Here, the term *kyriarchy,* instead of patriarchy, is helpful in revealing the complex system of domination and subordination in a contemporary neoimperial, empire-building situation. As noted in chapter 7 above, kyriarchy means "the rule of the emperor/master/ lord/father/husband over his subordinates."[30] It is also important to note that neither are women the pure victims nor men the pure

28. Albert Memmi, *The Colonizer and the Colonized* (Boston: Beacon, 1967), 82.
29. Ibid., 85.

victimizers. The exclusive gender dualism doesn't reveal the power imbalance among women of different races, ethnicities, classes, abilities, or sexualities. By adopting the term *kyriarchy,* I would like to reveal the underlying epistemology of empire building in relation to women's subjugation and, furthermore, to emphasize the fact that not all men dominate and exploit all women without difference. Not all women are oppressed by men simply on the ground of women's biology.

Some Asian intellectuals and social activists who have criticized the supremacy of the West often overlook their own supremacy in relation to Asian women. In this sense, Asian women are colonized not only by Western imperialist power but also by Asian kyriarchal domination. Those whom Western neoimperialism has treated as the other are practicing their own hegemonic powers on women and the powerless in their own local context. In this sense, localist opposition to Western empire-building may be politically well intentioned but rests on false assumptions and is therefore damaging. It assumes that the local is outside of empire-building. However, it is important to note that the local cannot represent a stable barrier against the emerging Western empire. Any locale is rarely unproblematic and any simple, blind celebration of local culture against the Western hegemony for its own sake cannot be the solution to the problem of empire. Asian men, for instance, can be those colonized by the Western empire, but at same time they can be the colonizers in practicing their kyriarchal power in their local culture. It is also true that Asian middle- and upper-class women can be the colonizers of lower-class men and women. One should also scrutinize the locality from the perspective of the marginalized, from those below, from the least in multiple contexts.

---

30. Elisabeth Schüssler Fiorenza, *Jesus—Miriam's Child, Sophia's Prophet: Critical Issues in Feminist Christology* (New York: Continuum, 1995), 14.

Here I would suggest differentiating, strategically, the Empire with a capital "E" from empire with a lowercase "e" to identify the Empire with the West as a master narrative and the empire in one's own locale as a small narrative. In this context, the real question would not be "*whether* Empire but *whose* Empire."[31] And this question is not only to check the abuses of power by others, but also to check our own abuses of power, and therefore to bring us into critical awareness of and engagement with the interests of all our relations.

In this context, Asian women in religion, generally speaking, have experienced multiple colonizations: colonization by socio-politico-cultural hegemony of the West; colonization by discursive hegemony of feminists in the West; colonization by kyriarchal hegemony of Asian men; and colonization by kyriarchal value systems in religions. Empire from a feminist perspective should not be in a singular form but a plural one, simply because there is not only one form of empire but many different forms of empire. Asian women must be alert to the multiple faces of Empires: not only Empire-out-there, but also empire(s)-in/among-us. A comprehensive discourse of empire helps us to figure out not just what to do but who we are. It would help Asian women to identify their sociopolitical and religious location in terms of power relations: who is the oppressor, who is the oppressed, and in what sense one can be both the oppressor and the oppressed at the same time. The comprehensive empire discourse helps us further to understand the multidimensionality and complexity of oppression. It also highlights the multiple and often contradictory elements of who *we* are as–Asian women. The we–they binarism is not as self-evident as we usually suppose: the *they* would disguise itself as *us* and is secretly invading us. It is important to acknowledge colonization by *them*, the West,

31. Sharon Welch, *After Empire: The Art and Ethos of Enduring Peace* (Minneapolis: Fortress Press, 2004), xvi.

but also colonization by *us*—Asian men, feminists in the West, and fellow men and women within a same religion. The once-colonized is not immune to becoming the colonizer on another level.

Glocal Feminist Theology:
Critical Theology as Resistance and Solidarity

Feminist theological movements are threatened by feminists who refuse to critically change themselves, even as they are trying to change the world. Many, either men or women, and either Western or Asian, exist in a painful ambiguity both as colonizers and colonized. Those who ignore the multiple power relations involved in various form of empire building fail to provide an epistemology for the task of transforming existing reality. In an era of globalization and neoempire, one cannot deny that "'We' do not quite know who is 'us' and who is 'them'" and "neither race nor language can any longer define nationality."[32] Although an Empire by one nation's hegemony dominates the rest of the world, it is our reality that we in fact are both a part of the Empire and have our own empires within and among ourselves.

In this context, one's geographical location is no longer as critical a parameter in constructing feminist theological discourse as it once was. Rather, a feminist theological construction today need not be in accordance with only a specific geographical territory. In an era of globalization, geographical boundaries have begun to blur through displacement of peoples. Through dislocation, relocation, and translocation of peoples with diverse cultures and religions, the old context for feminist theology has changed. Feminist theologians should radically redirect the direction of this theology, which has

---

32. Keller, Nausner, and Rivera, "Introduction," in *Postcolonial Theologies*, 1.

invested so much in geographical locations, fixed identity of *as-ethnic-women*, and Asian indigenous cultures and resources. The old paradigm of feminist theology based on one's ethnicity has been a localist and nativist position, in which theologians direct the major resources for theological construction only at local culture and tradition. In this localist and nativist approach, feminist theological discourses have had a tendency to romanticize, idealize, and glorify the local, the indigenous, and at the same time discredit the West. A binary contrast between Asia and the West has been a typical approach. I would argue that this kind of theological nativism functions and continues to imprison not only the other culture but also its own vernacular culture within entirely geographically deterministic and culturally essentialist discursive boundaries.

Feminist theological discourse in Asia must commit itself to two simultaneous projects: (1) an internal critique of the hegemonic kyriarchy of the theologians' own local cultures and societies; and (2) the formulation of historically and contextually grounded feminist theological concerns and strategies for overcoming gender injustice in theological discourse, theological and ecumenical institutions, and the church, which can provide an alternative vision of the world and of Christianity. While the first project is a process of deconstruction, the second is a process of reconfiguration of theological discourses. Feminist theological discourse has a further task on a global level: articulating and presenting the complex reality and hybrid experience of Asian women in their respective context and their feminist theological quest, inquiries, and hopes to the peoples of the globe.

I propose, finally, a *glocal* feminist theology, in which one critically combines the *global* context and the *local* context to resist empires of all forms and to strengthen solidarity with the marginalized, who are dislocated and displaced, either physically or ontologically, and whose lives have been destroyed and diminished by the power of various forms of empires. What I envision for a *glocal* feminist theology is transnational, transregional, transcultural, and transreligious. In order to carry out this vision for a glocal feminist theology, feminist theologians should take the following tasks into their account.

First, *glocal* feminist theology needs to articulate a comprehensive empire discourse that recognizes that feminist theologians' local activities are interlinked with a global geopolitical reality. Feminist theologians must not give up the claim that material life not only structures but sets limits on the understanding of social relations, and that, in systems of domination and subjugation, the vision available to the emperors and rulers will be both partial and will reverse the real order of things. The ruling empires, in terms of gender, race, class, or sexuality, actively structure the material-social relations in which we all are forced to participate, wittingly or unwittingly. We have to acknowledge, as Antonio Gramsci points out in his theory of hegemony, that empire-building has been possible not just by force but by our consent as well: "It seems clear . . . that there can, and indeed must be hegemonic activity even before the rise of power, and that one should not count only on the material force which power gives in order to exercise an effective leadership."[33] His theory of hegemony shows how dominant groups or individuals can maintain their hegemony by persuading the governed to accept, adopt, and internalize their hegemonic values and norms. Therefore, one cannot dismiss the vision of ruling empires as simply false or misguided. A binary position of *we* versus *they* can mislead our ambivalent reality. The colonized or the oppressed group must struggle for their own understandings, which will represent achievements requiring both

---

33. Antonio Gramsci, *Selections from the Prison Notebooks of Antonio Gramsci*, ed. Quintin Hoare and Geoffrey Nowell Smith (London: Lawrence & Wisher, 1971), 57.

theorizing and the education that grows from political struggle and engagement.

Second, *glocal* feminist theology needs to fiercely engage in the historical, sociopolitical, and theoretical process of constituting women as both subjects as well as objects of our specific history—both local and global, which are inextricably interlinked especially in an era of globalization. Glocal feminist theology needs to sort out who women really are: we ethnicized women need to dissolve the false *we* into its real multiplicity and variety. And out of this concrete multiplicity of I's, feminist theologians need to build an account of the world as seen from the margins, an account that can expose the falseness of the view from the top and can transform the margins as well as the center. The history of marginalization of Asian women will work against creating a totalizing discourse both by Asians and non-Asians, both by Westerners and non-Westerners. Feminist theologians continually and persistently need to name and present/represent women's diverse experiences of multiple colonization and struggle.

Third, *glocal* feminist theology needs to construct a power discourse, not only for women but also for the colonized of various types, which is a call for transformation and participation in altering power relations of domination and subjugation in multiple forms. Through the comprehensive power discourse, the glocal feminist theology is able to offer better illustrations of how neoimperialism works, and how neo-Empire and -empire(s) as ideological domination succeed the best without physical coercion, without territorial invasion, without actually capturing the bodies and the minds of women and the colonized/marginalized. The apparent absence of the enemy in an era of neo-Empire(s) as such requires more sophisticated and comprehensive power discourse.

Fourth, *glocal* feminist theology needs to shift from politics of identity to politics of solidarity, from as-discourse to with-discourse. With-discourse requires adopting we-hermeneutics, which interprets life and its opportunities and challenges in light of the self and community.[34] We-hermeneutics is a challenge to acknowledge our embeddedness in community without dismissing the significance of I-ness: "I am because we are; and we are because I am."[35] Here *we* is not based on hierarchical, vertical relationship nor is it an absence of a sense of individuality, but it rests on an egalitarian, horizontal, democratic relationship between and across gender, age, race, ethnicity, class, sexual orientation, and religious or cultural background.

Constructing feminist theological discourse as a theopolitical discourse of resistance and liberation is not just for identifying common victimizers, for self-justification as-women-the-victimized, or mutual recognition among women-as-victims under patriarchy. Instead, it should be for an ongoing contestation and change, ongoing learning, unlearning, and delearning, to work for change for an alternative world. *Asian* feminist theologians are those who are in-between. They are in-between the West and Asia, in-between women and men, in-between Christians and people of neighboring faiths, and eventually in-between the world of *already* and the world of *not-yet*. Their in-between consciousness makes them daydream. They dream of an alternative world where people can overcome all forms of domination and subjugation and where people alienate no one on the ground of sex, race, ethnicity, class, age, religion,

---

34. Jace Weaver, *Other Words: American Indian Literature, Law, and Culture* (Norman: University of Oklahoma Press, 2001), 303–304.
35. Karen Baker-Fletcher and Garth Kasimu Baker-Fletcher, *My Sister, My Brother: Womanist and Xodus God-Talk* (Maryknoll, NY: Orbis, 1997), 203–204.

sexuality, physical or mental ability, or appearance, and where an authentic peace prevails.

Feminist theologians are permanent resident aliens with a "'doubled' insider/outsider position"[36] who reside in this existing world but are alien because of their daydream. Through the daydreaming, they can form the solidarity in multiplicity and diversity, which is necessary for the survival of *Asian* feminist theology as a revolutionary discourse and movement.

---

36. Elisabeth Schüssler Fiorenza, *Discipleship of Equals: A Critical Feminist Ekklesia-logy of Liberation* (New York: Crossroad, 1994), 335. Also see, Janet Wolff, *Resident Alien: Feminist Cultural Criticism* (New Haven: Yale University Press, 1995).

8

Transethnic Feminist Theology in an Era of Globalization

Globalization begins at home.
—Homi K. Bhabha[1]

Global and local are two faces of the same movement from one epoch of globalization, the one which has been dominated by the nation-state, the national economies, the national cultural identities, to something new.
—Stuart Hall[2]

1. Homi K. Bhabha, *The Location of Culture* (New York: Routledge, 2006 [1994]), xxv.
2. Stuart Hall, "The Local and the Global: Globalization and Ethnicity," in *Culture, Globalization, and the World-System: Contemporary Conditions for the Representation of Identity*, ed. Anthony King (Minneapolis: University of Minnesota Press, 1997), 27.

Whose Globalization?
Discursive Location in a Global Space

Today the word *globalization* is an all-purpose catchword both in popular and scholarly discourse; it is "on the lips of politicians, professors, and pundits alike."[3] People in different areas use the term in highly disparate ways and its meaning often is elusive. Globalization easily risks becoming a cliché as different people use and misuse it for their purposes. The most common interpretation of globalization is the idea that the world is becoming more uniform, homogenized, standardized, and compressed through a technological, commercial, and cultural synchronization emanating from the West. Corporations, markets, finance, banking, transportation, communication, and production increasingly cut across national boundaries. It is obvious that the West (i.e., its culture, discourse, values, lifestyle) is moving to the center of the world through this process of globalization. The rise of the globalization paradigm in the 1970s became consolidated at the Seventh (1973–79) Tokyo Round of negotiations of the General Agreement on Tariffs and Trade (GATT), which was established in 1947.[4] This Tokyo Round coincided with the emergence of the Washington Consensus, a global economic model based on the principles of privatization, free trade, and deregulation (i.e., neoliberalism). Economic globalization, therefore, refers to neoliberal internationalization and the spread of capitalized market relations. The most prevalent view of globalization comes from those who see it in the light of increased economic interdependence and the integration of all national economies into one economy within the framework of a capitalist market, initiated by those countries in the global North. According to this analysis, the

3. Jeremy Brecher and Tim Costello, *Global Village or Global Pillage: Economic Reconstruction from the Bottom Up* (Boston: South End, 1994), 4.
4. Malcolm Waters, *Globalization* (New York: Routledge, 1995), 68ff.

world economy has been transformed and "has already changed—in its foundations and in its structure—and in all probability the change is irreversible."[5]

The most important aspect of this change entails a shift in commodities, from capital and materials to knowledge, and with this, the price of raw materials has collapsed, causing a drastic change in the mode of production from industry to information technology. The power of technological communications has changed the nature of finance and trade, transcending time and geographical borders. In economic globalization, the information holder becomes a power holder and economic profit becomes the highest virtue. National interest is geared toward maximum economic interest, which has created multiple forms of conflict, violence, and war in many regions of the globe. It is undeniable that much of the United States' foreign policy now targets the oil wealth of the Muslim states in the name of the war on terror, and that the war on terror has more of an impact on poor countries in the global South than on affluent countries in the global North. Who benefits from economic globalization is, of course, a complex and controversial issue. While some people argue that economic globalization improves living standards of people in all parts of the world, others maintain that the entire neocapitalist project of economic globalization benefits only certain groups of people but harms the majority of people in the global South. This contradictory assessment of economic globalization is also true of Asia, which long ago adopted the world capitalist system. Thus, most Asian countries are also a part of the problem.

The political world has "moved from a First/Second/Third World division to a multi-polar condition,"[6] and the focus is on the

---

5. Peter F. Drucker, "The Changed World Economy," *Foreign Affairs* 64, no. 4 (1986): 768.
6. Robert J. Schreiter, *The New Catholicity: Theology between the Global and the Local* (Maryknoll, NY: Orbis, 2004), ix.

increasing density of interstate relations and the development of global politics. What divides the world now is not the old political ideology, but the huge discrepancy between the rich and the poor. According to Robert D. Kaplan,

> We are entering a bifurcated world. Part of the globe is inhabited by Hegel's and Fukuyama's Last Man, healthy, well fed, and pampered by technology. The other, larger, part is inhabited by Hobbes's First Man, condemned to a life that is 'poor, nasty, brutish, and short'. Although both parts will be threatened by environmental stress, the Last Man will be able to master it; the First Man will not.[7]

This change makes us think that the end of ideology[8] has already arrived, especially in the post–Cold War era, and that "the universalization of Western liberal democracy is the final form of human government," as Francis Fukuyama argues in his *The End of History*.[9] But it would be naïve to affirm that "there is a fundamental process at work that dictates a common evolutionary pattern for all human societies—in short, something like a Universal History of mankind in the direction of liberal democracy,"[10] as he also optimistically predicts. This is because so many polities are democratic only insofar as they adopt democratic processes and institutions. However, they fail to share the underlying value system that ensures human rights and the freedom of individuals regardless of race, ethnicity, gender, class, ability, or orientation. We hear one of the pessimistic voices in the following observation:

> The American diplomat Richard Holbrooke pondered a problem on

---

7. Robert D. Kaplan, "The Coming Anarchy," *Atlantic Monthly* 273, no. 2 (1994): 60.

8. Daniel Bell, *The End of Ideology: On the Exhaustion of Political Ideas in the Fifties* (New York: Free Press, 1966).

9. Francis Fukuyama, "The End of History," *The National Interest* 16 (Summer 1989): 4. Here Fukuyama attributes the origin of the notion of "the end of history" to Karl Marx and then to G. W. F. Hegel, both of whom interpret history as a purposeful and dialectical process.

10. Francis Fukuyama, *The End of History and the Last Man* (New York: Free Press, 1992), 48.

the eve of the September 1996 elections in Bosnia, which were meant to restore civic life to that ravaged country. 'Suppose the election was declared free and fair', he said, and those elected are 'racists, fascists, separatists, who are publicly opposed [to peace and reintegration]. This is the dilemma.' . . . Democratically elected regimes, often ones that have been reelected or reaffirmed through referenda, are routinely ignoring constitutional limits on their power and depriving their citizens of basic rights and freedoms.[11]

Perception of good and evil is formulated in terms of national interest in many parts of the world and gives way to parochial tribalism. In this process, "technology will be used toward primitive ends."[12] Transnational trade and legal organizations, such as the United Nations, the IMF, the World Bank, WTO, and so on, are now replacing the state in claiming the rights to control the affairs of global cities and even the economies of sovereign nations. The links between politics and economics are becoming ever stronger. Therefore,

> Firms will be motivated not by productivity, but by *profitability*, for which productivity and technology may be important means, but certainly not the only ones. And political institutions, being shaped by a broader set of values and interests, will be oriented, in the economic realm, towards maximizing the *competitiveness* of their constituent economies. *Profitability* and *competitiveness* are the actual determinants of technological innovation and productivity growth.[13]

This pursuit of profitability and competitiveness has propelled a new international division of labor, and more people, especially women in poor households, become workers. A large number of people in Asia immigrate, legally or illegally, to economically developed areas within and outside Asia.

---

11. Fareed Zakaria, "The Rise of Illiberal Democracy," *Foreign Affairs* 76, no. 6 (1997): 22.
12. Kaplan, "The Coming Anarchy," 73.
13. Manuel Castells, *The Rise of the Network Society* (Cambridge: Blackwell, 1996), 81 (italics mine).

The discourse of cultural globalization mostly focuses on global communications and worldwide cultural standardization (e.g., "CocaColonization" and "McDonaldization").[14] If we adopt Clifford Geertz's definition of culture in the sense that it "denotes an historically transmitted pattern of meanings embodied in symbols, a system of inherited conceptions expressed in symbolic forms,"[15] then culture not only helps humans define themselves but also can be the means of communication, perpetuation, and development of knowledge about human life. Globalization has no doubt removed visible barriers in the way of cultural interaction. But the practical problems of seemingly intercultural communication increase the problem of power issues among and between different cultures, as it shifts toward a cultural standardization of the West in the guise of multiculturalism as the new tribalism. The most serious problem in this cultural standardization of the West is that one unmarks and thereby naturalizes the hegemony of whiteness, which results in "an almost total lack of theoretical discourse that relates 'race' to gender and sexuality,"[16] even within politically and culturally progressive groups. Capital, information, products, and people flow through the networks of information and transportation of the new global structure. These various kinds of flows "produce fundamental problems of livelihood, equity, suffering, justice, and governance."[17] For example,

> Media flows across national boundaries that produce images of well-being that cannot be satisfied by national standards of living and

---

14. Jan Nederveen Pieterse, "Globalization as Hybridization," in *Global Modernities*, ed. Mike Featherstone, Scott Lash, and Roland Robertson(London: Sage, 1995), 45.

15. Clifford Geertz, *The Interpretation of Cultures* (New York: Basic, 1973), 89.

16. Michele Wallace, "Multiculturalism and Oppositionality," in *Between Borders: Pedagogy and the Politics of Cultural Studies*, ed. Henry Giroux and Peter McLaren (New York: Routledge, 1994), 182–84.

17. Arjun Appadurai, "Grassroots Globalization and the Research Imagination," *Public Culture* ("Globalization" issue) 12, no. 1 (Winter 2000): 5.

consumer capabilities; flows of discourses of human rights that generate demands from workforces that are repressed by state violence which is itself backed by global arms flows; ideas about gender and modernity that circulate to create large female workforces at the same time that cross-national ideologies of 'culture', 'authenticity', and national honor put increasing pressure on various communities to morally discipline just these working women who are vital to emerging markets and manufacturing sites.[18]

All these issues are relevant if we view globalization as a complex, multidimensional process. But one should acknowledge many *discursive diasporas*, whose existence the mainstream/"malestream" scholars exclude from their discourses on globalization: women and children. For instance, in their book *Empire*, Michael Hardt and Antonio Negri do not discuss women's labor in sweatshops or as migrant workers.[19]

What would it then mean to be Asian women or gendered, racialized, and ethnicized persons in the age of globalization, when globalization is not strictly Asian or Euroamerican but a planetary phenomenon? What would it mean to *do* feminist theology *as* Asian women? To construct a feminist theological discourse, we must make a decision about whose opinion of globalization we adopt: Do we adopt the one by those who maintain that globalization offers new opportunities for development and accumulation of wealth for humanity? Or the other, by those who argue that globalization makes the discrepancy between the rich and the poor greater than ever? It is time for feminists to rethink their 1970s slogan, "The personal is political," because doing feminist theology involves being political. In the age of globalization, however, the meaning of being political is often distorted. We must therefore remind ourselves of the difference between being political and being politicized: "Being political is

18. Ibid.
19. Michael Hardt and Antonio Negri, *Empire* (Cambridge: Harvard University Press, 2000).

different from being directly and blatantly politicized—being made to serve interests and ends imposed by militant groups, whether in the name of heightened racial awareness, true biblical morality, androgyny, therapeutic self-esteem, or all the other sorts of enthusiasms in which we are currently awash."[20]

Being political in feminist theology gives rise to public awareness and responsibility for what is going on in reality, while being politicized leads to blind extremism. As politics cannot be just politics, religion cannot stay within the holy tower of religion. As Elizabeth Cady Stanton prophetically pointed out in 1895, "Let us remember that all reforms are interdependent, and that whatever is done to establish one principle on a solid basis, strengthens all."[21] Doing feminist theology in the age of globalization requires us to be more passionately political, because the purpose of doing feminist theology is "not to carry one fragmentary measure in human progress, but to utter the highest truth clearly seen in all directions."[22] I understand doing feminist theology as a theological commitment both to interpreting new realities from a feminist perspective and to engaging in a common vision for the betterment of humanity that God creates and is in the ongoing process of creating.

Interpreting our reality of globalization as an initial stage of doing theology is itself a political act because the way we see reality seriously indicates whom we stand for and where we stand. Needless to say, neutral or objective reading and interpretation of reality is impossible. The precondition for doing feminist theology is making a constant commitment to the art of representing and standing "on the same side with the weak and unrepresented,"[23] on whatever ground

20. Jean Bethke Elshtain, *Democracy on Trial* (New York: Basic, 1995), 81.
21. Elizabeth Cady Stanton, "Introduction," in *The Woman's Bible,* ed. Elizabeth Cady Stanton and the Revising Committee (New York: European Pub. Co., 1898), 11.
22. Ibid.
23. Edward Said, *Representations of the Intellectual* (New York: Vintage Books, 1996 [1994]), 22.

(i.e., gender, race/ethnicity, nationality, class, sexuality, or ability, and so forth). All forms of discrimination and exclusion begin with one epistemological ground: the logic of domination based on dualistic modes of thinking, which justifies, reinforces, and perpetuates the pattern and practice of domination/subjugation. In this regard, when feminist theologians try to comprehend globalization, the question of whose globalization they look into and whom they stand for becomes a significant issue in doing feminist theology. Clearly, powerful homogenizing forces nations affect and reshape the day-to-day lives of the underrepresented, and a fundamental contradiction between "placeless power and powerless places"[24]exists.

Asian Women at Multiple Crossroads

From its outset, feminism used the phrase "Women are marginalized." By this phrase, the movement meant simply that the mainstream, or "malestream," to be specific, marginalizes women. But it is becoming more and more difficult to answer the question, Marginal to what/whom/where? The place where people exercise and privilege the hegemonic power often seems invisible and unnoticeable. Due to the invisibility of the center, one can hardly draw a clear line between the center and the margin and thereby the center seems to be always out there or over there but not in here. On a global level, the center is usually Euro/U.S., white, male, middle-upper class, heterosexual, and Christian. Although each of these characteristics bears different weight and connotation, their combination describes a status that most people recognize. However,

24. Jeffrey Henderson and Manuel Castells, "Techno-economic Restructuring, Socio-political Processes and Spatial Transformation: A Global Perspective," in *Global Restructuring and Territorial Development,* ed. Jeffrey Henderson and Manuel Castells (London: Sage, 1987), 7.

this fixed pattern of who the center is seems to be too simplistic and monolithic to reveal the tremendously complex reality of how the rise of globalization affects the lives of women in different parts of the world in very complicated ways. It would be all too easy for a white, female, heterosexual professional, for instance, to claim victimhood as an outsider on the margin in a patriarchal society, while forgetting that her race, class, and sexuality still confer on her power and privilege.

The issue of the center and the margin, therefore, cannot be just a matter of women versus men, for instance, nonwhite versus white, or Asia versus the West. Asian countries, especially East Asian countries, long ago adopted neoliberal capitalism to catch up with the West. East Asian countries and regions, such as South Korea, Hong Kong Special Administrative Region (SRA), Japan, Singapore, and Taiwan, have been causing a lot of problems in violating human rights of migrant workers, for instance. We cannot, therefore, simply say that Asia, as an umbrella ethnic category, is entirely the pure victim of the Western, dominating powers of globalization. Identifying the victimizer and the victimized in the age of globalization requires both micro- and macro-approaches and multiple angles.

Asian women today embody the complexities, contradictions, and ambivalences that have shaped Asian women's identity in the last few years as they grapple with the multiple and divergent issues of globalization. I am not using the category of "Asian women" to engage in naturalization of cultural and geographical boundaries or nostalgic homogenization. Constructing the similarity of Asian women as a discursive category through homogenization, when histories between them indicate otherwise, is problematic and even dangerous because doing so ignores and distorts the difference of their material reality. Therefore, whenever one uses a politics of location in a manner of all innocence and cultural purity, such politics of location becomes more problematic than useful.

However, a politics of location, in my case using Asia as a primary location, can be useful when one uses it to destabilize stereotypical and culturally essentialist images of a certain group of people and, further, to establish a geopolitical coalition. This new politics of location that I employ is therefore "neither simply oppositional in contesting the mainstream (or *male*stream) for inclusion," but a discursive articulation in order to "empower and enable social action and, if possible, to enlist collective insurgency for the expansion of freedom, democracy, and individuality."[25] What scholars often overlook in the name of communitarian harmony is this power of collective insurgency among the women of Asia and also people across ethnic and racial boundaries, who become aware of the serious problems of Euro/U.S.-centrism, white supremacy, Western monoculturalism, or English linguicism[26] in an era of globalization. One should avoid a mono-factor analysis whenever one adopts a politics of location of as-Asian, because such discourse has the danger of losing sight of and touch with the complexities and diversities of the material reality of the group for which one tries to stand.

One reaction to globalization in non-Western countries is a nativist attempt to reshape and reclaim traditional cultural or national identity. People in non-Western countries often interpret West-centered globalization as a fundamental threat to their own ethnic and national identity. The fear of assimilation to the Western norms and culture urges them to seek and reclaim their ethnic, cultural,

---

25. Cornel West, "The New Cultural Politics of Difference," in *The Cultural Studies Reader*, 2d ed., ed. Simon During (New York: Routledge, 1999), 257.
26. The English language, in the age of globalization, is becoming more and more an unavoidable tool of power, domination, elitism, and communication across the continents, in a manner of neoimperialism. For an extensive discussion regarding linguicism and linguistic imperialism, cf. Robert Phillipson, *Linguistic Imperialism* (New York: Oxford University Press, 1992).

national identity. Women's questions, for example, once received central attention in the arena of social reform in many non-Western countries, but have now become secondary to the issues of ethnic, cultural, or national identity. So the issues of cultural and national identity and women's questions are in serious conflict. People in Asia often regard feminism as fundamentally foreign, and consider feminists as those who destroy, at worst, or dismiss, at best, their own cultural and national virtue, only to follow the individualistic lifestyle of the West. Asian women must often take a stance between nation and gender. In this context, it seems natural that the so-called Asian values discourse emerged in reaction to the threats of West-centered globalization.

Those who defend Asian values start by challenging Western-style civil and political freedoms, and strongly emphasize the significance of family and social harmony as uniquely Asian.[27] Lee Kuan Yew, a former prime minister of Singapore and one of the prime defenders of Asian values, argues that Asians believe that a "society with communitarian values where the interests of society take precedence over that of the individual suits them better than the individualism of America."[28] In this Asian values discourse, binarism between Asia and the West, and communitarian Asia versus individualistic West, become unavoidable, and those who emphasize Asian values exalt and idealize the traditional Asian family, which often means a patriarchal family where men/sons are the head of the household. This Asian values discourse has created a huge controversy, especially over the issue of human rights as to whether there is a universal notion of human rights that can be applied to the entire world. People expand this Asian values discourse to the issues of the universality versus

27. Joanne R. Bauer and Daniel A. Bell, eds., *The East Asian Challenge for Human Rights* (Cambridge: Cambridge University Press, 1999), 5ff.
28. *International Herald Tribune*, Nov. 9–10, 1991, quoted in ibid., 6.

particularity of human rights. One of the criticisms of Asian values discourse is that "culture is often no more than a convenient excuse deployed by authoritarian leaders to violate rights."[29]

One of the serious problems of the nationalist/regionalist/ethnic claim for Asians' own identity is their tendency to internalize orientalism. Non-Western nationalism or regionalism continues to project itself in a we–they binarism, but reverses the role of the Orient. The difference between the orientalism of the West and the orientalism of the Orient is that the Orient in non-Western nationalism becomes an active subject, rather than a passive object. The politics of Asian authentic identity is not only by Asians but also projected by Western feminists. Gayatri Chakravorty Spivak criticizes Julie Kristeva's ethnocentric projection of Chinese women in Huxian Square, for instance.[30] In her *About Chinese Women*, Kristeva naturalizes Chinese women in her ethnocentric, privileged, feminist view of Asian women: "An enormous crowd is sitting in the sun: they wait for us wordlessly, perfectly still. Calm eyes, not even curious, but slightly amused or anxious: in any case, piercing, and certain of belonging to a community with which we will never have anything to do."[31]

Here, Kristeva stereotypes and fixes Asian women in timeless space. When Asian women no longer stay in this fixed frame, people often regard those Asian women as inauthentic or Westernized. The fascination with the image of authentic Asian women is becoming stronger in the age of globalization and is often used as a rallying point by nationalists in Asia with their explicit nativism. In this context, contemporary nationalism in Asia tends to be more cultural

29. Bauer and Bell, *East Asian Challenge*, 12.
30. Gayatri Chakravorty Spivak, "French Feminism in an International Frame," in *In Other Worlds: Essays in Cultural Politics* (London: Methuen, 1987), 136.
31. Julia Kristeva, *About Chinese Women*, trans. Anita Barrows (New York: Marion Boyars, 1977), 11.

than political and thus is geared toward the defense of a traditional culture, which is, in most cases, strongly patriarchal. So, in the case of Japan, for instance: "Cultural nationalism aims to regenerate the national community by creating, preserving, or strengthening a people's cultural identity when it is felt to be lacking, inadequate, or threatened. The cultural nationalist regards the nation as the product of its unique history and culture and as a collective solidarity endowed with unique attributes. In short, cultural nationalism is concerned with the distinctiveness of the cultural community as the essence of a nation."[32]

Thus, the resurgence of nationalist identity becomes very evident in the age of West-centered globalization. For Asian culture, in the process of formulating a national identity in response to the threats of the West-centered globalization, women function as a signifier in many ways in the contrary dialectic of stasis and change in the imagining of Asia. Women become a site for mystic unity in the face of fragmentation, and a site for countering the challenge posed by Westernization. Women become the dream of a unified nation and "an infinite untrodden territory of desire which at every stage of historical deterritorialization, men in search of material for utopias have inundated with their desires."[33] In this process of claiming national/ethnic identity, women and the land become identical. Like the land, people often regard women as eternal, patient, ever-giving, and essential. In this regard, it is not surprising to see that nationalist claims have always accompanied claims to the soil.

In Korea, for instance, the agricultural associations first popularized the term *Shin-to-bul-e*, which means literally "the human body and the soil cannot be two." After the 1989 Uruguay Round, the

32. Kosaku Yoshino, *Cultural Nationalism in Contemporary Japan: A Sociological Inquiry* (New York: Routledge, 1992), 1.
33. Klaus Theweleit, *Male Fantasies* (Minneapolis: University of Minnesota Press, 1987), 294.

government used this as propaganda to substantiate a national identity, combining it with the phrase, "The most Korean is the most global," which was employed against the invasion of West-centered globalization. In this moment of rearticulating and reclaiming a national identity in the face of the threat of globalization, the linking of "mother" with the "land" gained exceptional popularity and people began using the words *woman* and *mother* as powerful metaphors for land and soil. People portray women, regardless of their marital status, as caring, ever-giving, ever-embracing, and ever-enduring, following Asian virtues and the ideal image of motherhood, which are allegedly different from Western values. People replace motherhood as an *experience* with motherhood as an *institution* in which they idealize stereotypes and fixed roles of women-mothers as the great virtues that constitute authentic women in society. Asian women are thus frozen to the past tradition and culture as the keepers of our culture, protecting our own tradition and virtue against the threat of assimilation to the West. Therefore, "*woman,* symbol of Hindu nationalism, covers real *women* in India, heterogeneous, various, of many castes, religions, and geographical regions."[34]

The tension between cultural homogenization as a desire to go back to the unpolluted locality and cultural heterogeneity as a reality of globalization is a serious dilemma in Asia today. Most Asian countries have positioned themselves in an ironic, paradoxical situation. On the one hand, they are afraid of Westernization, and thereby try to go back to their tradition and culture, claiming their own cultural homogenous identity. In their desire to go back to the unpolluted past, men often portray women as bearers of intact culture and custom. On the other hand, however, they ironically want to

---

34. Nalini Natarajan, "Woman, Nation, and Narration in *Midnight's Children,*" in *Scattered Hegemonies: Postmodernity and Transnational Feminist Practice,* ed. Inderpal Grewal and Caren Kaplan (Minneapolis: University of Minnesota Press, 1994), 85.

be more globalized, Westernized, and heterogenized by trying to catch up with America, meaning the United States of America.[35] The desire to catch up with the USA is explicit in commercialized sectors of music, movie, technology, fashion, food, sports, lifestyle, and also in educational systems and institutions. In this context, men in most Asian countries place women in this paradoxical situation of two conflicting national desires and women are often caught in the intersection of sexism, nativism, commercialism, capitalism, nationalism, or Asian regionalism.

The Internet in an era of globalization also contributes tremendously to the production and reproduction of stereotypes of Asian women, and people have used the Internet as a means of perpetuating and globally disseminating distorted stereotypes of Asian women. Websites frequently depict Asian women, for instance, as "'naturally feminine,' 'beauty queens,' 'sexual objects,' 'consumptive agents' and always an integral but subordinate component in the 'normal and nuclear modern' family."[36] The global male gaze on the Internet eroticizes Asian women as a collective entity without individuality. In the intersection of all these complex problems, it is not difficult to imagine Asian women, whom people have located in this uncontrollable paradoxical situation of globalization. The following quotation reveals the internal contradiction that Asian women experience:

> What kind of a self am I to myself if all I can be interested in is pleasing someone else's demands of me? What kind of self am I if in my

35. I notice that many people whom I have met in non-Western countries use the word *America* to indicate the United States, without thinking that there are many countries that can use the word *America*, in both North and South America. The powerful image of the United States in the world overshadows so many countries in the Americas.

36. Loong Wong, "Colour-Blind and Exclusive: The Internet and Asian Women," 2003, available at
http//:www.mngt.waikato.ac.nz/ejrot/cmsconference/2003/proceedings/
exploringthemeaning/Wong.pdf.

encounter with the other I am always the one who is named, framed, looked at? What kind of a self am I if my very ontological reality is the absolute function of the other's gaze? What kind of a self am I that I am not able to influence the other through my self-image or persuade the other to see himself as a function of my gaze?[37]

In this context, what globalization brings to us through the Internet is twofold, both positive and negative: a space for ongoing empowerment and solidarity among like-minded people who are seeking a better world,[38] and, at the same time, a space of re/production and dissemination of the essentialist homogeneity of a certain ethnic group of people. This negative function of cyberspace contributes to dissemination and perpetuation of distorted stereotypes of Asian women. If we define an identity politics as "a social practice in which a person or persons who identify with or are identified with a recognizable group such as 'women' or 'gays' make arguments or take action with the purpose of affecting social, economic, or educational policy relative to that group,"[39] what will happen when one's multiple identities coexist or are in conflict? Is there a hierarchy of identities, or a hierarchy of marginalities, such that one's gender identity, for instance, subsumes ethnic or national identity, or does this relationship produce an endless hyphenated identity, such as Asian-Korean-woman/man-lesbian/gay-Christian/Muslim/

---

37. R. Radhakrishnan, *Theory in an Uneven World* (Malden, MA: Blackwell, 2003), 55.

38. I used to have my Web homepage in the Korean language. I activated this homepage after I left Korea for the United States, to stay in close touch primarily with my former Korean students. To my surprise, this homepage has been used, not just as a means of communication, but more as a transgeographic space of solidarity and empowerment, especially among women in theological studies and ministry both in and outside Korea. I have come to realize that these correspondents share not only their intellectual, theological issues but their day-to-day experiences as a whole through this cyberspace. By providing an opportunity for mutual sharing of life as the marginalized, this e-space functions as a space of healing of inner wounds and pains, mutual empowering, affirming and reaffirming what they do, and ongoing solidarity with one another, which most of them, as the marginalized group in church and society, rarely find elsewhere.

39. Paula Moya, *Learning from Experience: Minority Identities, Multicultural Struggles* (Berkeley: University of California Press, 200), 103n.7.

Buddhist/Hindu? This question of the *multi*valent, if not just *ambi*valent, nature of one's identity becomes more and more anguished in the age of globalization.

Asian Women and Displacement

Disparity is the most striking feature of the world in the age of globalization. According to 2003 statistics, 10.6 million children die each year before they reach the age of five, and a fifth of these due to the lack of access to basic immunizations. Furthermore, eight hundred million people severely suffer from undernourishment, while 1.3 billion do not have access to drinking water.[40] The UN statistics also shows that nearly three million children under 5 years of age in Asia and the Pacific died in 2011.[41] An effect of the globalization of capital is increased disparity between the rich and the poor. Those who suffer the most when these disparities grow, in both industrialized and developing countries, are women and children, especially single mothers. The well-known concept of the *feminization of poverty* captures this phenomenon that an increasing proportion of the world's poor are female. The poor people in poor countries must leave their hometown and homeland to find financial resources for their day-to-day survival.

In this regard, it seems natural that a significant phenomenon to which economic globalization has contributed is the flow of both people and capital. World trade implies this flow, which makes international division of labor between nations more visible. Under neoliberal capitalist economic globalization, Asian countries and

40. *Asian Migrant Yearbook 2005* (Hong Kong: Asian Migrant Centre, 2005); see also, York W. Bradshaw and Michael Wallace, *Global Inequalities* (Thousand Oaks, CA: Pine Forge, 1996).
41. *Statistical Yearbook for Asia and the Pacific 2013* (Bangkok: United Nations, 2013), ix. Available at http://www.unescap.org/stat/data/syb2013/ESCAP-syb2013.pdf.

regions such as Hong Kong SRA, Singapore, South Korea, Taiwan (the so-called four dragons of Asia), and Malaysia and Thailand have generally used export-oriented measures, therefore requiring cheap labor for their own interests, and have become major receiving countries of migrant workers. They produce sophisticated consumption items and components, often at the leading edge of technology as well as traditional labor-intensive items, such as clothing. In this neoliberal economy, corporations practice inhuman exploitation of migrant workers, and women migrant workers are the most vulnerable victims.

Neoliberal globalization has produced millions of displaced workers and women in Asia, especially after the Uruguay Round (1986–94). According to statistics provided by the United Nations ESCAP (Economic and Social Commission for Asia and the Pacific), there are about fifty three million laboring migrants in Asia and Pacific region in 2010.[42] There are also millions of so-called undocumented migrant workers without visas or work permits, who are more vulnerable to multiple forms of exploitation by the receiving countries. Many less-developed Asian countries, such as Indonesia, Vietnam, the Philippines, and Bangladesh, become major sending countries of migrant workers. These workers are doing "3-D" (dirty, dangerous, difficult) work in factories, plantations, fisheries, construction, domestic situations, and as sex workers. One of the serious problems in many receiving Asian countries is that there are no standard employment contracts for migrant workers, and no institutionalized channels for consultation or representation on policies directly affecting them.[43] For instance, one of the top migrant–importing countries and regions in Asia is Hong Kong SAR,

42. Ibid., 20
43. *Asian Migrant Yearbook 2004* (Hong Kong: Asian Migrant Centre, 2004).

where 495,200 foreigners constituted at least 7.1 percent of its total population in 2000.[44]

One of the striking changes in the global workforce during the age of globalization is its composition. Since the 1970s, an increase in service-sector jobs has resulted in the increased recruitment of women. It is, therefore, a big mistake if we speak about globalization "without center-staging women of color,"[45] because they are the ones who have been an important source of the global labor market as low- or underpaid workers. Since globalization has encouraged industrialization in many Asian countries, women workers in Asia have been increasingly drawn into the new international division of labor. But they are the extremely exploited class of workers due to their lower level of skill training and lack of organized representation, as well as the patriarchal value system that tends to devalue works by women. With higher productivity expected from the new working system, women workers feel more pressure, leading to greater stress and tension at the workplace. As a result of the population growth due to the influx of workers, as well as a rise in the birth rate, the demand for housing and other basic amenities has increased in these areas.

Part of the economic plan developed by the International Monetary Fund (IMF) and World Bank for many Asian countries during the late 1960s and '70s was labor export. In this flow of labor, trafficking in Asian women emerged as a serious problem. Asian women become part of the globalization of the world's economy through various forms of trafficking. Asian women constitute 49 per cent of the global migration stock and 21.4 million domestic workers in the world are from the Asian and Pacific region.[46] The United

44. *Asian Migrant Yearbook 2000* (Hong Kong: Asian Migrant Centre, 2000).
45. Delia D. Aguilar, "Introduction," in *Women and Globalization*, ed. Delia D. Aguilar and Anne E. Lacsamana (Amherst, NY: Humanity Books, 2004), 16.
46. *Statistical Yearbook for Asia and the Pacific 2013*, 20.

Nations estimated that thirty million women and children in Asia were trafficking victims.[47] As goods to be shipped across borders, they are shipped all over the globe. For instance, the Philippines Department of Labor and Employment estimates that every day over two thousand people leave their country to look for work abroad. Over eight million Filipino/a migrant workers also work in over 186 countries, 65 percent of whom are women, excluding trafficked women or illegally recruited or those who migrated for marriage.[48] The victims come from poverty-stricken or conflict-ridden areas of Asian countries.

There are several categories of trafficking, but the first and largest in Asia is that of the transnational sex industry, including the mail-order bride industry. Websites frequently portray an Asian woman as an ideal bride for a man in the West. So the websites for the mail-order Asian bride market boom with advertisements such as, "Use these Asian bride dating sites and international marriage services to find a beautifully young and sexy Asian wife,"[49] or "Asian women seeking American and European men for dating and marriage,"[50] with photos of an elderly Anglo man holding a young, innocently smiling Asian woman. GABRIELA Network, a U.S.-based, Philippine–U.S. Women's Solidarity organization, estimates that since the 1980s there are annually at least five thousand Filipina mail-order brides in the United States alone moving through mail-

47. UNICRI (United Nations Interregional Crime and Justice Research Institute), Thirteenth Coordination Meeting of The United Nations Crime Prevention and Criminal Justice Programme Network. Courmayeur, Mont Blanc, Italy, 23–24 September 1998. Prepared by UNICRI.
48. Grace Chang, "Globalization in Living Color: Women of Color Living Under and Over the 'New World Order,'" in Aguilar and Lacsamana, eds., Women and Globalization, 242.
49. See http://www.trudating.com/asian-bride.html. There are countless websites on Asian brides or Asian wives, such as http://www.asianeuro.com, http://www.asiankisses.de, http://www.blossoms.com, and so on.
50. CleanAsia.com (2001–08), available at http://www.cleanasia.com. This website has individual boxes to click for Filipino, Thai, Chinese, Japanese, Korean, Indonesian, Vietnamese, Taiwanese, and Malaysian women so that people can pick the nationality of woman they wish.

order bride agencies or international matchmaking agencies, a multimillion-dollar business. Those mail-order brides, classified as "MOBs" in the ads in U.S. newspapers such as the *San Francisco Bay Guardian*, get married to Anglo, often elderly, males as their sex partners and housemaids. Furthermore, about 25,000 Filipinas have been brought into the United States to work in various sex industries.[51]

The trafficking of Asian women happens within Asian countries as well. Offering Asian women and young girls for sale to prospective husbands is a serious violation of human rights in Asian countries. In China from 1991 through 1996, for instance, Chinese police freed 88,000 kidnapped women and girls from other Asian countries and arrested 143,000 people for participating in this new form of slave trade.[52] At a fair in Singapore in 2005, Blissful Heart Marriage Center set up a booth at the Golden Mile Complex trading center in Singapore for a public exhibition of Vietnamese brides for instant marriage with single men in China. And people put Vietnamese women on display like products, who are there "to give potential clients [Singaporean men] an idea how Vietnamese girls look and to give them a feel of the on-the-spot selection process."[53] In South Korea, marriages to foreigners, especially Vietnamese women, are advertised on billboards and subway fliers, promising, "Marry Vietnamese virgins, they will never flee. If they do, we will return your money back." Another business that emerged in the late 1990s

---

51. GABRIELA Network USA (2005-08), available at http://www.gabnet.org/campaigns.php?page=2.2.
52. For more details, see the website of the Coalition Against Trafficking in Women (CATW), http://www.catwinternational.org/factbook. Founded in 1988, CATW is a nongovernmental international organization to combat sexual exploitation of women, especially focusing on sex trafficking. The CATW has regional networks in Asia, Latin America, Europe, Africa, and Australia. CATW obtained Category II Consultative Status with the United Nations Economic and Social Council in 1989.
53. Tran Dinh Thanh Lam, "Singapore Fair Puts Brides on Display," *Asia Times*, April 2, 2005, available at http://www.atimes.com/atimes/southeast_asia/gd02ae01.html.

targeted South Korean farmers or physically disabled men, matching them with women from other underdeveloped Asian countries. There were two to three thousand matching agencies in Korea in 2005. The major reason for this phenomenon is allegedly twofold: the shortage of Korean women and the increase of their educational and employment opportunities, which can also be factors in the rising divorce rates.[54] Since the 1980s, the widespread availability of ultrasound technology, through which one can screen the sex of the fetus, has resulted in the imbalance of ratio between male and female in South Korea.

In 2006, the *Chosun Daily*, a leading Korean newspaper, published an article entitled "Vietnamese virgins coming to Korea—a Nation of Hope," with a photo of eleven Vietnamese women whose faces were unconcealed.[55] Under the photo were the words, "Korean princes, please take me home." The article described a matchmaking process whereby a Korean suitor called Kim went to see his would-be brides and browsed through "a chorus line of 11 Vietnamese women." The paper also wrote that "he [the suitor] is also shown a catalogue on CD-Rom containing just the pictures of the [150] would-be brides—just scanning them all would have taken an hour and a half." Those 150 Vietnamese women, tagged with number tickets on their breasts, appeared on the computer screen, which sometimes zoomed in on their faces, sometimes on their whole bodies. According to this article, it cost US $8,000 and took seven days and six nights for this Korean man to get married to the Vietnamese woman he chose. The newspaper did not criticize this act, and Korean social activists harshly protested. The Vietnam Women's Union also asked the *Chosun Daily* to apologize publicly for the article. On July 11, 2006, thirty Korean

54. Norimitsu Onishi, "Korean Men Use Brokers to Find Brides in Vietnam," New York *Times*, February 22, 2007.
55. *Chosun Daily*, "Vietnamese virgins coming to Korea—a Nation of Hope," April 21, 2006. Available in Korean.

NGOs filed this case with the National Human Rights Commission of Korea to ban bride advertisements that violate women's human rights and perpetuate sexism, classism, and racism.[56] A list of incidents of this kind, showing an extreme violation of women's human rights, would be endless in Japan, Hong Kong SAR, and Taiwan. Women have become a commodity of exchange.

But this is just a surface issue. A more fundamental issue as to why this kind of unthinkable arrangement exists is the extreme poverty in many Southeast Asian countries after economic globalization. Poverty makes possible human trafficking in a "benign" form through matching agencies, if not through the overt use of force. Thus, it is little wonder why these Southeast Asian women seem to volunteer and give consent to this unbearably humiliating deal. They come from extremely poor families and take a risk to escape poverty. They are willing to try their luck even with the potential dangers. Neoliberal globalization has destroyed the self-sufficient system of the agricultural sector, which has led to the bankruptcy of farming areas. This bankruptcy of rural areas has forced residents in farming areas to leave their homes for the cities to look for jobs, but they end up in extreme poverty and are victims of various forms of crime, for the urban sector is also in trouble. In Vietnam, for example, 75 percent of the population is classified as farmers.[57] According to a study on the trade in Asian women: "Transnational marriages strengthen the internationalization of capital by (1) stabilizing the reproduction of cheap domestic labor in core and semi-peripheral states, as well as by offering a new source of cheap labor; (2) enhancing the primitive accumulation of capital in the peripheral countries; and (3) personalizing the abstract international division of labor."[58]

56. Available at http://www.viewsnnews.com/article/view.jsp?code=NCF&seq=4214 (in Korean).
57. Vu Thi Thanh Huong, "Policy and Measures to Promote ICT Application and Deployment for Business Development in Rural Areas in Vietnam," Technical Report on the Progress of Project. Ministry of Science and Technology, July 2006.

Transnational marriage for women in Southeast Asian countries is a way out of poverty and bankruptcy. Displaced women, especially from Southeast Asia, who are either in the mail-order bride pool or working as migrant workers, are driven by extreme poverty after their nation's adoption of a neoliberal capitalist system of globalization. Structural adjustment imposed by the First World on many Asian countries has caused the massive displacement of Asian women.

Transethnic Feminist Theology in an Era of Globalization

In order to do theology in the age of globalization, feminist theologians may have to ask a fundamental question about the role of feminist theologians in the public world. Outside of a small number of readers and audiences, few members of our own guild may know what we do or who we feminist theologians are. Are feminist theologians mere commentators on Christianity and religions? Given the analytical tools that feminist theologians employ in their wide-ranging research, studies, writing, teaching, and lecturing, I have come to believe firmly that feminist theologians have a role to play in helping to decide issues in the public world as the intellectuals. Edward Said remarks: "The intellectuals are individuals with a *vocation for the art of representing*, whether that is talking, writing, teaching, appearing on television. And that vocation is important to the extent that it is publicly recognizable and involves both commitment and risk, boldness and vulnerability. . . . The intellectual belongs on the same side with the weak and unrepresented."[59]

---

58. Hsiao-Chuan Hsia, "Internationalization of Capital and the Trade in Asian Women: The Case of 'Foreign Brides' in Taiwan," in Aguilar and Lacsamana, ed., *Women and Globalization*, 219.

Feminist theologians analyze and criticize religious institutions, traditions, scripture, and rituals from a feminist perspective. They equip themselves to scrutinize the ideological sleight of hand that leads to a seemingly perfect fit between the models constructed and divinely sanctioned by the society or congregations in question. In this regard, feminist theologians have clearly played the role of social critic. What type of reality do feminist theologians, then, expect to find represented? If the reality that feminist theologians expect to find represented and envisioned is something apart from concrete reality, this can encourage us as theologians to settle their public concern by enacting the divine will only within our religious circle. Therefore, such questions as to whether or not women can be ordained, for instance, can be reduced to a fundamentally religious reality, not a sociopolitical reality, because "the answer has everything to do with discerning and then enacting the will of God, and nothing to do with the rights of women."[60] In this context, feminist theologies in the age of globalization need to reaffirm that the personal is not just political; the personal is religious and theological as well. What happens in the world should become a serious feminist theological issue, and this is why feminist theologies in the light of globalization should reshape their theological identity as a "vocation for the art of representing" and reaffirm that feminist theologians belong "on the same side with the weak and unrepresented,"[61] as public intellectuals in Said's sense.

Feminist theologies in the age of globalization are to expose the ways in which people construct norms in politics, economics, culture, and religion and to display the ways people employ these norms in the contest over power, privilege, and control. Along the issue of the interrelatedness of the personal, political, religious, and theological,

---

59. Said, *Representations of the Intellectual*, 13 (italics mine).

60. Stephen Carter, *The Culture of Disbelief: How American Law and Politics Trivialize Religious Devotion* (New York: Doubleday, 1993), 77.

61. Said, *Representations of the Intellectual*, 13, 22.

feminist theology in the era of globalization needs to wrestle critically with the issue of the interconnectedness between the local and the global, the universal and the particular, and the macrodimensional and the microdimensional. Some examples of the macrodimensional aspects can be as Jacques Derrida describes:

1. The hundreds of millions of illiterate people: the massive scale of malnutrition, rarely taken into account by the media champions of human rights; the hundreds of millions of children who die every year because of water; the 40 to 50 percent of women who are subject to violence, and often life-threatening violence, all the time—and so on. The list would be endless;

2. The way that capitalist powers are concentrated into transnational and cross-state monopolies in the appropriation of the media, multimedia, and productions of the tele-technologies and even the languages that they use.[62]

Feminist theologians are critical of and do not value religious traditions and discourses for their own claims to truth and authority; rather, they value the ways in which these traditions and discourses may serve to liberate and enlarge human freedom and possibilities. For religion is about living in a concrete daily reality of people, not just about what people claim and proclaim or confess and profess.

Among different feminist discourses today, a strong tendency toward compartmentalization in the name of respecting difference, locality, and particularity of one's context exists. This tendency is clearly to avoid being falsely universal. But I would argue that such a thing as purely particular/local is impossible to exist especially when the *particular/local* is inextricably interlinked to the universal/

---

62. Jacques Derrida, *Paper Machine*, trans. Rachel Bowlby (Stanford: Stanford University Press, 2005 [2001]), 39.

global dimension in people's daily lives. It is becoming harder than ever to draw the rigid line between the particular and the universal, between the local and the global. In this sense, the term *glocalization*, as discussed in the previous chapter, captures this interconnectivity and entanglement of the local and the global well, in the sense that the local is "an aspect of globalization."[63] Celebrating the local and the particular should not be an excuse for ghettoization and compartmentalization of feminist theologies from various regions.

In any fragmentation among feminist discourses, a danger of developing an invisible discursive hierarchy can arise. Chandra Talpade Mohanty contends that Western feminists exercise their power through "discursive homogenization and systemization of the oppression of women in the third world,"[64] which creates a discursive hierarchy among feminists from different regions of the world. In this context, feminist scholars in the United States define international feminism "as feminism in England, France, West Germany, and the part of the Third World most easily accessible to American interests: Latin America."[65] Feminist scholars in the West categorize feminism in countries other than these as "Third-World feminism," which freezes "third world women in time, space, and history."[66] So a discursive rankism emerges in feminist scholarship in which scholars regard feminism in the United States as normative, the first rank, which does not need any adjective. International feminism is

---

63. Roland Robertson, "Glocalization: Time–Space and Homogeneity–Heterogeniety," in *Global Modernities*, ed. Mike Featherstone, Scott Lash, and Roland Robertson (London: Sage, 1995), 30.

64. Chandra Talpade Mohanty, "Under Western Eyes: Feminist Scholarship and Colonial Discourses," in *Third World Women and the Politics of Feminism*, ed. Chandra Talpade Mohanty, Ann Russo, and Lourdes Torres (Bloomington: Indiana University Press, 1991), 54.

65. Spivak, "French Feminism," 134.

66. Chandra Talpade Mohanty, "Introduction: Cartographies of Struggle: Third World Women and the Politics of Feminism," in Mohanty, et al., eds., *Third World Women*, 6. Although the term *Third* in Third World may mean an alternative to the First or Second Worlds, ever since the term was employed by the nonaligned nations at the Bandung Conference in 1955, one cannot deny that its connotation has been the *third-rank*, or *third-class*.

the second-rank feminism, and Third-World feminism takes up the third rank. Furthermore, those feminisms considered international or normative tend to denote the global, while other feminisms denote the local or the indigenous. However, all discourses are in fact local, in the sense that each discourse reflects one's situatedness in a specific time and space. Mary John calls for feminists in the West to travel and engage with the East: "Western feminists need to reconsider what they are out to learn from the distant places they visit. Instead of developing ever more theoretically sophisticated twists on the cross-cultural construction of gender, why not attend also to *feminist* voices from elsewhere?"[67]

Today, no one has the luxury to live just locally. What is happening in one place is interlinked to what is happening in the rest of the world. This inter-affectivity shows the transregional or transethnic aspect of globalization. In the age of globalization, one's ethnic identification serves only as a provisional starting point, not as what I would call a theologicaltribalism. In the age of globalization, feminist theologies from non-Western regions should shift their gaze from cultural contextualization, which focuses primarily on ethnic/cultural difference from the West as an ethnic group of people, toward geopolitical contextualization, which emphasizes the interconnectivity of our destiny across the regions of the world. Asian feminist theology has focused more on the Asian culturalcontext than on geopolitical context. But now the geopolitical context of Asia and its relationship to the rest of the world needs to come to the fore to construct feminist theological discourse and alliances. Theology can no longer reside only in the castle of religion.

I propose a transethnic feminist theology of Asia, where one's ethnicity can be an entry point but where one moves beyond

---

67. Mary E. John, *Discrepant Dislocations: Feminism, Theory, and Postcolonial Histories* (Berkeley: University of California Press, 1996), 144.

geographic, cultural, or ethnic boundaries and interests. This transethnic perspective requires a radical ecumenical spirit that adopts a very dialectical approach to race, ethnicity, and culture, and a fundamental awareness that the local, the particular, or the ethnic has always been shaped by the global and the global by the local. This transethnic perspective ought to produce not a blind universalism but a relational and dialectical universalism that promotes shared sensibilities across the boundaries of class, gender, race, ethnicity, ability, or orientation without sacrificing the particular situatedness of one's geopolitical and discursive location. This transethnic positionality that I propose further establishes a firm ground for the "recognition of common commitments" and will "serve as a base for solidarity and coalition"[68] among those who work for the betterment of our society.

In this regard, transethnic feminist theology should be, first, a discourse and practice of social and geopolitical criticism. Feminist theologians have to rearticulate and retheologize the histories of how the spread of capitalism and the neoliberal market interlink people in different geopolitical locations and circumstances. The failure to see that people repeat the patterns of dominance in global settings can account for the failure in obtaining equality between the genders, classes, or racial/ethnic groups in this uneven world of globalization. Furthermore, any theologies that do not take into account the power play between the macro- and micro-level, between the dominant and the dominated, would not have theological accountability. Second, transethnic feminist theology should be a discourse and practice of world traveling, through which one acknowledges and experiences multiple locations and realities. This is not merely physical travel but engaged, discursive travel through which one is able to get

---

68. bell hooks, "Postmodern Blackness," in *Yearning: Race, Gender and Cultural Politics* (Boston: South End, 1990), 27.

politically engaged in the reality of different religions/contexts of the world. In this sense, world traveling is different from world tourism, which lacks one's political engagement in the places where one travels: "Through travelling to other people's 'worlds' we discover that there are 'worlds' in which those who are the victims of arrogant perception are really subjects, lively beings, resistors, constructors of visions even though in the mainstream construction they are animated only by the arrogant perceiver and are pliable, foldable, file-awayable, classifiable."[69]

This world traveling makes possible the acknowledgment of different intersections of multiple spatio-temporalities of struggles and resistances, and it offers an epistemological and theological space of connections and solidarity between people of different gender, class, race, ethnicity, ability, sexuality, or language in the realm of materialized history and politics. Here, feminists need to construct a new conception of travel—travel between "third-world nations, for instance, or between third-world spaces in the West. . . in both the third world and in the first."[70]

Third, transethnic feminist theology should be a discourse and practice of geopolitical alliances across the globe, transcending borders between nations, cultures, and ethnicities. As Homi Bhabha relevantly illustrates, "what is crucial to such a vision of the future is the belief that we must not merely change the *narratives* of our histories, but transform our sense of what it means to live, to be, in other times and different spaces, both human and historical."[71] Doing theology in the age of globalization would mean world traveling in order to know, to feel in what kind of life situation marginalized

---

69. María Lugones, "Playfulness, 'World'-Travelling, and Loving Perception," in *Haciendo Caras/Making Face, Making Soul*, ed. Gloria Anzaldúa (San Francisco: Aunt Lute, 1990), 402.
70. John, *Discrepant Dislocations*, 144.
71. Bhabha, *The Location of Culture*, 256 (italics original).

people are positioned, what kind of theological implications these new contexts of globalization have, and how feminist theology can offer a vision for a better world to the religious communities and societies. Feminist theologians are to play a role of world travelers as social critics who raise a countervoice and counterhegemonic theological discourse in existing society, envisioning an alternative reality through the lens of post-kyriarchy.

In the age of globalization, vulnerable groups of people in global society have emerged and reflect serious problems not just in Asia and the West but also all over the world. The emerging problems are poverty, inadequate housing and living conditions, lack of access to medical care, environmental destruction, and extreme violation of basic human rights for dislocated people. These problems are inextricably interlinked from nation to nation and from region to region. The global and the local, the international and the national overlap and inextricably intersect, while strategically operating in mutually exclusive conditions. This new context of globalization points to the mandate for a new approach to feminist theological issues and concerns, an approach based on a recognition of fundamental mutuality and interconnectivity of nations and regions, and a desire for transnational, transregional, and transethnic cooperation, alliances, and solidarities, rather than the balkanization or theological tribalism of feminist theological discourse and issues based on national, cultural, regional, or ethnic divide.

9

Negotiating the Alternative

Women's Choice of Christianity in a Non-Christian World

> How is freedom measured in individuals and people? According to the resistance which must be overcome.
> —Friedrich Nietzsche[1]

Beyond *Ecumenical Taboo*

In most countries in Asia, one chooses to become, rather than happens to be, a Christian. When one makes a religious choice for a foreign religion such as Christianity, one bases the choice on the difference from, not the similarity with, the existing indigenous religions. In this chapter, I will illustrate the critical differences, as the ground of women's *religious choice-in-difference* between

1. Friedrich Nietzsche, *Twilight of the Idols*, in *The Portable Nietzsche* (New York: Viking, 1954), 542.

Confucianism and Christianity. Challenging the status quo of religions and moving toward a more just and transformative religion require breaking what I would call an ecumenical taboo, which discourages one from addressing critical differences between religions. I will also examine the discursive and institutional shift of Christianity in Korea from a liberative to a patriarchal religion in which women's marginality has been naturalized in theological discourses and practices as the divine order under the guise of the false egalitarianism of "equal but different." In reclaiming the theological significance of women's religious choice-in-difference in Korea, I would like to highlight the significance of a liberative and transformative function of religion in general, and of Christianity in particular, for those who are marginalized and voiceless in society, because otherwise the very existence of religion would be pointless in the daily lives of ordinary people.

One of the problems I have encountered in my longstanding involvement in ecumenical interreligious dialogue is its methodological dilemma: ecumenical methodology of religious similarities, which constructs dialogical ground on the similarities between religions. Most people who come to the ecumenical table for interreligious dialogue hardly talk about differences between religions out of fear of receiving criticism and challenges from other religions. Rather than examining the critical difference in epistemological frameworks and practices, they focus on the religious similarities or commonalities between their own religion and others so that they do not have to go through the possible painful experience of challenging or being challenged. A number of scholars of Korean religions focus on the similarities between Confucianism and Christianity as "religions of father and son" without offering a critical difference between the two.

For instance, Sung Bum Yun, a pioneering theologian for developing so-called Korean indigenous theology, in his book *Theology of Sung*, contends that the relationship of Jesus Christ with the Heavenly Father [sic] resembles Confucian filiality, that is, the earthly, cultural father-son relationship.[2] According to Yun, both in Judeo-Christianity and Confucianism, the father-son relationship is the essential norm for an integral approach to what it means to be human. He argues that "both Christianity and Confucianism are religions of the East, and the ethics of both begin with the family,"[3] which is in fact a typically patriarchal family. Yet, he fails to see the critical difference in the notion of family in Christianity and Confucianism. Whereas Confucian family is grounded on patrilineal bloodlines, Christian family moves beyond biological ties. When Jesus raises such a fundamental question as "Who is my family?" and goes on to say that "Anyone who does the will of God, that person is my sister, my brother, my mother" (Mark 3:33, 35, *The Inclusive Bible*), he makes clear that Christian notions of family should move beyond biological lines, unlike the Confucian system. While Sung Bum Yun sees only the terminological commonality of father-son in the two religions, he overlooks the significant difference in their construction of the notion of family. The father-son relationship in Confucianism is exclusively biological and socially conventional. In Christianity, however, it is theological, symbolic, counterconventional, and transbiological. Therefore, one should not equate the accidentality of the maleness of Jesus and the symbolic use of the masculine for God with the Confucian way of understanding the biological father-son relationship. Equation of the two sacralizes

---

2. Sung Bum Yun, *Ethics East and West: Western Secular, Christian, and Confucian Traditions in Comparative Perspective*, trans. Michael C. Kalton (Seoul: Christian Literature Society, 1977 [1973]), 16.
3. Sung Bum Yun, *Theology of Sung* (Seoul: Sungkwangsa, 1973), 125.

and reproduces traditional patriarchal constructions of theological/ religious discourse and institutions.

David Chung also emphasizes the similarity between the two religions by contending that there are common theological and ethical principles between Confucianism and Christianity in Korea: a theological belief in the Supreme Deity, ethical principles of sincerity, righteousness, altruism, just human relations, a sense of good and evil, and so forth. He goes on to talk positively about following the Five Orders of Relationship (also called the Confucian Five Relationships), as an example of the commonality between these two religions.[4] However, he fails to see the critical difference between these two by overlooking the fact that in the Confucian Five Orders of Relationship, it is impossible for women to attain an equal and just relationship with men as beings created equally in the image of God, as in Christianity. He also overlooks a critical epistemological difference between the two religions in terms of their understanding of individual persons, and thereby misses that the epistemological framework of the Confucian Five Orders of Relationship is extremely hierarchical and patriarchal.

As one of the most militarized regions in the world today, Korea has masculinized the so-called Korean tradition, which Korean scholars define as "what Korean people thought and think" and "what contributes to the development of Korean thoughts,"[5] in which people have come to regard men as more legitimate than women. Here we must ask the question as to what kind of Korean people those scholars refer when they define the Korean tradition, as Korean people are not a unitary entity, genderless, classless, ageless, or religionless. The Ministry of Education and the state intellectuals

4. David Chung, *Syncretism: The Religious Context of Christian Beginnings in Korea* (Albany: State University of New York Press, 2001), 112–19.
5. *The Identity of the Korean People: A History of Legitimacy on the Korean Peninsula* (Seoul: Research Center for Peace and Unification, 1983), 129–30.

under the regime of the President Park Chung Hee, who led the 1961 military coup d'état and called for the inevitability of military revolution and patriotism[6] after his takeover of the state through military force, depict the ethos of Tan'gun, whom Koreans regard as the founder and origin of the Korean nation, the attitude of *Silla* chivalry (*Hwarang*), state-protecting Buddhism, and Confucianism as the essential elements of Korean tradition. Korea has used the Tan'gun myth to portray the image of a timeless Korean nation, which appeared in *Samguk Yusa* ("Memorabilia of the Three Kingdoms") in the eleventh century, written by a Buddhist monk, Ilyon. The Tan'gun myth has been taught in the public schools as an explanation of the foundation of Korea as a state and carries within itself the practice of the marginalization and stereotyping of women as bearers of endurance and of womb, and the message of the androcentric construction of Korea as a state of extraordinary men—the heavenly male (*Hwanung*) and the earthly male (*Tan'gun*). The Tan'gun myth becomes the androcentric and patriarchal subtext of the authentic discourse of Korean national history and tradition.[7]

All these essential elements contain a strong desire to build a fully masculine Korea and contribute to reinforcing the interests of the male ruling elite. One can find this kind of androcentric construction of national tradition also in other nationalistic discourses, such as in India, in which Indian tradition is equated with the Hindu scriptures, the tradition of the male Indian elites.[8] This androcentric

---

6. Cf. Sejin Kim, *The Politics of Military Revolution in Korea* (Chapel Hill: University of North Carolina Press, 1971), 93–94.
7. Cf. James H. Grayson, *Korea: A Religious History* (Oxford: Clarendon, 1989).
8. Cf. Uma Chakravarti, "What Happened to the Vedic Dasi?: Orientalism, Nationalism, and a Script for the Past," in *Recasting Women: Essays in Colonial History*, ed. Kumkum Sangari and Sudesh Vaid (New Delhi: Kali for Women, 1989). Also, for the androcentric construction of German national identity that hinges on bourgeois German masculinity, see George Mosse, *Nationalism and Sexuality: Respectability and Abnormal Sexuality in Modern Europe* (New York: Howard Fertig, 1985).

construction of Korean tradition permeates every sector of Korean society through textbooks on national history and national language, media, and all means of education. It has also contributed to essentializing the difference between women and men, and to naturalizing the androcentric construction of Korea as a nation. The Korean brand of humanism, combining elements of Tan'gun's humanism (*hongik ingan*) and the Confucian notion of the basis of ruling in the people(*minbon juui*), has emerged from the state intellectuals.[9] Here, the concept of heaven's imperatives or heaven's mandate (*chon myong*) within Confucianism becomes significant, a way to legitimate the ruling power as a heavenly given and politics as taking care of the ruled. Some scholars tend to interpret heaven's imperatives analogously to the Western notion of natural rights.[10]

However, the problem Confucian scholars overlook is that in the notion of the basis of ruling in the people(*minbon juui*), there are no specific guidelines as to who gets to decide what kind of needs are to be taken care of and how. This absence of concrete guidelines both for the ruled and the ruler depoliticize the ruled and uncritically sacralize the power of the ruler, even when the ruler is manipulative or dictatorial. In the political intermingling of Confucian humanism with the spirit of heaven's mandate and the basis of ruling in the people, grassroots people easily become passive subjects, ruled without the possibility of active participation in the political processes of decision making. When the ruler does not ground the basis of ruling in the people or heaven's mandate of an epistemological acknowledgment of the dignity and equality of every individual person, Confucian humanism becomes a typical example of abstract

---

9. Cf. Han Sung-jo, "Hanguk minjujuuiui kukkaronjok kijo" ["A State Theory of Korean Democracy"] in *Hanguk Kukkaui gibbon Songgyokgwa Gwaje* [*A Basic Nature of the Korean State and Its Task*] (Sungnam: Institute of Korean Mental Culture Research, 1988).

10. Cf. Wm. Theodore de Bary, "Introduction," in *Confucianism and Human Rights,* ed. Wm. Theodore de Bary and Tu Weiming (New York: Columbia University Press, 1998), 18.

universalism, which is fundamentally different from *concrete universalism* that has emancipatory potential.[11] Here, abstract humanism can hardly serve the interest of the people and promote the human rights of the individual person, regardless of position or social class.

As we have seen, emphasizing the external similarities between religions, in this case Confucianism and Christianity, without scrutinizing the fundamental differences as to what it means to be human, can be theopolitically and theoethically misleading and distorting. In this context, first, the methodology of religious similarities is problematic because of its inability to provide an explanation for why people choose to become Christians in a religiously pluralistic world. If ecumenical interreligious dialogue focuses only on the similarities between religions, or ignores the differences in discourse and practice in the name of religious tolerance, it cannot provide an explanation as to why and how people come to change from one religion to other. Unless people are able to find critical differences between religions, they would not have any desire to change their religious affiliation. Examining the differences between religions in a specific context that lead women to change from one religion to another enables one to construct a religious discourse that scrutinizes the multiple roles of religion in a given society.

Second, the methodology of religious similarities is problematic because of its tendency to maintain the status quo of religious discourse and practice by accepting and naturalizing the religious reality-as-it-is. What I attempt to address here is especially the

---

11. For the further discussion about the "abstract universality" and "concrete universality," see David Couzens Hoy, *Critical Resistance: From Poststructuralism to Post-Critique* (Cambridge: MIT Press, 2004), 4–5, 132–35. Alessandro Ferrara also differentiates "generalizing universalism" from "exemplary universalism" in his book *Reflective Authenticity: Rethinking the Project of Modernity* (London: Routledge, 1998).

fundamental question of *why* women in a non-Christian world turn away from their traditional indigenous religions and convert to Christianity as an alternative religion. If one focuses only on similarities between religions, as many ecumenical scholars of religions often tend to do, one can overlook the transformative aspects that a particular religion has in a given time and space. By critically attending to differences among and between religions in specific socio-politico-cultural contexts, one can envision a *religious reality-as-it-ought-to-be*. I would argue that the ecumenical reluctance in acknowledging the critical difference between religions for the sake of ecumenical unity of religions has created an ecumenical taboo that I believe has hindered people from constructing a transformative ecumenicity among and between religions, the prophetic ecumenicality that would function as a channel for mutual challenge, reciprocal self-criticalism, and transformation for the betterment of humanity.

Addressing the issue of Christianity and women in Korea, where religious plurality and co-existence of multiple religions are a daily reality, means to critically challenge and move beyond this ecumenical taboo that discourages people from wrestling with such critical issues as patriarchy, sexism, heterosexism, classism, racism, imperialism, or homophobia that fundamentally challenge the very framework through which people continue to constitute and practice religions. Revisiting and reclaiming the liberative power of Korean women's religious choice for Christianity are extremely significant and urgent ways to reframe and reconstruct theological vision for a more accountable and relevant Christianity in the contemporary world. Challenging the status quo of religions and moving toward more just and transformative religions require critically breaking the ecumenical taboo. Otherwise, inter- or intrareligious dialogues and interactions are nothing but self-amusing and resource-consuming activities, amounting to just having tea together without being seriously challenged about the ways a religion can be concretely harmful to millions of people, especially women and the marginalized.

Christianity and Women under Confucianism

In order to understand Christianity in Korea, one must scrutinize the impact of Confucianism on the formation of the religious and social value systems of Korea since the Yi Dynasty (1392–1910), as Korea is considered the most Confucian country in the world today. The Yi Dynasty made Confucianism the national religion and basis of ethics, and since then, feudalistic Confucianism has had a pervasive influence on Korean society in general and on Korean women in particular. Confucianism introduced into Korean society the principle of *agnation*, which made men alone the structurally relevant members of society and relegated women to social dependence. Women were not always marginal and dependent members within Korean society. During the Koryo Dynasty (918–1392), before Confucianism came to Korea, women were, in a relative sense but to a great extent, in command of their own lives. Patrilineage, for example, was not the primary practice; daughters received family inheritance as equally as sons; female lines were regarded as being as important as male lines; and the remarriage of women was not a taboo, as in the Yi Dynasty.[12]

The introduction of Confucianism, however, brought a drastic change in women's status in Korean society. Only sons inherited the

---

12. Mark Peterson, "Women without Sons: A Measure of Social Change in Yi Dynasty Korea," in *Korean Women: View from the Inner Room*, ed. Laurel Kendall and Mark Peterson (New Haven: East Rock Press, 1983), 42.

family line and received an inheritance, the largest portion going to the eldest son. People considered daughters outsiders once they got married, and usually considered a man who had only daughters to have no children.[13] Even after marriage, Korean women still retain their maiden name, but this custom does not mean that society respects their identity. Retaining a maiden name after marriage in Korea has not been based in a feminist rationale, as some women have practiced in the West since the women's rights movement. Rather, women are conceptually permanent outsiders, who cannot become an authentic full member in the husband's family due to the lack of blood connection with the husband's household. Women are destined to become in-between beings, who do not have an authentic family membership either in their own natal family or their husband's family. They become an outsider-who-left-the-household (*chulga oein*), who belong nowhere.

The idea of "men are honored/women are abased" (*namjon yobi*) has become gradually naturalized and institutionalized since the introduction of Confucianism as part of the state religion and political ideology in the Yi Dynasty. Sons are of overwhelming importance to the family because of their potential role as providers of the family income. Even after death, it is the sons, as sole performers of the Confucian ancestor rites, who are responsible for the welfare of departed parents in the world of spirits. Daughters are not allowed to participate in the ancestral rites. In the Confucian context, ancestor worship/rites has a strong religious meaning because of its acknowledgment of the human relationship to the spiritual, transcendental world. Ancestor worship not only symbolizes human respect for the revelation of the spirit, but it also plays an indispensable role in reinforcing the cohesion of the family and its

13. Ibid., 36.

lineage. Some assumptions in Confucian ancestor worship are: first, the rite presupposes continuance of personality in some form after the death of the physical body; second, it assumes the possibility of continued contact between the dead and the living family members; third, in the sense of the family system and its hierarchical structure, the fact that original relationships remain in full force, despite the death of a senior, is clearly assumed.[14]

So, from the day of her marriage, a woman is under pressure to conceive and bring forth healthy males because the family lineage is acknowledged only through the male line. Without sons, people would have no heads of household to offer the ancestral worship. In the Confucian notion of filiality (hsiao), which people regard as the virtue of all virtues, the existence of a son in the household is inevitable. Korea, still a Confucianized nation today, received a nickname, "abortion paradise," because women tend to have sex-selective abortions, due to the resiliently "overarching Confucian culture of son-preference" there, which has created a severe disparity between the numbers of male and female children. Abortion in Korea is not an issue of women's choice or rights, in contrast to the feminist-oriented right of choice in the West, but is about destroying the life of female fetuses and perpetuating the Confucian culture of male-preference.[15]

In this context, Confucianism has played a crucial role in degrading the status of Korean women and perpetuates kyriarchal ideologies that have made male hegemony in Korea natural. The term kyriarchy, discussed in previous chapter above, reveals the complexity of domination and subjugation that run through the

14. Cf. Laurence Thompson, *Chinese Religion: An Introduction* (Belmont, CA: Wadsworth, 1989 [1979]), 46.
15. Cf. Sasha Hampson, "Rhetoric or Reality?: Contesting Definitions of Women in Korea," in *Women in Asia: Tradition, Modernity and Globalisation*, ed. Louise Edwards and Mina Roces, Women in Asia Publication Series (St. Leonards, Australia: Allen & Unwin, 2000), 174–75.

Confucian practice under the Yi Dynasty. Patriarchy, by contrast, is a rather limited term because the social network of domination and subordination often instantiated in Confucianism is rather multilayered. However, it is significant to note that Confucianism has practiced hegemonic power not only over women but also over lower-class people. Thus, in this context, one needs to redefine and complexify the concept of patriarchy, usually regarded as simply the rule of men over women, based on an assumed gender dualism.

According to Antonio Gramsci,[16] hegemony is like a naturalized ideology, which presents itself as the way the world is. Through naturalized ideology, one perceives the way things are as natural, and thus one cannot gain the distance or leverage needed to disagree with or change the reality. Michel Foucault contends that discourse constitutes and spreads hegemony.[17] Foucault's understanding of discourse points to the ways in which discourse serves as a form of surveillance and as a means of producing knowledge, reencoding/ recreating all of society. In order to implant and maintain Confucian hegemony, the Yi Dynasty produced various discourses that constituted and naturalized the kyriarchal hegemony of Confucianism, and its impact continues to be felt today. From 1392 to 1485, the Yi government encouraged people to achieve Confucian virtue by publishing *The Three Principles of Virtuous Conduct* [*Samgang Haengsildo*] in 1432. The three principles were loyalty to the crown, filial piety, and chastity.

Between 1486 and 1636, Confucianism became firmly entrenched in Korean society, especially in terms of its systemic control and subjugation of women with the promulgation of the Code of Laws

16. Cf. Antonio Gramsci, *The Prison Notebooks 1948–1951*, trans. Joseph A. Buttigieg and Antonio Callari (New York: Columbia University Press, 1992).
17. Cf. Michael Foucault, *The History of Sexuality, Vol. I: An Introduction*, trans. Robert Hurley (New York: Random House, 1990).

(*Kyongguk Taejon*) in 1485.[18] This set of laws codified proscriptions and prescriptions of every aspect of life. The Yi Dynasty launched various legal regulations to reinforce the Confucian view of the so-called virtuous women. The government regulated and prohibited women's outdoor activities in the name of public order, as the rulers of Yi Dynasty were convinced that the disorder in the Koryo Dynasty was due in part to women's frequent social activities. This regulation forbade women, especially from the noble family (*yangban*), from playing games and sports or enjoying feasts in the public place. Women also needed permission either from their husband or the head of the household for any kind of social activities. The regulation also prohibited the remarriage of widows at all, and did not allow the sons and grandsons of remarried women to take the government service examination (*kwago*),[19] which was a sociopolitical and institutional punishment upon women who dared to violate the regulation.

Hierarchical and androcentric discourses of Confucianism permeated political theory and the way society conceived of all social relationships, including ruler and subject, father and son, husband and wife, as natural. The Yi government enshrined the family as a sacred community. The family provides the matrix of three of the Five Cardinal Relationships (or Five Orders of Relationships), and society generates the other two. The Five Cardinal Relationships are to teach people human relations, that "between father and son, there should be affection; between ruler and minister, there should be righteousness; between husband and wife, there should be attention to their separate functions; between old and young, there should be a proper order;

18. Kim Chol-jun, "Backwardness of Korean History," *Korea Journal* 6, no. 3 (March 1966): 20.
19. The Committee for the Compilation of the History of Korean Women, *Women of Korea: A History from Ancient Times to 1945*, ed. and trans. Yung-Chung Kim (Seoul: Ewha Womans University Press, 1976), 84–85, 98.

and between friends, there should be faithfulness."[20] In the Confucian Five Cardinal Relationships, women's subordination thus becomes inevitable and natural.

Confucius is believed to have said the following of women: "Women indeed are human beings, but they are of a lower state than men and can never attain to full equality with them. The aim of female education therefore is perfect submission, not cultivation and development of the mind."[21] Hence, in both Confucian ideology and practice, to be a virtuous woman is to submit.[22] The ideology of three obediences (sam-jong-ji-do) is grounded on this Confucian discourse on family: before marriage, to obey the father; after marriage, to obey husband; and in the event of the husband's death, to obey her son.[23] Confucian construction and reinforcement of the normative discourse about virtuous women have also produced and perpetuated other hegemonic discourses such as the ideology of wise mother and good wife (hyun-mo-yang-che), the special rank of women who faithfully follow their husbands into death (yul-nea), and the ideology of chastity (jung-cho) that would make Confucian kyriarchy a naturalized ideology.

Confucianism has played a foundational and pervasive role in establishing and institutionalizing a kyriarchal value system in East Asian society, and its influence has had a formative impact on East Asian culture. In spite of its seemingly egalitarian complementary cosmology of yin and yang,[24] Confucianism has played a pivotal

20. Mencius, in A Source Book in Chinese Philosophy, trans. and compiled by Wing-Tsit Chan (Princeton: Princeton University Press, 1963), 69–70.

21. Margaret E. Burton, The Education of Women in China (New York: Revell, 1911), 19.

22. Li Chi: Book of Rites, trans. James Legge, ed. C. C. Chai and W. Chai (New York: University Books, 1967), IX:24.

23. Cf. David Robert Mace and Vera Mace, Marriage: East and West (Garden City, NY: Doubleday, 1959), 67.

24. In the structure of the family upon which Confucianism based its conception of society, relationships between members were ordered by the yin and yang cosmological principle. Although the yin and yang are not necessarily attributed to the biological male and female,

role in degrading the status of women in traditional East Asian society both in the private and public sector. Although Confucius himself wrote a limited amount about women, his patriarchal views of women, along with other Confucian philosophers such as Mencius, has had a significant influence on naturalizing women's status as second-class citizens. When one's role and place in a society is naturalized, one can hardly ask the root question of *why*. Confucius bases his entire body of teaching upon the patriarchal family, ancestor worship, and the duties of filial piety. The role and task of women within this Confucian teaching and its practice are simple: it is to obey.[25] In Confucian teaching and practice, women are born to obey and to submit to the fathers of the family and society.

One of the unique features of Confucian teaching is its sanctification of the family, although emphasis on the family is not unique to Confucianism because Christianity, for instance, regards marriage as sacrament. However, in Confucianism, the family is the very center of Confucian teaching and practice. According to Confucian teaching, the family is a natural basis for all moral and political behavior, and the most biologically rooted of all human institutions. Mencius posits that "the root of the empire is in the state, and the root of the state is in the family."[26] This statement implies that

people in Confucianism, unlike in Taoism, have used them to confine males and females to socially stereotyped roles with a strong sense of male superiority:

Yin and *Yang* are different in nature;
Men and women are different in behavior;
Yang is powerful [virtuous] because he is hard [firm];
Yin is functional because she is soft;
Men are worthy because they are strong;
Women are beautiful because they are weak.

Cf. Pan Chao of Later Han, *Ts'ao Ta-chia Nu Chieh*, chap. 3, 2b9-3al, quoted in Diana Paul, "Portraits of the Feminine: Buddhist and Confucian Historical Perspectives," in *Studies in History of Buddhism*, Papers presented at the International Conference on the History of Buddhism at University of Wisconsin, ed. A. K. Narain (Delhi: B.R. Pub. Corp., 1980), 212.
25. Mace and Mace, *Marriage: East and West*, 67.

the family is a model for all human social organizations, including government.

Here, the family means a biological family, which requires a direct blood connection exclusively with the fathers, not mothers. Due to an absolute emphasis on the patriarchal family, continuing the family lineage is the most significant duty of the family, and only the male child can maintain the family lineage. This exclusive notion of biological family results in discrimination against female children and women. Mencius's statement, "there are three things which are unfilial, and to have no posterity is the greatest of them,"[27] still affects the mindset of many contemporary Koreans. Posterity in Mencius's teaching means exclusively the male child. All the Confucian classics praise filiality as the root of Confucian ethics and familism, and the *Book of Filiality* (or *Hsiao Ching*), one of the Confucian classics, is exclusively dedicated to the topic of filiality. Filiality is defined as "while [the parents] are living, serve them with *li* [*principle*] when they die, bury them with *li* sacrifice to them with *li*."[28] Confucians consider filiality as the virtue of all virtues.

My criticism here is not the Confucian emphasis on filiality per se but the very nature of filiality because Confucian filiality requires the existence of a son and its primary emphasis is on the relationship between fathers and sons. K'ung Jung (153–208 C.E.), a descendant of Confucius, reportedly made the following remarks about the parent-child relationship solely as that of the father-son: "Why should there exist a special kind of affinity between father and son? Originally

---

26. *Mencius* in *The Four Books: Confucian Analects, the Great Learning, the Doctrine of the Mean, and the Works of Mencius*, trans. James Legge (New York: Paragon, 1966 [1923]), bk. IV, pt. I, chap. V.

27. Ibid., bk. IV, pt. 1, chap. XXVI.

28. Ibid., bk. II, pt. 5, chap. III. The word *li* (principle) originally had the meaning of order or pattern. There are various views on this concept in accordance with some different perspectives on Confucian philosophy. For further explanation, see Chan, *Source Book in Chinese Philosophy*, 766–68.

the father merely intended to satisfy his desire. What exactly is the relationship between mother and son? A son in his mother's womb is no different from a thing in a bottle. Once the thing comes out of the bottle, the two become separate and no longer related."[29] Confucian misogyny equates women with inferior persons even in the reproduction process, considering mothers just a bottle, bearing striking similarity to Aristotelian biology that sees women as mere containers or incubators.

Whether or not Confucianism supports human rights is a controversial issue, especially in relation to the Universal Declaration of Human Rights adopted by the United Nations in 1948. What I see in various works on Confucianism and its relation to human rights is not only inattentive to gender and class, but seriously lacks sensitivity to gender or class consciousness without a lived experience on the margins under Confucianism. Religion is not just about theory or philosophical/theological framework but is primarily about people's daily lived experience. By people, I mean to be socioculturally specific in terms of their gender, social class, marital status, age, familial status, and so forth. By using this socioculturally specific approach, one takes a partularized standpoint to how religion functions concretely in people's lives. Wm. Theodore de Bary, one of the editors of *Confucianism and Human Rights*, contends:

> It is significant . . . that several East Asian countries (Japan, South Korea, Taiwan) have not found their Confucian past an obstacle to the acceptance of Western-style constitutions and guarantees of human rights. Cultural diversity did not prevent Chinese representatives from actively participating in the formulation of the 1948 Declaration of Human Rights, as they found no incompatibility between the essential

29. *Hou-Han shu* [*History of the Latter Han*], punctuated ed., 12 vols. (Peking: Chung-hua Shu-chu, 1961), 8:2278, quoted in Ying-shih Yu, "Individualism and the Neo-Taoist Movement in Wei-Chin China," in *Individualism and Holism: Studies in Confucian and Taoist Values*, ed. Donald J. Munro (Ann Arbor: Center for Chinese Studies, The University of Michigan, 1985), 124.

humanistic values of Confucianism and these new human rights initiatives.[30]

Here we must ask whose perspective and whose lived experience under Confucianism the scholars adopted in de Bary's volume, whose human rights Confucianism was compatible with, and whose life experiences under Confucianism the "Chinese representatives" represented, those who were "actively" participating in the formulation of the 1948 Declaration of Human Rights. I doubt that the "Chinese representatives," whom the Chinese government must have selected from the high-rank officers, could have fully represented the human rights of women from all classes and male commoners, for instance, in Confucian society in East Asian countries such as Korea. The oversimplification of Confucian influence on East Asian societies, like de Bary's comment in relation to human rights, is extremely misleading, in spite of its half-truth, because it misrepresents and distorts the reality of how the human rights of women and the lower classes are violated under Confucian practice.

Confucianism entirely excluded women, for example, from participating in the Confucian ancestral rites, which is the most essential component of practicing Confucian filial piety. Since only sons could offer ancestral rites in Confucianism, a woman has been under pressure from the day of her marriage to conceive and bring forth healthy males. Without sons, there would be no heads of household to offer the ancestral rites and the family would acquire a secondary status, lacking the authentic posterity of family. The husband had the right to send his wife back to her family and divorce her if she failed to bear a son for his family. The failure of a wife to bear a son used to be one of the seven evils/offenses (*chil-go-*

---

30. de Bary and Weiming, eds., *Confucianism and Human Rights*, 24.

ch-iak), which could be the grounds for divorce by her husband, among other grounds such as disobedience to a husband's parents, promiscuity, jealousy, having an incurable disease, talking too much, and stealing.[31] Such treatment exemplifies the violation of women's human rights under Confucian influence in Korean society during the Yi Dynasty. Women, along with men from commoner and lower-class families, were barred from any kind of public education and the government-service examination(*kwa-go*), which examined the degree of expertise in the Confucian classics and was used for selecting upper-class (*yangban*) men for government office. The saying often quoted from the Confucian Analects to support universal human rights, "all men are brothers," [32] fundamentally lacks inclusivity in terms of gender and social class.

Scholars hold two contrasting views on whether to regard Confucianism as a humanist religion that promotes human rights for all.[33] My major criticism of Confucianism in Korea involves its lack of an epistemological perspective for granting women human rights just as it lacks a perspective for granting human rights to anyone as simply human. Instead, it grants rights based on one's occupation or position in society, such as daughter-in-law, wife, or mother. Due to its fundamental lack of affirmation of the individuality of a human being regardless of one's gender, class, age, or position in family and society, Confucianism in Korea has promoted and defended the interests and privileges of males and of the middle-upper class (*yangban* and royal families). One can, of course, argue that the

---

31. Theresa Kelleher, "Confucianism," *Women in World Religions*, ed. Arvind Sharma (New York: State University of New York Press, 1987), 137. For a further detailed discussion about "seven evils," also see Committee for the Compilation of the History of Korean Women, *Women of Korea*, 52–53, 89.

32. de Bary and Weiming, eds., *Confucianism and Human Rights*, 7.

33. For an example of these two contrasting views, see Joanne R. Bauer and Daniel A. Bell, eds., *The East Asian Challenge for Human Rights* (Cambridge: Cambridge University Press, 1999); and de Bary and Weiming, eds., *Confucianism and Human Rights*.

Neo-Confucian movement emphasizes the worth of individual self-development and the importance of an independent, critical attitude toward the Confucian texts and encourages free critical discussion.[34] However, one should note that this attitude applies only to men from the noble family(*yangban*), not to women and men from the lower class. Neo-Confucianism in Korea has not contributed to liberation and the interests of women and the lower-class people (commoner and lowborn, slaves [*chonmin*] families) as independent individual human beings. Instead, it has justified, perpetuated, and reinforced the *kyriarchal* status quo in which extreme sexism and classism are naturalized.

Furthermore, it has institutionalized and sanctioned male hegemony both in the private and public sector. Confucian male hegemony in family and society in Korea is manifest in the Family Registry System (*hoju-je*) in Korea, in which any male, regardless of his age, takes precedence over any females as the head of the household (*hoju*). When a husband, the head of the household, dies, for example, his first son becomes the legal head of the household, not his wife, even if the son is one year old. Each family member is to define oneself in terms of his or her relationship to the *hoju*. Although the Korean cabinet approved a bill to abolish the *hoju-je* in 2003, as a result of a longstanding protest from feminist and civic groups, Korea legally practiced this *hoju-je* until the Supreme Court eventually issued the details of the implementation of the new family registration law, effective as of January 2008. Proponents for this *hoju-je* used Confucian ideology and family value, in opposition to the arguments for abolition of the *hoju-je* by feminist and civic groups. This incident shows the powerful influence of Confucianism

---

34. Wm. Theodore de Bary, *The Liberal Tradition in China* (New York: Columbia University Press, 1983), 67–90.

on every sector of Korean society until today.[35] It is not surprising to see that the male-only society of Confucian practitioners (*yoo-rim*) in Korea has been the strongest opponent of the feminist and civic movement for gender equality in the family registry system and inheritance law.

From a liberationist perspective, Confucianism in Korea has failed not because of its lack of cosmological principles of harmony or humanistic philosophy, but because of its extremely kyriarchal praxis that has entirely limited, rather than enlarged, human freedom and liberation, particularly for women and lower-class people in Korean society. It has failed to provide even the minimum degree of freedom for women and lower-class people. How can we measure one's freedom as an individual or a group? Friedrich Nietzsche answers: "According to the resistance which must be overcome."[36] Freedom and resistance are deeply interlinked, because if there is no minimum space of freedom, ironically, resistance would be impossible. Where people live in absolute constraint and unfreedom, they can hardly even resist, socially becoming an absolute victim. Following Nietzsche's way of measuring freedom, the sheer fact that women under Confucianism have never been able to establish any form of Confucian feminist liberation resistance to Confucian domination, like Christian feminist liberation resistance to Christian domination within Christianity, reveals the failure of Confucianism and its absolutely patriarchal praxis in Korean society.

I do not believe in discursive or institutional purity within a religion, because religion is a complex and often self-contradicting institution in terms of its oppressing and, at the same time, liberating function in human reality. We must, therefore, ask context-specific

35. Cf. Jae-Won Kim, "The Confucian Tradition and Its Impact on the Family Law Reform in Korea," an unpublished paper presented at the annual meeting of the Law and Society Association, Chicago, May 27, 2004.
36. Nietzsche, *Twilight of the Idols*, 542.

questions: To whom does a religion play the role of oppressor or liberator? and Whose freedom and liberation does it limit or enhance? For, to be human means to live with the specific social markers of identity, either by force or by choice, based on sex, sexuality, class, race and ethnicity, age, nationality and citizenship, religion, and so forth. Where people live in a total absence of freedom, resistance can never happen. Confucianism in Korean society has rarely offered women a space of freedom that would permit even minimal women's resistance. Sharon Welch rightly posits: "The dangerous memory expressed in liberation theology is not only a memory of conflict and exclusion. . . . It is also a memory of hope, a memory of freedom and resistance. This memory of hope is a significant element of the experience of resistance. . . . Domination is not absolute as long as there is protest against it."[37]

Do women under Confucianism in Korea have the dangerous memory, the memory of freedom and resistance to kyriarchal domination? When we deal with religion, it is insufficient to talk about only texts, principles, doctrines, philosophies, or theologies. Instead, we must ask specific, power-sensitive questions as to whether the religion has implemented a liberating practice in a concrete reality and whose privileges and interests it has served. A religion in a given society can be liberative for some people but oppressive for others. In the case of Confucianism in Korea, it has privileged upper-class men but has constricted women from all classes and lower-class men. Overlooking the extreme power disparity between different social and familial groups results in misrepresentation of the concrete reality of the people. One should note that the Confucian emphasis on family and harmony through Confucian rites and teaching could mean one's total subordination to the interests of the stronger party

37. Sharon Welch, *Communities of Resistance and Solidarity: A Feminist Theology of Liberation* (Maryknoll, NY: Orbis, 1985), 39.

in the social and familial relationship. The hierarchical nature of community means the domination of the fathers over mothers, husbands over wives, sons over daughters, older over younger, and ruler over ruled.

Negotiating the Alternative:
Women's Religious Choice-in-Difference

Christianity arrived in Korea in 1784 (Catholic) and 1884 (Protestant) and did not come as a part of Western colonial power as it did in other parts of the world. From the beginning, people in Korea associated Christianity with modern education and medicine, not with Western colonialism. Christianity made a remarkable contribution in Korean modern history by breaking down the rigid social barriers based on one's class and sex through its teaching and practice of the basic human equality of every individual person regardless of sex or class.[38] By that time, most Korean women in general or men from the lower class, for instance, could hardly imagine sitting together with men or people from a noble family(*yangban*) in any public sphere. Church became the physical space of border crossing between different sexes and classes, albeit in a relative sense, because people still practiced gender segregation in the pew. Furthermore, Christian teaching of the creation story in which God created male and female equally in the image of God offered a revolutionary idea of human equality regardless of one's sex or class.

It would be impossible to produce a universal theory for how one encounters a specific religion because of the heterogeneity, hybridity, and complexity of one's social, cultural, personal, political, or spiritual context. It is pointless, therefore, to make a universal claim, such as a particular religion X is simply either liberating or oppressing

---

38. Cf. Committee for the Compilation of the History of Korean Women, *Women of Korea*, 197.

for women, without taking a specific historical context into its consideration. No single religion in human history has maintained its nature as such in one solid form. Needless to say, a religion, both as an institution and a movement, changes its functions in diverse ways according to the power dynamics that it plays in a given historical situation. In this sense, religion has been always historically and socioculturally situated. Therefore, we need to see the specific context in which Korean women encountered Christianity and why they were drawn to Christianity in Korea under Confucianism.

When Korean women encountered Christianity, it was not through systematized doctrines but through praxis of equality. Due to the extreme limitations of linguistic skills of missionaries from the West, the missionaries had to simplify the Christian messages. The messages that they proclaimed were extremely simple narratives, which were like "Jesus-heaven" (*Yeasu Chundang*), "Hell without faith" (*Bulsin Jiok*), "We all are the children of God" (*Woori modu Hananim Janoe*), and so forth. However, the radical equality embedded in Christian teaching that all those who believe in Jesus Christ can go to heaven regardless of their sex or class, for instance, offered sufficient grounds to attract many women and lower-class people to Christianity. Christianity then became an alternative religion to Confucianism, especially for those who were on the margins of Korean society due to their sex or class, and whose full humanity society denied under the Confucian structures.

John Nevius, who was a missionary in China, came to Korea in 1890; following his advice, the Council of Missions produced the so-called "Nevius Missionary Policy," which stressed self-sufficiency in outlining the basic rules for the mission policy of Korean Christianity. Among these rules, the priority of evangelism in Korea was given to the working class and women, unlike in China.[39] In this context, Christianity made a contribution for the emancipation of Korean women from the Confucian confinement and degradation and taught them the radical idea of equality that they were created in the image of God and therefore they were the children of God with full dignity as human beings with men.[40] The notion of equality in the creation story, in which God created humans, both male and female, in the image of God, laid the epistemological ground of the infinite worth and dignity of the individual human being and led to the construction of natural law and human rights in Western civilization.[41] One's human rights are innately granted, not by one's position or role in society and family as in Confucianism, but simply by one's being created in the image of the divine. It is true, as one can see in the spirit of the French Revolution, that "[t]o claim a right simply on the basis that one is a human is already a revolutionary act."[42]

Mary Scranton, a Methodist woman missionary from the United States, started public women's education in Korea by founding Ewha School (*Ewha Hakdang*) with one student in 1886. But by 1904, less than twenty years later, ten other Christian schools for women were founded.[43] It is noteworthy that women missionaries had conservative ideals for the education of Korean women, with the aim not of developing the full humanity of women but to train them to be good wives, mothers, and educators of their own children. However, opening the door of public education to women was itself a revolutionary act, whether or not the missionaries intended or

39. Cf. Min Kyong-Bae, *Hanguk ui kidokkyohoe-sa* [*History of Christian Church in Korea*] (Seoul, 1968), 68; and Hwang Song-mo, "Protestantism and Korea," *Korea Journal* 7, no. 2 (February 1967): 5.
40. Cf. Committee for the Compilation of the History of Korean Women, *Women of Korea*, 197–98.
41. Cf. Leonard Swidler, "Human Rights: A Historical Overview," in *The Ethics of World Religions and Human Rights*, ed. Hans Küng and Jürgen Moltmann, *Concilium*, 1990/2 (London: SCM, 1990).
42. Swidler, "Human Rights," 12.
43. *Ewha Hakpo* [*Ewha School Paper*], June 20, 1975: 3.

expected it, through which Korean women were able to develop their own world in spite of the missionaries' conservative educational ideals . The Nevius Missionary Policy reflected a similar conservative perspective on women's education, emphasizing the significance of women's education, not for women's self-development as humans but to build their role as mothers responsible for children. Despite this conservative tendency, this mission policy, which targeted women and the working class, rather than the upper class as in China, was meaningful because those who were on the margins of the Korean society accepted the Christian gospel as a liberating message for themselves, which gave impetus for the rapid growth of Christianity in Korea.[44]

Korean women were enlightened not only through the public schools the missionaries from the West founded but also through the churches' educational programs. The churches provided Bible schools and classes, and women were able to extend their lives beyond the Confucian confinement of women to the private sphere.[45] In this way, churches became the first public sphere in which Korean women exposed themselves. It is interesting to note that the first student of Ewha School, now the world's largest women's university, was a concubine of a high official, and that most students who joined the school later were from the commoner class, because Confucian culture did not allow families, especially of *yangban* class, to send girls into the public sphere.

Therefore, women and girls from the noble class (*yangban*) experienced restrictions more severe than those from the commoner or lower class because the noble class was expected to follow Confucian values and practice more strictly than others.[46] It was

44. Hwang, "Protestantism and Korea," 5.
45. "Wife" in Korean is *Anhae* or *gipsaram*, which means literally one who is "inside." This shows the cultural perception of wife's proper social location in the private sector of society.
46. Committee for the Compilation of the History of Korean Women, *Women of Korea*, 218–19.

unthinkable under Confucianism for women to learn organizational skills by participating in the public activities of the church, such as Sunday schools and various women's societies. Regarding the church's educational programs, Helen Kim, the first Korean president of Ewha Woman University, made the following statement: "They helped to wipe out illiteracy by teaching women to read the Bible and to sing the hymns. Ideas such as democracy and world brotherhood [sic] were introduced to the rank and file of the people through Christian churches. Wiping out superstition, bringing about social class consciousness, and contributing to the women's own discovery of themselves as well as to the raising of their status are contributions brought about by these pioneer Christian missions."[47]

She also testified to her experience of God's calling, which led her to commit herself to the liberation of women. While she was praying in a dark prayer room at night, she began hearing some "crying and appealing voices" and then there was a gentle voice saying to her:

"Do you hear it?"

"Yes, I do."

"That's the crying from Korean women. How can you sit here calmly and comfortably hearing that cry? Only that is your mission."

The voice was a distant one.[48]

For Kim, the most important mission of Christianity was to liberate Korean women from Confucian oppression and patriarchal convention. Like Kim, many Korean women who were living in an extremely androcentric Confucian culture were drawn to the

---

47. Helen Kim, *The Role of Women in the Next Half Century* (Seoul: Ewha Woman University, 1968), 23.
48. Helen Kim, *Ku pitsoge chagun saengmyong* [*Autobiography: A Small Life in that Light*] (Seoul, 1965), 56–58. Quoted in Committee for the Compilation of the History of Korean Women, *Women of Korea*, 221.

Christian message, which contained a spirit of a radical equality, even though the nature of liberation was limited from a twenty-first-century feminist perspective. In the Confucian view of men and women, one could hardly imagine such a notion of equality of women with men as humans. The message that even women could be equally qualified with men to become children of God and to enter heaven was an extremely revolutionary idea at that time. In this context, Christianity provided a space for women to become equal members of the church with men, a space for women to affirm that they were as human as men, and an opportunity to learn how to read and write, which Confucian culture discouraged by prohibiting women from learning and studying the Confucian texts.

In the nineteenth century, a missionary observed: "The Gospel has been a large factor in liberating women in Korea. . . . The Korean woman had everything to gain and nothing to lose by becoming a Christian. Her circle of social contacts was immediately widened and enriched. Christianity taught a higher status for women than what she had known."[49] This rather simplistic statement by an early missionary does not, of course, show the ambivalent role that Christianity in Korea played in terms of women's liberation if we apply a contemporary feminist standard; after all, Christianity was unable to make a fundamental challenge to the core of Confucian kyriarchal structures, due to its own patriarchality and the conservativism of missionaries. Most missionaries who came to Korea were themselves the product of the eighteenth- and nineteenth-century Western patriarchal worldview, where women were still struggling to attain rights of suffrage and equal education. This nineteenth-century statement by a missionary shows us, however, the visible change in women's activities and their social engagement

49. Charles Allen Clark, *The Korean Church and the Nevius Methods* (New York: Revell, 1930), 234.

through the public programs and education that Christianity then provided, in contrast to women's lives under Confucianism in Korea. The church organized the enlightenment movement and trained women to be leaders for the group activities and Bible schools. Catholic women formed a Catholic community of women, for instance, among those who decided to remain celibate or single. Remaining celibate or single was then an unthinkable and the most unfilial act under Confucianism, because having posterity through marriage was the most significant duty of women. Women's choice to rebel against the conventional Confucian norm by voluntarily being the members of a celibate Christian community was itself a revolutionary and liberative movement.[50] Through the organization of women's societies by Christian missionaries, a large number of Korean women began to participate in public life, which Confucian practice fundamentally prohibited. The beginning of collective activities among women in public sphere, both as leaders and members, was possible through the various Christian women's societies, after the first Protestant women's society, called the House Missionary Society, was started in 1897 in Pyongyang province.[51] It is also important to note that Christian women and men formed a patriotic movement, called the Independence Club, at Chungdong Methodist Church in Seoul, in 1897, and debated gender equality. The founding members of this Independence Club were twenty-five males from Paejae School (*Paejae Haktang*) and eleven females from Ewha School.

Another significant role that Christianity played in nineteenth-century Korea was raising women's consciousness of individuality by providing them proper names. Korean women did not have their

---

50. Ok Hee Kim, *Chunjukyo Yesung Woondongsa* I [*History of Catholic Women's Movement*] (Seoul: Hankuk Inmun Kwahakwon, 1983), 120–24.
51. Committee for the Compilation of the History of Korean Women, *Women of Korea*, 249.

own name for various stages of life. Before marriage, people would call them simply by their nickname, such as "pretty girl," "happy girl," "older girl," "disappointing girl" (meaning it is so disappointing that you are not a boy), "younger girl," "daughter of Kim," or "the last girl." After marriage, people would address women only by the surname of their husbands' family, such as "wife of Kim" or "wife of Lee" before they gave a birth to a child. After a woman had a child, people would call the married women by their childrens' name plus the word for mother, for instance, "mother of Chulsoo." Within the household, people would address women by a kinship term denoting their position in the family relations. Being an authentic member of the family required a blood tie with the family, which women did not have.[52] Missionaries were shocked to find that Korean women did not have their own names, and missionaries began to give individual names to those women who came to church. The missionaries thought having no name was like being a slave. So women, who had no unique name for themselves in the Confucian structure, began to have their formal given names in the church. Although the names those missionaries gave were mostly Western names or names from the Bible, the experience of being addressed with their unique proper names gave women a sense of independence and self-awareness as independent human beings.[53] That women get to have their names is significant for the emancipation of women from patriarchy because

52. In Chinese language, there are more than one hundred terms for various family relationships, which have no equivalent in the Western languages. Cf. Fung Yu-Lan, *A Short History of Chinese Philosophy* (New York: Free Press, 1948), 21. The Korean language also has many terms referring to various relatives of the family. For example, every term relating to relatives is differentiated according to whether they are related to the father or mother, or to husband or wife. In the case of the mother's side, the term *oe* (outer) is added to the regular terms, indicating that anyone not on the father's side or husband's side is not part of the "inner circle" but, rather, is considered an outsider, e.g., *oe samchoon* (outer-uncle), *oe halmuni* (outer-grandmother), or *oe halabugi* (outer-grandfather), etc. In this way, Korean language naturalizes women's inferior status in the household.

53. Cf. Lee Woo Chung, *Hankuk Kidogkoe Yesung Baknundi Baljachi* [*A Hundred Years of History of Korean Christian Women*] (Seoul: Minjung, 1985) 41–42.

an awareness of human individuality is fundamental in being able to claim one's rights as humans, and having one's own proper name is essential for gaining a sense of individuality and singularity.

Through its egalitarian and liberative message of creation and redemption, and its democratic practice of inclusion of gender and class, Christianity in nineteenth-century Korea played a role of an alternative religion to kyriarchal Confucianism, which had reinforced and institutionalized oppression of women and lower-class people. While Confucian ancestor worship, for instance, did not allow women's participation, Christian worship was open to everybody in society regardless of one's gender or social class. When Confucianism was fostering the ideology of men are honored/women are degraded (*Namjon Yobi*), Christianity was then teaching the message that God created men and women in God's image and therefore all humans, both male and female and lower and upper class, were created equal as the children of God and could go to heaven as long as they believed in Jesus Christ. This simplified Christian message of radical equality, inclusion, and redemption was one of the major factors of women's religious choice-in-difference. The Christian message of radical equality in creation and redemption transformed the existing reality of women and lower-class people, offering them a sense of high self-esteem as humans. Christian women launched the Praise Society (*Chan-yang-hoe*) in 1898, which was the first women's rights organization in Korean history. They grounded the Society in the spirit of human dignity and equality granted by the divine and thus demanded women's rights in Korean society.[54]

---

54. Cf. Committee for the Compilation of the History of Korean Women, *Women of Korea,* 249–50; and Bae-yong Lee, "'Chan-yang-heo,'" The First Women's Organization," at http://www.womennews.co.kr/news/12989.

Making Religion:
Creating a Liberative Religion
of Radical Inclusion

One of Christianity's contributions in eighteenth- and nineteenth-century Korea was making women aware of their ontological individuality as humans created in the image of God regardless of who or what they were. Although most missionaries were theologically and politically conservative and therefore may not have had such feminist intentions, the notion of radical equality through the messages of divine creation and redemption contributed to raising women's consciousness of their I-ness as individual human beings with full dignity and their own proper names. Korean women's religious choice of Christianity was in fact the first religious choice that they had made throughout the history of Korea. All other religions, such as Confucianism, Shamanism, Buddhism, and so forth were given by the state or the society or were just there in their household or community to which they belonged, which did not necessarily require women's conscious choice, or a so-called religious conversion experience to become affiliated.

Yet, for women to make up their minds to become Christians under the strong Confucian context then meant taking an enormous risk and responsibility for the consequences of their choice. Therefore, this decision was a decisive, voluntary, dramatic, emancipatory, and revolutionary act that women took as individual human beings with dignity and rights, not as collective, unified, nameless people of roles as merely mothers, daughters-in-laws, wives, or slaves without proper names of their own. Christian women made numerous testimonies, including those women who endured physical and verbal violence in their household due to their decision or conversion to become Christians. They were able to endure the hardship because the joy that they came to have after becoming Christian. One of the testimonies revealed the experience of emancipation and joy that a Christian woman had:

> The day that I was baptized was the happiest day of my life. We *Chosun* [Korea's name in the Yi Dynasty] women have lived under the men's oppression for thousands of years. If the lights from Jesus had not come to *Chosun*, women in *Chosun* would have not lived a life that we have now. The *Chosun* women's liberation movement started from the day Christ came to our peninsula.[55]

The experience of joy and liberation, as this *Chosun* woman had at that time, and of suffering and oppression, as women in the history of witch burning in the West, are two edges of women's experience in Christianity due to its paradoxical nature—egalitarian and kyriarchal—of theology and practice. A large number of feminists have perceived institutionalized religions as a source of patriarchal conservatism in their belief system and practice. Once the religions become established and institutionalized in a society, most institutionalized religions tend to defend the status quo by deriving their legitimacy from the past tradition and practice, rather than promoting change and transformation, as is the case in Christianity in Korea.

When a religion bases its legitimacy on past tradition, it assimilates rather than resists the existing value system and inevitably becomes kyriarchal and oppressive because the existing system is still grounded in sexism, classism, racism, ableism, homophobia, and so forth. As one of the dominant religions in Korea today, Christianity has incorporated with the Confucian culture in Korea, instead of challenging and contesting its kyriarchal value system. Christians

---

55. Mr. Noble, ed., *Seong-li-ou-sang-hwal* [*Life of Victory*] (Kyung Sung: Christian Window, The year 2, *So-wha* [1926]), 72. Cited in Woojung Lee, *Hankuk Kidogkoe Yesung Baknundi Baljachi* [*A Hundred Years of History of Korean Christian Women*], 75–76.

began to emphasize the kyriarchal messages of Pauline texts, for instance, and interpreted them in a way that perpetuated and reinforced Confucian patriarchal values and ethics. The Christian message of love and sacrifice became patriarchalized, which led women to accept uncritically their own victimization and oppression under kyriarchy in the name of Jesus' love and sacrifice for humanity.

In this way, Christianity in Korea became an ethically Confucianized Christianity after it became settled in Korean society, especially in terms of its androcentric, kyriarchal, and hierarchal teachings and practices. Men still monopolize the decision-making bodies and processes in most Christian denominations, for instance. As of the year 2013, the Korean Methodist Church, for instance, which people regard as one of the progressive denominations in Korea because it allowed women's ordination early in 1931, does not have a single woman bishop even though women comprise 70 percent of church members. No theological university or freestanding theological seminary has a woman president. This institutional practice of 100 percent male leadership in theological institutions and denominational offices has constituted Christianity in Korea with its proud growth in numbers. As a result, men monopolize the two fundamental sources of religious power and authority: sites for teaching and preaching. Women, who have laid the ground of the development of Christianity with their passion and commitment since its introduction to Korea, are now excluded from leadership roles of teaching and preaching, and they are welcomed only when they play roles that are an extension of what they are supposed to do in their household: assisting men, taking care of the kitchen and children, and doing church chores.

Confucianism has been making a significant influence on contemporary Korea. Although the intensity of Confucian influence may differ, the way Korean people perceive the political and social authority, interpersonal relationships in private or public spheres, and education is still strongly Confucian, in terms that the hierarchy between different gender, class, social and marital status, or age is extremely explicit. Although people may not read the Confucian texts and may have simplified and modified Confucian ancestral rites, the attitudes associated with them are still alive and still guide people's daily lives. Therefore, it is important to note that although only 2 percent of Koreans consider themselves Confucians today, nearly 90 percent of Koreans are in fact Confucians in the sense that they follow Confucian ethics, value systems, and teachings in their daily lives.[56]

What I am concerned about are two contradicting functions of religion: the liberative function of transformation and the role that religion can play in promoting human liberation and freedom; and at the same time the oppressive function in reinforcing, perpetuating, and maintaining pernicious oppression and discrimination based on one's gender, race, class, or sexuality. The significance of feminist theology and other forms of liberation theology lies in their content and vision for an alternative world. Various forms of liberation theologies talk about the crisis of Christian faith. The crisis, however, is not merely just theological or philosophical but practical. In this regard, the fundamental failure of Confucianism in Korea lies in its total absence of a liberative practice for women and lower-class people—a failure to establish in practice its teaching and vision of the community of human freedom and equality across gender and class barriers.

Christianity offered a transformative and liberative space and practice for the marginalized in the beginning of its introduction

---

56. Junshik Choi, *Hankuk Jongkyo Iyagee* [*Story of Korean Religions: Shamanism, Buddhism, Confucianism, and Taoism that Formed the Ethos of Korean People*], vol. I (Seoul: Hanwool, 1995), 93.

to Korea but lost its liberating function and eventually failed in transforming the oppression and injustice of Korean society. The task of Christianity today is to become the instrument of human liberation and freedom in a concrete reality, to revive the dangerous memory[57] of liberative and transformative roles that it once played in various societies. We must ask the question of legitimacy—especially who is qualified to speak for a Confucian or Christian tradition that is compatible with the spirit of the Declaration of the Universal Human Rights, and who determines the standards of the authenticity of one's religious choice when women make a religious choice-in-difference. What we need in Korea and other places today may be reintroduction of new Christianity, which is equipped with postpatriarchal and liberative perspective and practice of radical inclusion—a revival of the liberative spirit that once led Korean women to make a religious choice-in-difference, despite the huge risk of social ostracization.

Edward Said's description of the role of public intellectuals precisely echoes what I believe the role of scholars and practitioners of religions should be:

> The intellectual . . . is neither a pacifier nor a consensus-builder, but someone whose whole being is staked on a critical sense, a sense of being unwilling to accept easy formulas or ready-made clichés, or the smooth, every-so-accommodating confirmations of what the powerful or conventional have to say, and what they do. . . . This is not always a matter of being a critic of government policy, but rather of thinking of the intellectual vocation as maintaining a state of constant alertness, of a perpetual willingness not to let half-truths or received ideas steer one along.[58]

57. For the term *dangerous memory*, see Johannes Baptist Metz, *Faith in History and Society: Toward a Practical Fundamental Theology* (New York: Seabury, 1980), 66–67.
58. Edward W. Said, *Representations of the Intellectual*, The 1993 Reith Lectures (New York: Vintage, 1996 [1994]), 23.

The function, task, and role of theologians and scholars of religions have always been political. At the moment they write or speak, they are entering into the sphere of "politics," where a value neutrality is impossible and the personal, the political, the societal, the cultural, and the religious are inextricably interlinked in one way or another. Religion has never been in isolation from the world of politics in a broad sense. The theologians and scholars of religions speak and write from multiple angles as witnesses to the extreme pains of human suffering and oppression of reality-as-it-is and, at the same time, the hope, dream, and vision for the reality-as-it-ought-to-be, for the world of the impossible, and for the world of not-yet.

I believe that any kind of religious community ought to be a "community of resistance and solidarity"[59]—the community of resistance to any type of domination and the community of solidarity with those on the margins on whatever ground in society, culture, or religion. A resistance is not just a reaction to domination. The authentic resistance that I perceive is a resistance that both refuses domination and, at the same time, offers a vision of the reality-as-it-ought-to-be and of what needs to be achieved by social, political, ethical, religious transformation. Christianity in Korea today needs to redirect itself from a community of kyriarchal domination to being a community of resistance and solidarity. Korean women's religious choice-in-difference in the eighteenth and nineteenth centuries needs to be revisited from a liberationist perspective because it can be a constant reminder of the mandate role of a religion in a society. Revisiting and reclaiming the historical memory of those Korean women, who yearned for a world of human freedom and equality, is an act of what Cornel West calls "prophetic criticism" to keep "track of the complex dynamics of institutional and other related

---

59. For this phrase, I am indebted to the book title by Welch, *Communities of Resistance and Solidarity*.

power structures in order to disclose options and alternatives for transformative praxis."[60] This struggle to revisit the "earlier silences and margins" is, therefore, not to make an absolute truth-claim but to reorient ourselves in order to attend to what is beneficial to those on the margins and to "our liberation in the multiple voices, languages, her-and his-stories."[61]

60. Cornel West, "The New Cultural Politics of Difference," in *Out There: Marginalization and Contemporary Culture*, ed. Russell Ferguson, Martha Gever, Trinh T. Minh-ha, and Cornel West (New York: New Museum of Contemporary Art/Cambridge: MIT Press, 1990), 31,

61. Iain Chambers, *Border Dialogues: Journeys in Postmodernity* (New York: Routledge, 1990), 9–10.

10

Resurgence of *Asian Values*

Confucian Comeback and Its Embodiment in Christianity

Who determines the standards of conformity with cultural values and
'national' objectives?
—Abdullahi A. An-Naim[1]

The idea of Asian values derives its appeal from its anti–West-centric
stance.
—Inoue Tatsuo[2]

The debate on Asian values has expanded considerably in the last
couple of decades. At the core of Asian values lies Confucian
familism, with its emphasis on human-relatedness. Feminists have

---

1. Abdullahi A. An-naim, "The Cultural Mediation of Human Rights: The Al-Arqam Case in
Malaysia," in *The East Asian Challenge for Human Rights*, ed. Joanne R. Bauer and Daniel A. Bell
(Cambridge: Cambridge University Press, 1999), 149.
2. Inoue Tatsuo, "Liberal Democracy and Asian Orientalism," in ibid., 29.

exposed the oppressive potential of the resurgence of Confucian familism and challenged the Confucian concept of family. In this chapter, I first will juxtapose Confucian and Christian familism, and critically reevaluate them from a feminist perspective. In the process, I will explore the similarities and differences between the two concepts of familism. Second, I shall put Confucian familism under scrutiny, and show how people in Korea have practiced it in a concrete reality, and how Koreans misunderstood familism under the guise of the noble Asian values, emphasizing the importance of human-interrelatedness. Third, I shall carefully examine the social/religious embodiment of Confucian familism and its creation of male homosocial reality in Korean society and Christianity.

Confucian Comeback:
The Rise of *Asian Values*

Since the 1970s, numerous East Asian countries have experienced rapid economic and national developments, especially with the emergence of the Four Asian Dragons: Singapore, Korea, Japan, and Taiwan. People have referred to this phenomenon as the "Asian Miracle" and attributed it to Asian values. Dynamic emerging markets, rapid economic growth, increased economic power, and rising standards of living have characterized these Asian countries. People often regard Asian values as family values. Therefore, one of the simple descriptions of Asian values involves the connection of the individual to the family; the family to the whole society; and these links to the basis of the society. When Asian leaders stress the importance of Asian traditional virtues, most of them directly or indirectly refer to the traditional Confucian virtues. In this context, Asian leaders highly exalt Confucian familism and often attack feminism for its allegedly antifamily nature. And such statements as

"Confucian tradition is highly compatible with capitalism" or "Asian values are the alternative to the Western values" are increasingly being expressed in Asia.[3] In this era of globalization, people who do not want to lose their national/cultural identity tend to cling to the traditional values and customs in order to differentiate themselves from the West. Under the propaganda statement, "The most Korean is the most global," mass media and a group of allegedly progressive people in South Korea, for instance, have begun to emphasize the revival of Korean indigenous values and cultures. People even say that Asian values are universal, while Western values are only Western. Asians seek out local attachments to recover a sense of belonging and try to come to grips with a postcolonial identity while at the same time identifying, ironically, with larger, global movements.

Kuan-Yew Lee, a Senior Minister of Singapore, provoked the Asian values debate, and Prime Minister Mahathir of Malaysia further advocated for it. Those who advocate Asian values assert that a certain set of values, such as hard work, discipline, thriftiness, family solidarity, and a stress on the community rather than the individual, are uniquely Asian. Kuan Yew Lee argues that Asians have "little doubt that a society with communitarian values, where the interests of society take precedence over that of the individual, suits to them better than the individualism of America." They use Confucius as a weapon for their own purposes. People often refer the contemporary resurgence of Confucianism as the "Confucian comeback."[4] Interestingly, until recently, China has never attempted to revive

3. For the rise of Asian values, see Kuan-Yew Lee, "In Defense of Asian Values: Singapore's Lee Kuan Yew," *Time*, March 16, 1998; Fareed Zakaria, "Culture is Destiny: A Conversation with Lee Kuan Yew," *Foreign Affairs* 73, no. 2 (March-April 1994): 109–127; Marc F. Plattner and Larry Jay Diamond, "Hong Kong, Singapore, and 'Asian Values,'" *Journal of Democracy* 8, no. 2 (1997): 9–10.
4. Melinda Liu, "Confucian Comeback: China Remains Divided Over Reviving its Ancient Sage," *Newsweek*, September 10, 2012.

Confucius, even though he was Chinese. Rather, socialist leaders in China believed Confucius was holding China back. Since the new cultural movement of May 4, 1919, revolution has meant rejecting traditional Chinese culture, especially Confucianism, in modern China. And one of the most important aims of Mao Zedong's Cultural Revolution was to get rid of Confucianism. However, the Chinese regime has recently attempted to revive Confucianism in order to protect itself from the "influx of Western notions like universal suffrage" and hopes to mix Chinese nationalism and Confucian thoughts. Yet, the Chinese regime's attempt to revive and reinsert Confucianism into the lives of the Chinese people has encountered huge criticism from those who contend that this is nothing but "cynical nationalism" and that Confucius promotes a "social hierarchy in which roles are strictly defined: students defer to teachers, kids revere elders, wives serve husbands, and citizens obey rulers."[5]

In the course of developing a postcolonial sensitivity, not only political leaders but also many scholars in Asia began to claim their cultural/national identity by clinging to their own past tradition and values. Those Asian nationalist scholars tried to overcome their cultural, political, and intellectual dependence on the West by especially emphasizing so-called unique Asian values and Asian unity. There are also Asia admirers—both specialist and amateur—among both Asians and Westerners who tend to attribute to Asia absolute differences from the West. They believe that the "Wisdom of the East" and its spirituality offer a deep, ancient, penetrating wisdom that will overcome the destructive materialism and individualism of the West. In such a form of anti-West-centrism, they merely change the evaluative connotation of this Oriental essence from negative to positive while keeping its cognitive content unchanged. For a unique

5. Ibid.

Asian identity, they take the stereotype that orientalists imposed on Asia to establish a superior Western identity, and shift it to their newly revived identity as Asian in a positive sense. By upholding so-called Asian-owned cultural traditions, Asian valuers want to claim their right to self-determination. Furthermore, the conversion strategy can play the role of healing a people's wounded self-respect more powerfully than the strategy of destroying the stereotype, as one can see in some of the strategies among radical feminist groups.

Such rhetoric about Asian values versus Western values as the opposite, however, is not only an oversimplification but also a gross misrepresentation. Furthermore, as noted in earlier chapters, the underlying assumption that Asia has a cultural essence fundamentally different from the West is, in fact, a view originating from Western intellectual imperialism, what Edward Said calls "orientalism." As Said puts it, orientalism operates in the service of the West's hegemony over the East primarily by producing the East discursively as the West's inferior Other. It does so principally by distinguishing and then essentializing the identities of East and West through a dichotomizing system of representations embodied in stereotypes. Orientalism is, therefore, a collective notion identifying us-Westerners as against all those-non-Westerners, and "a Western style for dominating, restructuring, and having authority over the Orient."[6]

The West-centrism guides and misguides those arguments for Asian values by Asian political leaders and scholars, which Asians have criticized because their dualistic assumptions are the products of the Western intellectual and discursive imperialism that the Asian valuers are supposedly attacking. Furthermore, the sharp dichotomy between an individualist West and a communitarian Asia distorts Asian reality

6. Edward Said, *Orientalism* (New York: Vintage, 1978), 3.

and promotes Asians stereotyping themselves. The tendency to overvalue the East produces dangerous problems of neglecting and distorting the materiality of the daily life of contemporary Asian people. In this imagined East, invented by an orientalist mentality, people eternally freeze and fix the real people of Asia to the timeless past. In the logic of Said's argument about orientalism, both the Asian debaser, describing Asia in an extremely negative way characterized by backwardness, inequality, or degeneracy, and the Asian admirer, simply admiring and glorifying Asia as a space of beauty, virtue, and wisdom, alike follow the orientalist logic by defining the Orient only as different from the West. Both groups are, wittingly or unwittingly, reorientalizing Asia, and these overvalued qualities are as distorted as their negative counterparts. Furthermore, establishing Asian identity based only on its difference from the West makes Asians a more true subaltern group, establishing their identity only in a limited form of an "identity-in-differential."[7] One of the serious problems with this identity-in-differential is that it requires always a constitutive other to address who one is.

Here is a dangerous trap in the rise of Asian values that Asian politicians and scholars propose as the potential remedy for the disease of Western egoism and destructive individualism, especially when it exalts Confucian values as the basis of the ideal virtues of Asian culture. The rise of the Asian-values discourse is dangerous because, first, it overlooks not only the vices of communitarianism, such as the hierarchical and patriarchal communitarianism, but also the virtues of individualism, such as the ethical individualism that highlights the dignity and value of an individual human being, which are fundamental in promoting human rights. Second, it tends to blur the root causes of women's oppression under Confucian patriarchy

---

7. Gayatri Chakravorty Spivak, "Can the Subaltern Speak," in *The Post-colonial Studies Reader,* eds. Bill Ashcroft, Gareth Griffiths, and Helen Tiffin (New York: Routledge, 1995), 26.

by idealizing traditional patriarchal family structure and values that rigidly and hierarchically distinguish between women's and men's places and their respective roles. As a result, it freezes women in the patriarchal past, the traditional images, and the premodern reality. Third, it justifies and perpetuates classist sociopolitical structures that relegate the lower-class people, the commoner, to being second-class citizens. The Confucian culture theory seems to respect women by emphasizing the harmony of *yin,* the female and *yang,* the male, the two interacting universal elements. In its discourse, however, people tend to glorify patriarchal authoritarianism as a driving force of Asian economic development, and revive neoconservativism in which people justify gender discrimination under the name of the noble Asian values.

In this Asian-values emphasis, culture is often more than a convenient excuse to ignore women's issues as neither urgent nor relevant. Here people use culture as a culturalist alibi that takes culture as an excuse for violating the human rights of women and sexual minorities, for instance. As Gayatri Chakravorty Spivak relevantly points out: "The new cultural alibi, working within a basically elitist culture industry, insisting on the continuity of a native tradition untouched by a Westernization whose failures it can help to cover, legitimizes the very thing it claims to combat."[8] In this context, people often dismiss the demand for women's rights on the grounds of its foreign origin and blindly accuse feminists of ignoring their own culture and national identity and as being too Westernized. In this rhetoric of Asian values, rooted in Confucianism, people mystify, obscure, and conceal the real inequalities between different classes, genders, sexuality, and ages. The long tradition and history of Confucianism show that improving women's status in Confucianism

8. Gayatri Chakravorty Spivak, "Who Claims Alterity?" in *Remaking History,* ed. Barbara Kruger and Phil Marian (Seattle: Bay Press, 1989), 281 (italics mine).

has never succeeded. Confucianism did not bring about countersystemic transformation in women's conditions. On the contrary, it has perpetuated and reinforced women's oppression and inequality.

The rise of Asian values, therefore, is the rise of the spirit of antidemocracy because of its emphasis on the hierarchical human connection and community and because of its lack of the principle of actualizing and practicing universal human values, that is, justice, equality, power equity among different genders, classes, sexuality, and ages. It tends to silence depowered groups, especially women, minors, the poor, and the uneducated, which is unjust.[9] The rise of Asian values also is antifeminist because of its male-centeredness. It tends to disregard feminist issues as Western, not authentically Asian. Accordingly, it neglects the material praxis of women's lives in Asia today, and ignores how sexism and androcentrism distort, lessen, and marginalize women's lives under the Confucian patriarchal value system and its institutions.

People refer to Confucianism on different levels such as philosophy, political ideology, state politics and institutions, or religious practice. In this sense, Confucianism covers a broad spectrum. It is necessary, therefore, to make clear that I take Confucianism primarily as an ethical and religious discourse and practice which informs people about ways of life in their daily lives. Whether or not one regards Confucianism as a religion would depend on one's definition of religion. I take Confucianism as a religion and I believe religion is not just about philosophical frameworks and discourses, abstract cosmological principles, or doctrinal beliefs and confessions. Rather, "religion is, in reality,

---

9. Cf. Won-Shik Choi, "Experiences of Non-Western Colonies and the Ghost of Asianism," paper presented at the International Conference on Toward a New Global Civilization—The Role of Activists of People's Movement, Nationalist Movement, and Local Activism, in honor of the 30-year anniversary of Creation and Critique, April 24–26, 1996, Seoul.

'living.' . . . one's religion, then, is one's life, not merely the ideal life but life as it is actually lived. . . . All that we do and are is our religion."[10] In this regard, religion is about living together—with oneself and with others in dignity, equality, justice, and peace.

Views on Family: Confucian and Christian

Patrilineal Biological Familism: Confucian View on Family

If one asks Koreans what their religion is, only 2 percent of the population answers "Confucianism." But when one asks whether they practice or follow Confucian teachings in their daily lives, then 90 percent of Koreans answer "yes."[11] Confucian tradition in contemporary Korea is significant. While their adherence to Confucianism differs in intensity, most Koreans remain strongly influenced by Confucian values. In modern times, even though Confucian texts are not read and the rituals are becoming simplified or abandoned, Confucian values and ethics still guide Koreans' concrete lives. One can find the continued presence of Confucianism in Korea in how individuals respond to family, school, community, workplace, and the state. Contemporary Koreans obviously are not Confucians in the sense that their ancestors were, but Confucian values have deeply permeated and guided Korean people's daily lives.

---

10. Jack Forbes, *Columbus and Other Cannibals: The Wetiko Disease of Exploitation, Imperialism, and Terrorism* (Brooklyn: Automedia, 1979), 26–27. Quoted in Sharon D. Welch, "Beyond Theology of Religions: The Epistemological and Ethical Challenges of Inter-Religious Engagement," in *The Oxford Handbook of Feminist Theology*, ed. Mary McClintock Fulkerson and Sheila Briggs (New York: Oxford University Press, 2012), 353.
11. Choon-Sik Choi, *Han-Kuk Chongkyo Ijaki* [*A Story of Korean Religions*] (Seoul: Han Wool, 1995), 92.

In this sense, Confucianism probably has more influence on Koreans than does any other of the traditional religions or philosophies of Asia. Confucianism was the official state ideology, philosophy, and religion of the Yi Dynasty (1392–1910) in Korea, and the Korean regimes and institutions have continued to thoroughly institutionalize and systematically diffuse the Confucian code of conduct and ethics to the Korean people. This long-standing implementation of the Confucian way of life and practice contributes to making Korea the most Confucian society in the world today. Because of the strong influence of Confucianism on Korean people's everyday lives, I regard Christianity in Korea as ethically Confucianized Christianity.

In Confucianism, people enshrine the family as a sacred community, and an important aspect of Confucianism is the rational justification or theoretical explication of this family system. People under Confucian influence consider the family the natural basis for all moral and political behavior and the most biologically rooted of all human institutions. Mencius states that "the root of the empire is in the state, and the root of the state is in the family."[12] This statement resembles Aristotle's argument that the earliest form of political organization was an extension of the family.[13] People under Confucianism consider themselves, therefore, to be a model for all human social organization, including government. Thus, in the Chinese and Korean languages, people use more than one hundred terms for various family relationships,[14] none of which have any equivalent in Western languages. People differentiate those terms according to whether they relate to the father's side or the mother's

---

12. Mencius, trans. James Legge, *The Four Books: Confucian Analects, the Great Learning, the Doctrine of the Mean, and the Works of Mencius* (New York: Paragon, 1966 [1923]), Bk. IV, Pt. I, Chap. V.
13. Aristotle, *Politics*, 1252b, 1259b.
14. Fung Yu-Lan, *A Short History of Chinese Philosophy* (New York: Free Press, 1948), 21.

side, bestowing and denoting a more authentic status to the father's side.

Because of the emphasis on the family system in Confucianism, continuing the family lineage is the most significant duty of the family, which only the male child can perform. According to Mencius, therefore, "there are three things which are unfilial, and to have no posterity is the greatest of them."[15] Here posterity refers exclusively to a male child, not a female child. People often consider only the male child as a countable family member. Sons are still of overwhelming importance to the family because of their potential role as providers of the family income. Moreover, only sons can glorify the family through official appointment or perpetuate the family name. Even after death it is the sons, as sole performers of the ancestor worship, who are responsible for the welfare of their departed parents in the spirit world. Daughters cannot offer ancestral sacrifice. So, from the day of her marriage, a married woman is under pressure to conceive and bring forth a healthy male child because people acknowledge the clan lineage only through the male line. Without a son, there would be no head of the household to offer the ancestral sacrifices and the clan would acquire a secondary status, existing only along the female line. People regard the marriage as a sacred event in Confucianism, registered in the cosmic order and with the ancestral line, and people thereby consider it something that one should not dissolve. Yet, the importance of sons is so great that if a wife fails to bear a male child, according to Confucian teaching, the husband has the right to divorce her and send her back to her

15. Legge, trans., *The Four Books*, 725.

family.[16] A wife, however, never had any grounds for initiating a divorce against her husband under any circumstances.

Theoretically, the duty of the Confucian male child is to devote himself to the welfare of his parents. The duty of a son's wife is to share in this complete devotion to her husband's parents, not to her own parents. Here, the concept of filiality is of the most significance for understanding the Confucian family. The term *hsiao* (filiality or filial piety) presents one of the most basic social and religious concepts of Confucian society. The written symbol in Chinese for *hsiao* consists of the graph for the old supported by the graph for son placed underneath. Confucius gave this virtue of filiality a primacy in human moral development. Filiality, as the root of familism, is praised in all the Confucian classics. In fact, the Book of Filiality (or *Hsiao Ching*), one of the Confucian classics, is exclusively dedicated to this topic. The Book of Filiality describes filiality as follows: "while [the parents] are living, serve them with *li* [principle]; when they die, bury them with *li,* and sacrifice for them with *li.*"[17] Confucians consider filiality as the virtue of all virtues and the source, measure, and form of all the virtues and direct sons toward their ultimate end in ultimate aim of piety toward heaven.

The center of the Confucian family is found in the relationship between father and son. Consequently, the teaching of the filiality is mainly focused on the relationship between fathers and sons. Since the family lineage is patrilineal, people exclude the family of the wife

16. There were seven traditional grounds for divorce by husband—disobedience to a husband's parents, failure to bear a son, promiscuity, jealously, having an incurable disease, talking too much, and stealing. See Theresa Kelleher, "Confucianism," in *Women in World Religions*, ed. Arvind Sharma (New York: State University of New York Press, 1987), 137.

17. *Analects*, trans. James Legge, II. 5.3. The word *li* ("principle") originally has the meaning of order or pattern. There are various views on this concept in accordance with some different perspectives within Confucian philosophy. For further explanation, see Wing-tsit Chan, *A Source Book in Chinese Philosophy* (Princeton: Princeton University Press, 1963), 766–68.

from the family lineage. This aspect is the most significant flaw in Confucian notion and practice of familism.

Because of its significant emphasis on filiality, ancestor worship or rite is the oldest and most basic Confucian tradition. One should note that "ancestor" primarily means a male ancestor of the husband. The ancestor in Confucian ancestor worship is not a universal category that evenly includes the ancestors of both husband and wife. A woman born into a family will not be an ancestor at all, for she is born to join herself to another family's ancestor worship. Confucian exaltation of the authority of father and son made the unequal treatment of women appear natural. Society can see the subordination of wives to husbands and daughters to all men in the family, the denial of inheritance rights, the inequitable marriage laws, and the unequal treatment in genealogical records as proof of the sexual inequality fostered by Confucianism in a Confucian society such as Korea. In sum, the Confucian view of family is inevitably patriarchal, patrilineal, and patrilocal.

Critical Familism:
Christian View on Family

Focusing upon family discourse is significant for understanding a particular society because such discourse not only gives meaning to social life but also controls it. A monolithic image of family serves, as one can see in the conception of the Confucian family, not simply as an accurate reflection of reality but as an ideology prescribing one type of family as normative. People in a society take one's commitment to that type of family as evidence of one's normality and morality. In this sense, the family discourse "provides an important and ubiquitous social control rhetoric."[18] Unlike in Confucianism, for instance, Christianity offers no single concept of family. Within

Christianity, different views on family coexist: from the fundamentalist view to the Christian feminist one, and from the Catholic view to the Protestant one, for instance. Most of the traditional Christian teachings on the family tend to suggest only one normative model for the family, which sometimes seems incompatible with feminism. From this traditional view of family, Christians regard feminism as an anti-family ideology that would destroy so-called Christian family values. Conservative Christian groups such as the Christian Coalition in the United States use the term *antifamily* as a slogan. Conservative Christians have used such an understanding of family as a "conceptual and institutional fortress of patriarchy, sexism, and heterosexism."[19]

One of the more progressive Christian responses to the fundamentalist Christian view on family is an emphasis upon the formlessness of the family. According to John Platton and Brian H. Childs: "there is no ideal form for the Christian family toward which we should strive. There is, however, a normative function: Care."[20] For them, any form of family is acceptable as long as it comes with redemptive care, which one can characterize as a combination of appreciation, respect, compassion, and solicitude. Some argue that the Christian family should not be a haven of private separation from the public. In rejecting the public–private split that is typical of the modern bourgeois family, Rodney Clapp attempts to recover the notion of the Christian home as a mission base crossing over the split between the private and public, a concept that is consistent with the

18. Jaber F. Gubrium and James A. Holstein, *What Is Family?* (Mountain View, CA: Mayfield, 1990), 143.
19. Sally Purvis, "A Common Love: Christian Feminist Ethics and the Family," in *Religion, Feminism, and the Family*, ed. Anne Carr and Mary Stewart Van Leeuwen (Louisville: Westminster John Knox, 1996), 112.
20. John Patton and Brian H. Childs, *Christian Marriage and Family: Caring for Our Generations* (Nashville: Abingdon, 1988), 12.

pattern of home churches explicit in the process of the formation of early Christianity.[21]

Christian feminists also began to challenge the patriarchal understanding of family in fundamentalist Christianity, and to redefine the family and marriage based on gender equality and justice. Family is not only a biological but also "a social institution, affecting and affected by other social institutions in which it is located."[22] In this sense, the public–private split cannot adequately characterize the complexity of family and interconnectedness between the two spheres, as addressed in the well-known feminist slogan, "The personal is the political." Emphasis on the family only as a biological unit and confining it to the private sphere has reinforced and justified the male headship of the household and sexism. Jesus relativizes both the biological reality and the sociological reality of the family in his claim, "Whoever does the will of God is my brother and sister and mother" (Mark 3:35; Matt. 12:50; Luke 8:21). Jesus' nonbiological conception of family is important because it puts priority on the theological reality, not biological reality, of family. This theological and spiritual relativization of the traditional family as a biological or sociological unit can be a Christian principle of the renunciation of patriarchal value and the male-centered structure of family. The theological principle of family, of course, does not deny the biological and sociological families, but puts all other relationships in the service of a community that exists for the purpose of enabling and enhancing each person's relationship to God.

In this context, Christians need to evaluate the Christian concept of family in a new way to understand how the family provides for people's relation to God in a concrete reality. Christians can judge

---

21. Rodney Clapp, *Family at the Crossroad: Beyond Traditional and Modern Options* (Downers Grove, IL: InterVarsity, 1993).
22. Purvis, "A Common Love," 115.

the biological or sociological family as good, for example, only if it enhances the God-relation of its members and the community. Otherwise, one may need to rearrange or leave the family behind in light of the theological principle of family. Theologically speaking, Jesus' claim that only those who do the will of God are his family is a characterization of the demands of justice and equality in family. It deconstructs the patriarchal and homosexist family that has justified the subordination of women to men and the opposition to the civil unions or marriages of same-sex couples. It can also be a Christian feminist principle that criticizes the patriarchal aspects in the biblical and Christian tradition because practicing sexism or other forms of discrimination would not be the will of God. Jesus' view on who counts as family breaks from traditional social definitions and understandings of family, and especially contrasts with the Confucian understanding of family that people base exclusively on a male biological connection. Christians can therefore define family in terms of God-relation and doing the will of God—the deeds of justice and love, grounded in Jesus' teaching. Here, family as biological unit loses its status as family when it justifies unjust family relations, because such does not follow the will of God.

Christians have defined love in various ways, some associating it more with self-sacrifice (*agape*), and others with self-fulfillment (*eros*). But primarily, love means equal regard (*caritas*) that includes elements of both sacrifice and fulfillment. The Christian notion of family thus advocates "the committed, intact, equal-regard, public-private family" as a new family ideal in which both husband and wife respect each other and participate in both public and private realm. This Christian notion of family promotes not a narrow familism that endorses only one type of family but a "critical familism" that respects and supports those who live outside of a conventional family structure. A "love ethic of equal regard"[23] grounds this Christian family and places its value on mutuality, self-sacrifice, and individual fulfillment.

Critical Reevaluation of Two Familisms

On the surface, both Confucianism and Christianity seem to have one thing in common: an emphasis on the relationship of father and son. Sung Bum Yun, a Korean theologian who initiated Korean indigenous theology in 1960s, contends that the relationship of Jesus Christ with the Heavenly Father resembles Confucian filiality, that is, the father-son relationship.[24] According to Yun, both in Judeo-Christianity and in Confucianism, the father-son relationship is the essential norm for an integral approach to what it means to be human. He contends, "both Christianity and Confucianism are religions of the East, and the ethics of both begins with the family."[25] He goes on to argue that Christianity emphasizes the primary importance of the father-son relationship in the creation story and treats the husband-wife relationship as secondary. God first made Adam, and God was the Father and Adam God's first-born son. After God established the father-son relationship between God and Adam, God made Adam a wife, Eve. Accordingly, the father-son relationship is primary and inevitable, while the husband-wife relationship is contingent.

Second, in the New Testament, the relationship of God the Father and God's Son, Jesus Christ, is likewise primary. The essence of the relationship of the Father to Son is clearly manifested in the New Testament's christological thinking, which denotes that the

23. Don S. Browning, et al., *From Culture Wars to Common Ground: Religion and the American Family Debate* (Louisville: Westminster John Knox, 1997), 2, 3.
24. Sung Bum Yun, *Ethics East and West: Western Secular, Christian, and Confucian Traditions in Comparative Perspective*, trans. Michael C. Kalton (Seoul: Christian Literature Society, 1977 [1973]), 16.
25. Sung Bum Yun, *Sungeui Sinhak [Theology of Sung]* (Seoul: Sungkwangsa, 1973), 125.

triune God is grounded upon the Father-Son relationship.[26] In this sense, Yun argues, a similarity between Christian and Confucian ethics is obvious, because filiality is the essential norm in both. Yun regrets that the Western Christian tradition lost the meaning of authentic family that is the essence of Christianity by its adoption of individualism. Thus he unreservedly concludes that the most essential factor in both Judeo-Christianity and Confucianism is the father-son relationship.

However, Yun, as well as other scholars who share similar views on the relationship of Confucianism and Christianity, overlooks some critical differences between the Confucian notion of family and that of Christianity. First, Confucianism and Christianity have crucial differences in their understanding of what it means to be human, an understanding on which people have based the idea of human rights and equality. The idea of human rights requires "a certain level of individualism, wherein the individual person would be valued for her/his own sake, and not just as a relationship to others."[27] In Confucianism, unlike in Christianity, one can hardly find a sense of individuality because the family as a group precedes an individual person. In the Confucian tradition, no conception of individuality existed, and the underlying idea of Confucianism is "not individual liberty or equality but order and harmony, not individual independence but selflessness and cooperation, not freedom of individual conscience but conformity to orthodox truth" and "the purpose of society was not to preserve and promote individual liberty but to maintain the harmony of the hierarchical order."[28] In this

26. Yun, *Ethics of East and West*, 23–25.
27. Leonard Swidler, "Human Rights: A Historical Overview," in *Concilium* ("The Ethics of World Religions and Human Rights'), ed. Hans Küng and Jürgen Moltmann (London: SCM, 1990), 12.
28. Louis Henkin, "The Human Rights Idea in Contemporary China: A Comparative Perspective," in *Human Rights in Contemporary China*, ed. R. Randle Edwards, Louis Henkin, and Andrew J. Nathan (New York: Columbia University Press, 1986), 21.

vein, the feminist claim of woman as an individual, singular human being, not simply as a role or function, has no place in Confucian perception of human being. A number of Confucian scholars endorse the following understanding of human being and morality and use it as a rationale for rejecting universal human rights: "For the early Confucians there can be no *me* in isolation, to be considered abstractly; I am the *totality of roles*. I live in relation to specific others. I do not *play* or *perform* these roles; I am these roles. When they have all been specified I have been defined uniquely, fully, and altogether, with no remainder with which to piece together a free, autonomous self."[29]

In this Confucian context, therefore, the relationship between the family members is more important than the individual. The problem here is the fact that the relationship is hierarchical according to gender, age, and social status in a way that is antidemocratic and androcentric. Many regard Confucianism as a true humanism. But this idea is misleading because the human being in Confucianism has rights only if she or he has a certain position in a family. The individual person has rights not as an individual person, but as a brother, son, or father. There is no place for a woman to claim her human rights as an individual person, especially in the public sphere—not even as wife, daughter, or mother. This asymmetrical status among family members—between husband and wife, son and daughter, senior and junior—is not seen when one argues that Confucianism is a true humanism because of its exaltation of human relationship within a community.

Even though the Fifth Commandment in the Ten Commandments says, "Obey your parents," the place of filial piety

---

29. Henry Rosemont, "Why Take Rights Seriously? A Confucian Critique," in *Human Rights and the World's Religions*, ed. Leroy Rouner (Notre Dame, IN: University of Notre Dame Press, 1988), 177.

in Christianity and Confucianism is critically different. Paul teaches Christians, for instance, to obey parents *in the Lord* (Eph. 6:1) and if the biological parents instigate Christians to any transgression of God's law, such Christians may justly consider their biological parents not as parents, but as strangers who are attempting to seduce them from obedience to God.[30] In Confucianism, however, it is not possible for one to disobey one's parents, especially the biological father, in any circumstance. The concept of father as a symbol of God and of priest within the Christian community did not derive from the natural family as it is in Confucianism. Christianity claimed a higher right to be an authentic family than the natural/biological family. Christianity weakened people's loyalties to their traditional patriarchal clans by encouraging competing loyalties to Christian communities and Christian marriage ("A man shall leave his father and mother and be joined to his wife," Gen. 2:24), a fact that non-Christian Confucians may view as dangerous to the existing patrilineal social order.

In Confucianism, such a conception is not possible because a son never should leave his father.[31] From the Confucian view on family, the absence of a biological father in Jesus' birth, for instance, can be a serious problem because Jesus is a misbegotten child who does not have any biological father with a direct blood relation. Furthermore Jesus, as an unmarried man, is an unfilial son because he does not carry on his biological family line. Furthermore, Jesus relativizes the family, as the biological unit, by the claim that those who do God's will are his mother, brothers, and sisters, strangely omitting fathers. Therefore, one cannot bind Jesus' notion of family to the Confucian biological, patriarchal, and heterosexual notion of family.

---

30. Robert Bellah, *Beyond Belief: Essays on Religion in a Post-Traditionalist World* (Berkeley: University of California Press, 1970), 93.
31. Ibid., 91.

With its radical inclusivity, one can find some guiding principles not only for the heterosexual family but also for all forms of family today, for instance, a homosexual family, a single-parent family, a mixed-race family, a family with adopted children who have no biological connection to their parents, a family with no children, and so on. By contrast, the Confucian notion of family makes those people in allegedly nonstandard family forms marginal, abnormal, and deficient, thereby depriving their rights to be happy as normal citizens. Divorced women and their children, for instance, are among the most deprived people in Confucian society, not only legally but also socially and culturally, for they have no male head of household, which is the ideal of the Confucian family that people have legally practiced through various forms of institutions in Korea.

If one employs the method of reflection on praxis in examining a religion, then one ought to take a look at the concrete praxis of how each individual has rights as a human being under the particular religious/philosophical teachings in her or his everyday life. Academic discourse on Confucianism must take into account the serious violation of human rights in women's lives under Confucian teachings. Romanticizing and idealizing Confucianism as a true humanism will only blur the root causes of women's oppression under Confucianism and its practice, and will likely simply ignore the present problem of an extreme male-centeredness in Confucian culture and society. It is hard for one to find both the concept and the reality of human rights, especially for women in Confucian teachings and their practices in a concrete reality. Rather, widespread violations of the basic rights of women and children under Confucianism have prevailed even today.

One should also note that the Confucian concept of the person as a center of relationships, rather than merely an isolated individual, and its emphasis on family-centeredness and human-relatedness, have resulted in nepotism, favoritism, and provincialism in private and public sectors of Korea such as church, family, workplace, and politics. People establish most political and social relationships based on one's family relationships, one's hometown, or one's alma mater. Thus, people highly recommend and widely practice hiring someone because of personal ties and relations based on one's hometown, alma mater, personal acquaintance, and so forth. Confucian scholars have not fundamentally challenged the injustice resulting from these problematic social relations and values, which have raised major barriers to Confucian society's achieving a more advanced, mature form of democracy. Confucian scholars and practitioners should address not only the virtues but also the possible vices of Confucian communitarianism, especially in Confucian family discourse. The absence of the notion of individuality in Confucianism has exaggerated the vices implicit in egoistic family-centeredness and human-relatedness because of the lack of a sense of common justice and fairness, which one should apply to every single member of society regardless of age, gender, social status, natal origin, or similar factors.

The notion of individualism is in fact very complex. Generally speaking, one can view individualism in two ways. One view holds that individualism is destructive to an individual and to one's social interaction. People regard individualism as negative and destructive because it ignores the notion of human beings as social, communal, and interdependent beings, which has resulted in unscrupulous competition, an understanding of humans as self-contained and self-sufficient, and an alienation from self and society. Most contemporary feminists have criticized this negative view and practice of individualism. The other view of individualism maintains that this destructive individualism is a Hobbesian notion and is incompatible with true ethical individualism. The positive aspects of this ethical individualism are self-actualization, freedom of choice, personal responsibility, and universality, which involves respect for the well-being and rights of others because denying the rights of others would implicitly endorse the idea that one does not possess such rights for oneself as well.[32]

Despite the potential vices of individualism that many, including feminists, have pointed out, the initial stage of feminist consciousness nevertheless requires this positive notion of ethical individualism in order for women, the powerless, or the marginalized to acknowledge themselves as responsible and free agents not dependent on men, and to reject the patriarchal construction of men-the Subject and women-the Other. Failure to achieve sufficient autonomy, for instance, which is one aspect of individualism, can be a block to achieving a mature relationship and thus a full understanding of interdependence. Autonomy, in this feminist context, is not absolute self-sufficiency, as many too readily claim, but one's capacity for independent survival, thinking, and judgment. Autonomous persons recognize others' needs for freedom and their own lives. I do not see any inevitable dichotomy between individualism and communitarianism, or I-ness and we-ness. What we need is neither a total rejection of nor a blind acceptance, but an ongoing reconceptualization of the notion of individualism that requires a dialectical perspective.

Christian understanding of the human being implies a strong sense of ethical individualism on which people base the modern concept of human rights and equality in the name of natural rights. The Christian claim that God created each and every human being in God's image gave rise to the idea that we should treat all humans with the same reverence and respect because they equally bear God's

---

32. Cf. Alan. S. Waterman, *The Psychology of Individualism* (New York: Praeger, 1984).

image. All human beings are to have dignity and rights as humans created equal, regardless of their sex, class, or race. This ontological principle of human equality in Christianity became the conceptual framework for the nineteenth-century women's movement in the United States. When the first National Women's Right Convention in the United States took place in 1848 in Seneca Falls, New York, the delegates approved the Declaration of Sentiments, modeled on the Declaration of Independence. The following part of the declaration shows how the principle of ontological equality in Christianity became the vital force for the rise of the modern feminist movement in the United States, even though women activists harshly criticized patriarchal teachings and practices of Christian tradition at that time: "We hold these truths to be self-evident: that all men and women are created equal; that they are endowed by their Creator with certain inalienable rights; that among these are life, liberty, and the pursuit of happiness."[33] Following from this principle of human equality, justice becomes the necessary context for normative claims about the family and the norm of right relations both within and outside of biological and sociological family units. Because many feminists define justice as right relations, we have to ask how the members of the family, whether they are husband or wife or son or daughter, are relating to one another and to the context of their lives. When there are right, fair, just, equal relations among family members, one can judge the family as good. So, one should evaluate the family not just by a biological relationship but by deeds in accordance with God's will—justice and love.

People under the Confucian influence have used the lack of the concept of individuality in Confucianism, and the Confucian view of family as an exclusively biological unit, to justify the violation of

---

33. Elizabeth Cady Stanton, "Declaration of Sentiments," in *The Feminist Papers: From Adams to de Beauvoir*, ed. Alice S. Rossi (New York: Columbia University Press, 1973), 416.

women's basic human rights in the name of harmony and filiality. So many women have suffered because of its principle of agnation, which made men alone the structurally relevant members of family and society and relegated women to social/familial dependence. Most people have not seen women and the powerless as individual persons. Idealization of the Confucian concept of relatedness between humans without a reflection on the praxis of how women have actually lived under this Confucian concept of relatedness has resulted in the perpetuation of women's suffering under extreme androcentric values and institutions in Confucian society.

Researchers show that there had been not much discrimination of the paternal line against the maternal line dating back from the ancient times down to the mid-Yi Dynasty. The patrilineal system took shape later in the Yi Dynasty(*Chosun*), which adopted Confucianism as its founding ideology. When the Yi Dynasty firmly entrenched Confucianism in the period from 1486 to 1636, systemic control and subjugation of women started. So, the ideal Confucian family system made Korean women legally subordinated to men in accordance with the prevalent Confucian ethic. One can characterize the Confucian family system as follows: (1) people regard only the paternal line relatives as primary relatives; (2) society transmits social class and rights only from fathers to sons; (3) the sole authority in the family rests with the father who holds control over the children; (4) society allows marriages only with those outside the blood clan; and (5) first-born males held the right to lineal succession.[34]

Here, one can see the fundamental ironies and problems in Confucian familism. The ironies of Confucian familism are as follows: first, it absolutely requires the male to carry on the family lineage, which results in female infanticide and the extreme

---

34. Yung-Chung Kim, ed., *Women of Korea: A History from Ancient Times to 1945* (Seoul: Ewha Womans University Press, 1976), 84–89.

imbalance in the ratio between female and male children in Korea[35]; second, the ancestors for filiality are primarily the ancestors of the husband's family, which thereby disregards the wife's family. The system of family lineage (*chokbo*) and the male headship of the family have been the most powerful operating social system in Korean society, and they have influenced the androcentrism in Korean Christian churches today.

Homosocial Reality:
Embodiment of Confucian Familism in Christianity

In a patriarchal society, the relations between men, not between men and women, are the most important. Especially in Confucian culture, relations between men, both in the private and the public spheres, have been the center of all human relationships. The relations between men establish a firm solidarity among male members of society that enables them to dominate and hold power over women. Women isolated from the close-knit public relations among men cannot find their place except in small private sectors. To work in the public sphere, women must enter the exclusive network of men. However, it is extremely difficult for women to relate to men as coworkers because the Confucian tradition has defined the

---

35. A study shows that in South Korea, the birth ratio of baby boys to girls was 107:100 in 1983. It increased to 112:100 in 1988, 115.4:100 in 1994, thereby setting the world record. This imbalance of birth ratio between boys and girls implies the world's highest abortion ratio of female fetuses. Among these abortions are some cases of terminating unwanted pregnancies from rape, but most of the abortions done are of female fetuses following a sex test. The Korean *Sisa Journal* magazine reported in 1993 that some 620,000 babies were born every year in South Korea, while 1.6 million fetuses—or 2.5 times the number actually born—were aborted. According to the *Journal*, one can now estimate the number of abortions at two million per year, which averages to six thousand per day. The balance of male vs. female babies began to shift in the mid-1980s with the introduction of ultrasonography, which doctors use as a means to find out the sex of the baby. The ratio of boys to girls is 106:100 if the baby is the firstborn; 113:100 if it's the second child, and 196:100 if it is the third child.

relationship of women to men as that of a life spouse suited only for marriage. Furthermore, men easily exclude women from the shared information among male workers, which women would need for proper promotions and so on.

Various social/religious institutions also embody the Confucian emphasis on the homogeneity of the family lineage. For example, people neither encourage nor commonly practice adoption in Confucian cultural societies such as Korea. Since an adopted child has no homogeneity in terms of bloodline with the father, people would not consider the adopted child to be an authentic family member. So, most families try to hide the fact of the adoption and pretend so that people outside the family see the child as their real birth-child. In this context, it is not unusual that people extend this negative attitude toward interracial marriage and its offspring as well, for they also embody an impure marriage because of its lack of homogeneity in blood.

Another, initially paradoxical, example of the social embodiment of the Confucian emphasis on the homogeneous family line is that Korean women retain their maiden name even after marriage, which might seem to imply equality until one comes to understand the underlying androcentric view of family. Women after marriage still retain their maiden names not because their husband's family members respect women's independence but because they cannot accept women as a full member of their husband's household. Since the married women do not have a direct blood connection with the husband's family, women after marriage become absolute outsiders both in their natal family and husband's family: married women are in-between and belong nowhere. It is only when women give birth to a male child that they are able to claim their status as family members in their husband's family. So, it has been a survival issue for Korean women to give birth to sons, which has resulted in the extreme ratio imbalance between male and female children even today in Korea.

Christians have extended Confucian familism, with its emphasis on the homogeneity of family blood, to the religious sphere. Korean Christianity emphasizes a denominational homogeneity among Christians, which has resulted in a lack of ecumenical spirit. Because of this, one can hardly find a mutual interaction between denominations; instead, they are highly competitive and even hostile to one another. Consequently, mutual interaction among faculties and students of seminaries of different denominations is hardly possible or desirable. Faculties and students in denominationally affiliated theological schools are exclusively from the same denomination. Furthermore, among faculty members in a particular seminary, homogeneity also prevails, not only in terms of the denomination but also in the schools from which faculty members have graduated. Denominational or institutional nepotism creates an antiecumenical and antidemocratic ethos in theological educational bodies and practices.

Confucianism in Korea is not the only force for promoting the patriarchal reality in Christianity, but it justifies, reinforces, and finally perpetuates a strong patriarchal ethos in Christianity. Confucianism has tended to be extremely conservative, supporting the ruling elite and the status quo, providing theoretical justification for authoritarianism, and justifying inequality between the sexes and age groups. It strives to maintain the existing social hierarchical structure, and it reinforces and justifies women's subordination to men in family, society, and church in the name of harmony and peace of community. It has strongly influenced the contemporary patriarchal construction of Christianity in Korea. Of course, this has not taken place automatically, for men have been the primary social and religious engineers of Christianity, too. Yet, we should not overlook the fact that women also contributed to the development of early Christianity, and they were even equal partners with men.[36] Despite these problems, including the patriarchal tradition, Christianity—even Christianity in Korea—also has an egalitarian tradition that can engender a vital force for criticizing the patriarchal factors in Christianity and for fostering women's leadership in church and society. A large number of feminist theologians have attempted to recover the egalitarian principles in Christianity and reconstruct Christianity as a more just religion.

I wonder, however, if there is any possibility for the emergence of feminist theologians within Confucianism who could recover a Confucian egalitarian tradition and practice within the Confucian community in the same way that Christian feminists try to do within the Christian community and its institutions. I wonder about this issue because it is hard to find any historical trace of egalitarian community for different sexes, age groups, and social classes in the long history of Confucianism. I regret that Christians in Korea have made Christianity ethically Confucianized and armed with a stronger patriarchy than that of the Christianity practiced in the countries from which missionaries introduced Christianity to Korea. This combination of Confucianism with Christianity in Korea has resulted primarily in the exclusion of women from leadership roles in theology and the ministry. Furthermore, the Confucian exaltation of homogeneity in family lineage has resulted in a spirit of antiecumenism and exclusive denominationalism and has fostered a homosocial reality in the spheres of theology and ministry. As a result, Christianity in Korea is becoming more and more conservative and

---

36. Cf. Elisabeth Schüssler Fiorenza, *In Memory of Her: A Feminist Theological Reconstruction of Christian Origins* (New York: Crossroad, 1983). Here Fiorenza focuses on the important leadership role of women in the formation of the early church.

fundamentalist and is losing its prophetic voice and the possibility of transformation toward a more just and inclusive religion.

Confucian values, which people generally list as attachment to the family, respect for elders and authority, commitment to education, thriftiness, belief in order and stability, valuing consensus over confrontation, and so on, are likely to fail as political norms in the contemporary world, especially from a feminist perspective. Being *duty-oriented* rather than *rights-oriented* in people's relation to their communities, Confucian family-centeredness and human-relatedness force women to stay in private sectors, for Confucian teachings make a strict distinction between women's and men's places, between women's work and men's work, between women's roles and men's roles, a distinction that limits equal opportunities for jobs and justifies this limitation. Almost all social institutions in Korea presuppose women to be housewives and often fail to count the female labor force as a real economic factor.

Whenever someone attempts to defend Asian or Confucian values, one must ask, *Who* is defending the values, for *what* purposes, for *whose* benefits, and *from what* perspective? This is especially the case with regard to women's issues. Emphasizing a respect for authority and elders often serves as a road to underpinning established social and political hierarchies and as a ground on which people in power force women, minors, and the lower social class to endure an authoritarian community, in terms of family, school, religious community, and the nation. When Asians try to utilize resources from Asian traditions, the consequence of these efforts should be to enhance the quality of our lives. If the traditions do not provide the better lives for which contemporary women aspire, women should make use of other cultural and religious traditions and learn from them. The geographical origin of democracy or feminism is, in this sense, pointless. What matters here is whether the idea or the tradition can contribute to promoting the rights of women and the marginalized and to opening a new horizon for the good life to both men and women, not only in their metaphysical or spiritual world but also in their concrete material world. Therefore, when one makes judgments about certain values, such as Asian values or Confucian values, one should make the judgments on the ground of whether those values would contribute to betterment of the lives of the marginalized, not the lives of the already privileged. One can direct feminist criticism of Asian or Confucian values at the tendency of men to use those values to justify women's subjugation to men in all forms of social and religious institutions.

When people criticize the concept of individualism in the modern West, they should also problematize the concept of communitarianism and human-relatedness in Asia. The chain of corruption in many forms in contemporary Korea, for instance, has deep roots in the distorted notion of human interconnectedness, which has led to the social injustices of nepotism, favoritism, provincialism, and male dominance. Attempts to argue that the Confucian notion of *Jen*, which is often translated as benevolence, love, kindness, charity, compassion, humaneness, humanity, perfect virtue, goodness, true humanhood, and so on, is compatible with a feminist ethics of care[37] are misleading because the Confucian concept itself is characteristically patriarchal and therefore has persistently and deeply served as part of a patriarchal ideology for antifeminist traditions. Confucian scholars and practitioners have hardly implemented the concept of *Jen* for promoting the status and well-being of women, lower-class people, and the minor in Confucian society. Before glorifying Asian or Confucian human-relatedness as the alternative to the Western individualism, one needs

---

37. Chenyang Li, "The Confucian Concept of Jen and the Feminist Ethics of Care: A Comparative Study," *Hypatia* 9, no. 1 (Winter 1994): 70–89.

to ask first whether these philosophies base the notion of human-relatedness on the ideal of justice and fairness among its members, regardless of one's gender, age, social status, and so on. In so doing, one can point out not only the vices of individualism but also those of communitarianism. Discursive binarism of individualism versus communitarianism or of I-ness versus we-ness does not lead one to a proper reflection on what we need to preserve as a universal value for a more egalitarian, communal, and just society, for those two are neither indivisible nor identical. Individualism and communitarianism have both vices and virtues, when people practice and implement them in human reality. Suppression of either, however, will result in a greater oppression. What we need is a critically scrutinized balance of individualism and communitarianism that contributes to maximizing the interest and well-being of the marginalized and to establishing a healthy society of justice, equality, peace, and solidarity.

Bibliography

Abraham, Susan. *Identity, Ethics, and Nonviolence in Postcolonial Theory: A Rahnerian Theological Assessment.* New York: Palgrave Macmillan, 2007.

Adams, Mary Louise. "There's No Place Like Home: On the Place of Identity in Feminist Politics." *Feminist Review* 31 (Spring 1989): 22–33.

Adorno, Theodore. *Minima Moralia: Reflections from a Damaged Life.* Trans. E. F. N. Jephcott. London: Verso, 1974.

Aguilar, Delia D. "Introduction." In Delia D. Aguilar and Anne E. Lacsamana, eds., *Women and Globalization*, 11–24. Amherst, NY: Humanity Books, 2004.

Aichele, George, et al. *The Postmodern Bible: The Bible and Culture Collective.* New Haven: Yale University Press, 1995.

Allen, Ernest, Jr. "Ever Feeling One's Twoness: 'Double Ideals' and 'Double Consciousness' in the Souls of Black Folk." *Contributions in Black Studies: A Journal of African and Afro-American Studies* (Special Double Issue: African American Double Consciousness) 9/10 (1990–1992): 55–69.

Alexander, M. Jacqui, and Chandra Talpade Mohanty, eds. *Feminist Genealogies, Colonial Legacies, Democratic Futures.* New York: Routledge, 1997.

Althaus-Reid, Marcella. *From Feminist Theology to Indecent Theology: Readings on Poverty, Sexual Identity and God.* London: SCM Press, 2004.

Amour, Ellen T. *Deconstruction, Feminist Theology, and the Problem of Difference: Subverting the Race/Gender Divide.* Chicago: University of Chicago Press, 1999.

Anderson, Benedict. *Imagined Communities: Reflections of the Origins and Spread of Nationalism.* London: Verso, 1985 (1983).

Anthias, Floya. "Culture, Identity and Rights: Challenging Contemporary Discourses of Belonging." In Nira Yuval-davis, Kalpana Kannabiran and Ulrike M. Vieten, eds., *The Situated Politics of Belonging*, 32–41. London: Sage, 2006.

Anzaldua, Gloria. *Borderlands/La Frontera: The New Mestiza.* San Francisco: Aunt Lute, 1987.

Appadurai, Arju . "Grassroots Globalization and the Research Imagination." *Public Culture* (Globalization issue) 12, no. 1 (Winter 2000): 1–19.

Appiah, Kwame Anthony. *The Ethics of Identity.* Princeton: Princeton University Press, 2005.

Arendt, Hannah. *The Origins of Totalitarianism.* New York: Schocken, 2004 (1951).

———. "We Refugees." In Ron H. Feldman, ed., *The Jew as Pariah: Jewish Identity and Politics in the Modern Age*, 55–65. New York: Random House, 1978.

———. "The Jew as Pariah: A Hidden Tradition." *Jewish Social Studies.* 6, no. 2 (April 1944): 99–122. Also in Ron H. Feldman, ed., *The Jew as Pariah: Jewish Identity and Politics in the Modern Age*, 67–90. New York: Random House, 1978.

———, and Karl Jaspers. *Correspondence: 1926–1969.* Ed. Lotte Kohler and Hans Saner. Trans. Robert Kimber and Rita Kimber. New York: Harcourt Brace Jovanovich, 1992 (1985).

Ashcroft, Bill, Gareth Griffiths, and Helen Tiffin, eds. *The Post-Colonial Studies Reader.* 2d ed. New York: Routledge, 1995.

————, eds. *Key Concepts in Post-colonial Studies*. New York: Routledge, 1998.

Asian Migrant Yearbook 2000. Hong Kong: Asian Migrant Centre, 2000.

Asian Migrant Yearbook 2004. Hong Kong: Asian Migrant Centre, 2004.

Aviv, Caryn, and David Shneer. *New Jew: The End of the Jewish Diaspora*. New York: New York University Press, 2005.

Bachelard, Gaston. *The Poetics of Space*. Trans. Maria Jolas. Boston: Beacon, 1969.

Bahramitash, Roksana. "The War on Terror, Feminist Orientalism and Orientalist Feminism: Case Studies of Two North American Bestsellers." *Critique: Critical Middle Eastern Studies* 14, no. 2 (Summer 2005): 221–35.

Baker-Fletcher, Karen, and Garth Kasimu Baker-Fletcher. *My Sister, My Brother: Womanist and Xodus God-Talk*. Maryknoll, NY: Orbis, 1997.

Balibar, Etienne, and Immanuel Wallerstein. *Race, Nation, Class: Ambiguous Identities*. New York: Verso, 1991.

Barber, Daniel Colucciello. *On Diaspora: Christianity, Religion, and Secularity*. Eugene, OR: Cascade, 2011.

Baudrillard, Jean. *The Transparency of Evil: Essays on Extreme Phenomena*. Trans. James Benedict. New York: Verso, 1993.

Bauer, Joanne R., and Daniel A. Bell, eds. *The East Asian Challenge for Human Rights*. Cambridge: Cambridge University Press, 1999.

Bell, Daniel. *The End of Ideology: On the Exhaustion of Political Ideas in the Fifties*. New York: Free Press, 1966.

Bellah, Robert. *Beyond Belief: Essays on Religion in a Post-Traditionalist World*. Berkeley: University of California Press, 1970.

Benhabib, Seyla. *The Claims of Culture: Equality and Diversity in the Global Era*. Princeton: Princeton University Press, 2002.

————. "Feminism and Postmodernism: An Uneasy Alliance." In Linda Nicholson, ed., *Feminist Contentions: A Philosophical Exchange*, 17–34. New York: Routledge, 1995.

_____. "The Generalized and the Concrete Other." In Seyla Benhabib and Drucilla Cornell, eds., *Feminism as Critique: On the Politics of Gender*, 77–95. Minneapolis: University of Minnesota Press, 1987.

_____, and Drucilla Cornell, eds. *Feminism as Critique: On the Politics of Gender*. Minneapolis: University of Minnesota Press, 1987.

Bhabha, Homi K. *The Location of Culture*. New York: Routledge, 2006 (1994).

_____. "The World and the Home." *Social Text* (Third World and Post-Colonial Issues) 31/32 (1992): 141–53.

_____. "The Third Space: Interview with Homi Bhabha." In Jonathan Rutherford, ed., *Identity: Community, Culture, Difference*, 207–221. London: Lawrence & Wishart, 1990.

Bickford, Susan. "Anti-Anti-Identity Politics: Feminism, Democracy, and the Complexities of Citizenship." *Hypatia* (Citizenship in Feminism: Identity, Action, and Locale issue) 12, no. 4 (Autumn 1997): 111–31.

Blommaert, Jan, and Jef Verschueren. *Debating Diversity: Analysing the Discourse of Tolerance*. New York: Routledge, 1998.

Boyarin, Daniel, and Jonathan Boyarin. "Diaspora: Generation and the Ground of Jewish Identity." *Critical Inquiry* 19, no. 4 (Summer 1993): 693–725.

Bradshaw, York W., and Michael Wallace. *Global Inequalities*. Thousand Oaks, CA: Pine Forge, 1996.

Brah, Avtar. *Cartographies of Diaspora: Contesting Identities*. Gender, Race, Ethnicity series. New York: Routledge, 1996.

Brass, Paul R. *Ethnicity and Nationalism: Theory and Comparison*. London: Sage, 1991.

Braidotti, Rosi. *Nomadic Subjects: Embodiment and Sexual Difference in Contemporary Feminist Theory*. New York: Columbia University Press, 1994.

Braziel, Jana Evans. *Diaspora: An Introduction*. Oxford: Blackwell, 2008.

_____, and Anita Mannur, eds. *Theorizing Diaspora: A Reader.* Oxford: Blackwell, 2003.

Brecher, Jeremy and Tim Costello. *Global Village or Global Pillage: Economic Reconstruction from the Bottom Up.* Boston: South End, 1994.

Brown, Robert McAfee. *Spirituality and Liberation: Overcoming the Great Fallacy.* Philadelphia: Westminster, 1988.

Browning, Don S., et al., eds. *From Culture Wars to Common Ground: Religion and the American Family Debate.* Louisville: Westminster John Knox, 1997.

Brubaker, Rogers. "The 'Diaspora' Diaspora." *Ethnic and Racial Studies* 28, no. 1 (2005): 1–19.

Bulkin, Elly, Minnie Bruce Pratt, and Barbara Smith, eds. *Yours in Struggle: Three Feminist Perspectives on Anti-Semitism and Racism.* Brooklyn: Long Haul, 1984.

Burton, Margaret E. *The Education of Women in China.* New York: Revell, 1911.

Butler, Judith. *Gender Trouble: Feminism and the Subversion of Identity.* New York: Routledge, 2008 (1990).

_____. "Subjects of Sex/Gender/Desire." In Ann Cudd and Robin Andreasen, eds., *Feminist Theory: A Philosophical Anthology*, 145–53. Blackwell Philosophy Anthologies. New York: Wiley-Blackwell, 2005.

_____. *Undoing Gender.* New York: Routledge, 2004.

_____. *Excitable Speech: A Politics of the Performative.* New York: Routledge, 1997.

_____. "Performative Acts and Gender Constitution: An Essay in Phenomenology and Feminist Theory." *Theatre Journal* 40, no. 4 (Dec. 1988): 519–31.

_____, and Joan W. Scott, eds. *Feminist Theorize the Political.* New York: Routledge, 1992.

_____, Jürgen Habermas, and Charles Taylor. *The Power of Religion in the Public Sphere.* New York: Columbia University Press, 2011.

Cady Stanton, Elizabeth. "Declaration of Sentiments." In Alice S. Rossi, ed., *The Feminist Papers: From Adams to de Beauvoir*, 417. New York: Columbia University Press, 1973.

Calinescu, Matei. *Five Faces of Modernity*. Durham: Duke University Press, 1987.

Capra, Fritjof. *The Turning Point: Science, Society, and the Rising Culture*. New York: Simon & Schuster, 1982.

Caputo, John D. *The Prayers and Tears of Jacques Derrida: Religion without Religion*. Bloomington: Indiana University Press, 1997.

Card, Claudia. *Feminist Ethics*. Lawrence: University Press of Kansas, 1991.

Carr, Anne, and Mary Stewart Van Leeuwen, eds. *Religion, Feminism & the Family*. Louisville: Westminster John Knox, 1996.

Carroll, Noel. "The Return of the Repressed: The Re-emergence of Expression in Contemporary American Dance." *Dance Theatre Journal* 2, no. 1 (1984): 16–27.

Carter, Stephen. *The Culture of Disbelief: How American Law and Politics Trivialize Religious Devotion*. New York: Doubleday, 1993.

Castells, Manuel. *The Rise of the Network Society*. Oxford: Blackwell, 1996.

————. *The Power of Identity*. Oxford: Blackwell, 1997.

Castles, Stephen, and Alistair Davidson. *Citizenship and Migration: Globalization and the Politics of Belonging*. New York: Macmillan, 2000.

Chakrabarty, Dipesh. *Provincializing Europe: Postcolonial Thought and Historical Difference*. Princeton: Princeton University Press, 2000.

Chakravatri, Uma. "What Happened to the Vedic Dasi?: Orientalism, Nationalism, and a Script for the Past." In Kumkum Sangari and Sudesh Vaid, eds., *Recasting Women: Essays in Colonial History*, 27–87. New Dehli: Kali for Women, 1989.

Chambers, Iain. *Border Dialogues: Journeys in Postmodernity*. New York: Routledge, 1990.

Chang, Grace. "Globalization in Living Color: Women of Color Living Under and Over the 'New World Order.'" In Delia D. Aguilar and Anne E. Lacsaman, eds., *Women and Globalization*, 230–61. Amherst, NY: Humanity Books, 2004.

Chen, Kuan-Hsing, *Asia as Method: Toward Deimperialization.* Durham: Duke University Press, 2010.

Chen, Xiaomei. *Occidentalism.* New York: Oxford University Press, 1995.

Chivallon, Christine. "Beyond Gilroy's Black Atlantic: The Experience of the African Diaspora." *Diaspora* 11, no. 3 (Winter 2002): 359–82.

Choi, Choon-Sik. *Han-Kuk Chongkyo Ijaki* [*A Story of Korean Religions*]. Seoul: Han Wool, 1995.

Chopp, Rebecca S., and Sheila Greeve Davaney, eds. *Horizons in Feminist Theology: Identity, Tradition, and Norms.* Minneapolis: Fortress Press, 1997.

Chow, Rey. *Writing Diaspora: Tactics of Intervention in Contemporary Cultural Studies.* Bloomington: Indiana University Press, 1993.

————. "Postmodern Automatons." In Judith Butler and Joan W. Scott, eds., *Feminists Theorize the Political*, 101–117. New York: Routledge, 1992.

Christiansen, Flemming, and Ulf Hedetoft, eds. *The Politics of Multiple Belonging: Ethnicity and Nationalism in Europe and East Asia.* Research in Migration and Ethnic Relations Series. Burlington, VT: Ashgate, 2004.

Chung, David. *Syncretism: The Religious Context of Christian Beginnings in Korea.* Albany: State University of New York Press, 2001.

Chung, Hyun Kyung. *Struggle to be the Sun Again: Introducing Asian Women's Theology.* Maryknoll, NY: Orbis, 1990.

Clapp, Rodney. *Family at the Crossroad: Beyond Traditional and Modern Options.* Downers Grove, IL.: InterVarsity, 1993.

Clark, Charles Allen. *The Korean Church and the Nevius Methods.* New York: Revell, 1930.

Cliff, Michelle. *Claiming an Identity They Taught Me to Despise.* Watertown, MA: Persephone, 1980.

Clifford, James. *Routes: Travel and Translation in the Late Twentieth Century.* Cambridge: Harvard University Press, 1997.

_____. "Diasporas." *Cultural Anthropology* 9, no. 3 (1994): 302–338.

_____. "Traveling Cultures." In Lawrence Grossberg, Cary Nelson, and Paula Treichler, eds., *Cultural Studies,* 96–116. New York: Routledge, 1992.

_____. "Notes on Theory and Travel." *Inscriptions* 5 (1989): 177–88.

_____, and George E. Marcus, eds. *Writing Culture: The Poetics and Politics of Ethnography.* Berkeley: University of California Press, 1986.

Cohen, Ed. "Who Are 'We'? Gay Identity as Political (E)motion." In Diana Fuss, ed., *Inside/Out: Lesbian Theories, Gay Theories,* 71–92. New York: Routledge, 1991.

Cohen, Robin. *Global Diasporas: An Introduction.* Seattle: University of Washington Press, 1997.

_____, and Steven Vertovec, eds. *Migration, Diasporas and Transnationalism.* Cheltenham, UK: Edward Elgar, 1999.

The Committee for the Compilation of the History of Korean Women. *Women of Korea: A History from Ancient Times to 1945.* Ed. and trans. Yung-Chung Kim. Seoul: Ewha Womans University Press, 1976.

Cone, James H. *A Black Theology of Liberation.* Maryknoll, NY: Orbis, 1991 (1970).

_____. *Black Theology and Black Power.* New York: HarperCollins, 1969.

Connor, Walker. "The Impact of Homelands Upon Diasporas." In Gabriel Sheffer, eds., *Modern Diasporas in International Politics,* 16–46. New York: Harcourt, 1986.

Cox, Oliver C. *Caste, Class and Race.* New York: Monthly Review, 1959 (1948).

Crosby, Christina. "Dealing with Differences." In Judith Butler and Joan Scott, eds., *Feminists Theorize the Political*, 130–43. New York: Routledge, 1992.

Cutting-Gray, Joanne. "Hannah Arendt, Feminist, and the Politics of Alterity: What Will We Lose if We Win?" *Hypatia* 8, no. 1 (Winter 1993): 35–54.

Daly, Mary. *Beyond God the Father: Toward a Philosophy of Women's Liberation.* Boston: Beacon, 1985 (1973).

Davis, Dawn Rae. "(Love Is) The Ability of Not Knowing: Feminist Experience of the Impossible in Ethical Singularity." *Hypatia* 17, no. 2 (Spring 2002): 145–61.

Davis, Lennard J. "Nation, Class, and Physical Minorities." In Timothy B. Powell, ed., *Beyond the Binary: Reconstructing Cultural Identity in a Multicultural Context.* New Brunswick, NJ: Rutgers University Press, 1997.

Dean, Jodi. *Solidarity of Strangers: Feminism after Identity Politics.* Berkeley: University of California Press, 1996.

de Bary, Wm. Theodore. "Introduction." In Wm. Theodore de Bary and Tu Weiming, eds., *Confucianism and Human Rights*, 1–26. New York: Columbia University Press, 1998.

———. *The Liberal Tradition in China.* New York: Columbia University Press, 1983.

de Certeau, Michel. *The Practice of Everyday Life.* Berkeley: University of California Press, 1984.

de Lauretis, Teresa. *Technologies of Gender: Essays on Theory, Film, and Fiction.* Bloomington: Indiana University Press, 1987.

Deleuze, Gilles, and Felix Guattari. "What Is a Minor Literature?" In *Kafka: Toward a Minor Literature*, 16–27. Trans. Dana Polan. Minneapolis: University of Minnesota Press, 1986.

Derrida, Jacques. "Avowing—The Impossible: 'Returns,' Repentance, and Reconciliation." In Elisabeth Weber, ed., *Living Together: Jacques Derrida's*

Communities of Violence and Peace, 18–43. New York: Fordham University Press, 2013.

_____. Paper Machine. Trans. Rachel Bowlby. Stanford: Stanford University Press, 2005 (2001).

_____. Monolingualism of the Other; or, The Prosthesis of Origin. Trans. Patrick Mensah.; Stanford: Stanford University Press, 1998 (1996).

_____. Of Grammatology. Trans. Gayatri Spivak. Corrected Ed. Baltimore: Johns Hopkins University Press, 1997 (1967).

_____. "Critical Response: But, beyond . . . (Open Letter to Anne McClintock and Rob Nixon)." Critical Inquiry 13, no. 1 (Autumn 1996): 155–70.

_____. Points . . . Interviews, 1974–1994. Ed. Elisabeth Weber. Trans. Peggy Kamuf, et al. Stanford: Stanford University Press, 1995.

_____. The Gift of Death. Trans. David Willis. Chicago: University of Chicago Press, 1995 (1992).

_____. Other Heading. Trans. Pascale-Anne Brault and Michael B. Naas. Bloomington: Indiana University Press, 1992.

_____. Limited Inc. Trans. Samuel Weber. Evanston: Northwestern University Press, 1988.

_____. Spurs: Nietzsche's Styles. Chicago: University of Chicago Press, 1979.

Disch, Lisa Jane. Hannah Arendt and the Limits of Philosophy. Ithaca: Cornell University Press, 1994.

Donaldson, Laura E. Decolonizing Feminisms: Race, Gender, and Empire-Building. Chapel Hill: University of North Carolina Press, 1992.

Drucker, Peter F. "The Changed World Economy." Foreign Affairs 64, no. 4 (1986): 768–91.

Du Bois, W. E. B. The Souls of Black Folk. Rockville: Arc Manor, 2008 (1903).

duCille, Ann. "The Occult of True Black Womanhood: Critical Demeanor and Black Feminist Studies." *Signs: Journal of Women in Culture and Society* 19, no. 3 (1994): 591–629.

Dufoix, Stephane. *Diasporas*. Trans. William Rodarmor. Berkeley: University of California Press, 2008.

du Gay, Paul, Jessica Evans, and Peter Redman, eds. *Identity: A Reader*. London: Sage, 2000.

de Gruchy, Steve. "Human Being in Christ: Resources for an Inclusive Anthropology." In Paul Germond and Steve de Gruchy, eds., *Aliens in the Household of God: Homosexuality and Christian Faith in South Africa*, 233–69. Cape Town: David Philip, 1997.

Dumm, Thomas. "The Politics of Post-modern Aesthetics: Habermas Contra Foucault." *Political Theory* 16, no. 2 (May 1988): 209–228.

Dungey, Nicholas. "(Re)Turning Derrida to Heidegger: Being-with-Others as Primordial Politics." *Polity* 33, no. 3 (Spring 2001): 455–77.

Eder, Klaus, et al. *Collective Identities in Action: A Sociological Approach to Ethnicity*. Burlington, VT: Ashgate, 2002.

Edwards, Louise, and Mina Roces, eds. *Women in Asia: Tradition, Modernity and Globalisation*. Women in Asia Publication Series. St. Leonards, Australia: Allen & Unwin, 2000.

Edwards, R. Randle, Louis Henkin, and Andrew J. Nathan. *Human Rights in Contemporary China*. New York: Columbia University Press, 1986.

Eisenstein, Zillah. *Against Empire: Feminisms, Racism, and the West*. London: Zed, 2004.

Elshtain, Jean Bethke. *Democracy on Trial*. New York: Basic, 1995.

Epstein, Steven. "Gay Politics, Ethnic Identity: The Limit of Social Constructionism." In Edward Stein, eds., *Forms of Desire: Sexual Orientation and the Social Constructionist Controversy*, 239–93. New York: Routledge, 1992 (1990).

Fabella, Virginia , ed. *Asia's Struggle for Full Humanity*. Maryknoll, NY: Orbis, 1980.

————, and Sun Ai Lee Park, eds. *We Dare to Dream: Doing Theology as Asian Women*. Maryknoll, NY: Orbis, 1990.

————, and Mercy Amba Oduyoye, eds. "Final Statement: Asian Church Women Speak (Manila, Philippines, Nov. 21-30, 1985)." In *With Passion and Compassion: Third World Women Doing Theology*, 118–23. Maryknoll, NY: Orbis, 1988.

Fanon, Fanon. *The Wretched of the Earth*. Trans. Constance Farrington. New York: Grove, 1963.

————. *Black Skin, White Masks*. New York: Grove, 1952.

Ferguson, Russell, Martha Gever, Trinh T. Minh-ha, and Cornel West, eds. *Out There: Marginalization and Contemporary Cultures*. New York: The New Museum of Contemporary Art/Cambridge: MIT Press, 1990.

Ferrara, Alessandro. *Reflective Authenticity: Rethinking the Project of Modernity*. London and New York: Routledge, 1998.

Fischer, Michael J. "Ethnicity and the Post-Modern Arts of Memory." In James Clifford and George E. Marcus, eds., *Writing Culture: The Poetics and Politics of Ethnography*, 193–233. Berkeley: University of California Press, 1986.

Flax, Jane. "The End of Innocence." In Judith Butler and Joan W. Scott, eds., *Feminists Theorize the Political*, 445–63. New York: Routledge, 1992.

————. *Thinking Fragments: Psychoanalysis, Feminism, and Postmodernism in the Contemporary West*. Berkeley: University of California Press, 1990.

Forbes, Jack. *Columbus and Other Cannibals: The Wetiko Disease of Exploitation, Imperialism, and Terrorism*. Brooklyn: Automedia, 1979.

Foster, Hal. "(Post) Modern Polemics." *New German Critique* 33 (Fall 1984): 67–78.

Foucault, Michel. *The Essential Foucault: Selections from Essential Works of Foucault 1954–1984*. Ed. Paul Rabinow and Nikolas Rose. New York: The New Press, 2003 (1994).

_____. *Language, Counter-Memory, Practice: Selected Essays and Interviews*. Ithaca: Cornell University Press, 1993 (1977).

_____. *The History of Sexuality, Vol. I: An Introduction*. Trans. Robert Hurley. New York: Random House, 1990.

_____. *The Foucault Reader*. Ed. Paul Rabinow. New York: Pantheon, 1984.

_____. *Power/Knowledge: Selected Interviews & Other Writings 1972–1977*. Ed. Colin Gordon. New York: Pantheon, 1980.

_____. *Discipline and Punish: The Birth of the Prison*. Trans. Alan Sheridan. Harmondsworth, UK: Peregrine, 1979.

Fox, Matthew. "A Mystical Cosmology: Toward a Postmodern Spirituality." In David Ray Griffin, ed., *Sacred Interconnections: Postmodern Spirituality, Political Economy, and Art*, 15–33. Albany: State University of New York Press, 1990.

Friedman, Susan Stanford. *Mappings: Feminism and the Cultural Geographies of Encounter*. Princeton: Princeton University Press, 1998.

Fukuyama, Francis. *The End of History and the Last Man*. New York: Free Press, 1992.

_____. "The End of History." *The National Interest* 16 (Summer 1989): 3–18.

Fulkerson, Mary McClintock. "Feminist Theology." In Kevin J. Vanhoozer, ed., *The Cambridge Companion to Postmodern Theology*, 109–125. Cambridge: Cambridge University Press, 2003.

_____. *Changing the Subject: Women's Discourses and Feminist Theology*. Minneapolis: Fortress Press, 1994.

_____, and Sheila Briggs, eds. *The Oxford Handbook of Feminist Theology*. New York: Oxford University Press, 2012.

Fung, Yu-Lan. *A Short History of Chinese Philosophy*. New York: Free Press, 1948.

Gandhi, Leela. *Postcolonial Theory: An Introduction*. Sydney: Allen and Unwin, 1998.

Gedalof, Irene. *Against Purity: Rethinking Identity with Indian and Western Feminisms*. Gender, Racism, Ethnicity series. New York: Routledge, 1999.

Geertz, Clifford. *The Interpretation of Cultures*. New York: Basic, 1973.

Chan, Wing-tsit. *A Source Book in Chinese Philosophy*. Princeton: Princeton University Press, 1963.

Ghosh, Amitav. "The Diaspora in Indian Culture." *Public Culture* 2, no.1 (Fall 1989): 73–78.

Gilroy, Paul. *The Black Atlantic: Modernity and Double Consciousness*. Cambridge: Harvard University Press, 1993.

_____. "Cultural Studies and Ethnic Absolutism." In Lawrence Grossberg, Cary Nelson, and Paula Treichler, eds., *Cultural Studies*, 187–98. New York: Routledge, 1992.

Gitlin, Todd. "The Rise of 'Identity Politics': An Examination and a Critique." *Dissent* 40, no. 2 (Spring 1993): 172–77.

Giroux, Henry. *The Giroux Reader*. Ed. Christopher C. Robbins. Boulder, CO: Paradigm, 2006.

_____. *Border Crossing: Cultural Workers and the Politics of Education*. New York: Routledge, 1992.

_____, and Peter McLaren, eds. *Between Borders: Pedagogy and the Politics of Cultural Studies*. New York: Routledge, 1994.

Goldberg, David Theo, ed. *Multiculturalism: A Critical Reader*. Oxford: Blackwell, 1994.

Goodman, Nelson. *Of Mind and Other Matters*. Cambridge: Harvard University Press, 1984.

Gramsci, Antonio. *Selections from the Prison Notebooks of Antonio Gramsci.* Ed. Quintin Hoare and Geoffrey Nowell Smith. London: Lawrence & Wisher, 1971.

Grayson, James H. *Korea: A Religious History.* Oxford: Clarendon, 1989.

Grenz, Stanley J., and John R. Franke. *Beyond Foundationalism: Shaping Theology in a Postmodern Context.* Louisville: Westminster John Knox, 2001.

Grewal, Inderpal, and Caren Kaplan, eds. *Scattered Hegemonies: Postmodernity and Transnational Feminist Practices.* Minneapolis: University of Minnesota Press, 1994.

Griffin, David. *God and Religion in the Postmodern World.* New York: State University of New York Press, 1989.

Grillo, Trina. "Anti-Essentialism and Intersectionality: Tools to Dismantle the Master's House." *Berkeley Women's Law Journal* 10, no. 1 (1995): 16–30.

Grossberg, Lawrence. "Cultural Studies and/in New Worlds." *Critical Studies in Mass Communication* 10, no. 1 (March 1993): 1–22.

————, Cary Nelson, and Paula Trichler, eds. *Cultural Studies.* New York: Routledge, 1992.

Gubrium, Jaber F., and James A. Holstein, *What Is Family?* Mountain View, CA: Mayfield, 1990.

Habermas, Jürgen. "Modernity—An Incomplete Project." In Hal Foster, ed., *The Anti-Aesthetic: Essays on Postmodern Culture,* 3–15. Townsend, WA: Bay Press, 1983.

————. "Modernity versus Post Modernity." *New German Critique* 22 (Winter 1981): 3–14.

Hall, Stuart. "The Local and the Global: Globalization and Ethnicity." In Anthony King, ed., *Culture, Globalization and the World-System: Contemporary Conditions for the Representation of Identity,* 19–39. Minneapolis: University of Minnesota Press, 1997.

_____. "Old and New Identities, Old and New Ethnicities." In Anthony King, ed., *Culture, Globalization and the World-System: Contemporary Conditions for the Representation of Identity*, 41–68. Minneapolis: University of Minnesota Press, 1997.

_____. "New Ethnicities." In *Stuart Hall: Critical Dialogues in Cultural Studies*, 442–51. New York: Routledge, 1996.

_____. "Introduction: Who Needs 'Identity'"? In Stuart Hall and Paul du Gay, eds., *Questions of Cultural Identity*, 1–17. London: Sage, 1996.

_____. "The West and the Rest: Discourse and Power." In Stuart Hall and Bram Gieben, eds., *Formations of Modernity*, 275–320. Cambridge, UK: Polity. 1992.

_____. "The Question of Cultural Identity." In Stuart Hall, David Held, and Tony McGrew eds., *Modernity and Its Futures*, 273–377. Cambridge, UK: Polity, 1992.

_____. "Cultural Identity and Diaspora." In Jonathan Rutherford, ed., *Identity: Community, Culture, Difference*, 222–37. London: Lawrence & Wishart, 1990.

_____, and Paul du Gay, eds. *Questions of Cultural Identity*. London: Sage, 1996.

Han, Sung-jo. "Hanguk minjujuuiui kukkaronjok kijo" ["A State Theory of Korean Democracy"]. In *Hanguk Kukkaui gibbon Songgyokgwa Gwaje* [*A Basic Nature of the Korean State and Its Task*]. Sungnam: Institute of Korean Mental Culture Research, 1988.

Hand, Sean, ed. *Facing the Other: The Ethics of Emmanuel Levinas*. Richmond: Curzon, 1996.

Hardt, Michael, and Antonio Negri, *Empire*. Cambridge: Harvard University Press, 2000.

Hassan, Ihab. "The Question of Postmodernism." *Performing Arts Journal* 6, no. 1 (1981): 30–37.

Heidegger, Martin. *Identity and Difference.* Trans. and with an Introduction by Joan Stambauch. New York: Harper & Row, 1969 (1957).

Helmreich, Stefan. "Kinship, Nation, and Paul Gilroy's Concept of Diaspora." *Diaspora: A Journal of Transnational Studies* 2, no. 2 (Fall 1992): 243–49.

Henderson, Jeffrey, and Manuel Castells. "Techno-economic Restructuring, Socio-political Processes and Spatial Transformation: A Global Perspective." In Jeffrey Henderson and Manuel Castells, eds., *Global Restructuring and Territorial Development*, 1–17. London: Sage, 1987.

Heng, Geraldine. "'A Great Way to Fly': Nationalism, the State, and the Varieties of Third-World Feminism." In M. Jacqui Alexander and Chandra Talpade Mohanty, eds., *Feminist Genealogies, Colonial Legacies, Democratic Futures*, 30–45. New York: Routledge, 1997.

Hicks, Emily. "Deterritorialization and Border Writing." In Robert Merrill, ed., *Ethics/Aesthetics: Post-Modern Positions*, 47–58. Washington, DC: Maisonneuve, 1988.

Hollinger, David. *Postethnic America: Beyond Multiculturalism.* New York: Basic Books, 1995.

_____. *Cosmopolitanism and Solidarity: Studies in Ethnoracial, Religious, and Professional Affiliation in the United States.* Madison: University of Wisconsin Press, 2006.

Honig, Bonnie. *Democracy and the Foreigner.* Princeton: Princeton University Press, 2001.

_____. *Political Theory and the Displacement of Politics.* Ithaca: Cornell University Press, 1993.

_____. "Toward an Agonistic Feminism: Hannah Arendt and the Politics of Identity." In Judith Butler and Joan W. Scott, eds., *Feminists Theorize the Political*, 215–37. New York: Routledge, 1992.

_____, ed. *Feminist Interpretation of Hannah Arendt.* University Park: Pennsylvania State University Press, 1995.

hooks, bell. *Feminist Theory: From Margin to Center.* Boston: South End, 2000 (1984).

_____. *Yearning: Race, Gender, and Cultural Politics.* Boston, MA: South End, 1990.

_____. *Talking Back: Thinking Feminist, Thinking Black.* Boston: South End, 1989.

_____. *Teaching to Transgress.* New York: Crossing, 1984.

Howe, Irving. "Mass Society and Postmodern Fiction." *Partisan Review* 26 (Summer 1959): 420–36.

Hoy, David Couzens. *Critical Resistance: From Poststructuralism to Post-Critique.* Cambridge: MIT Press, 2004.

Hsia, Hsiao-Chuan. "Internationalization of Capital and the Trade in Asian Women: The Case of 'Foreign Brides' in Taiwan." In Delia D. Aguilar and Anne E. Lacsamana, eds., *Women and Globalization,* 181–229. Amherst, NY: Humanity, 2004.

Hutcheon, Linda. *The Politics of Postmodernism.* New York: Routledge, 2002 (1989).

_____. "Postmodern Problematic." In Robert Merrill, ed., *Ethics/Aesthetics: Post-modern Positions,* 1–10. Washington, DC: Maisonneuve, 1988.

_____, Homi K. Bhabha, Daniel Boyarin, and Sabine I. Goelz, "Four Views on Ethnicity." *PMLA* (Special Topic: Ethnicity) 113, no. 1 (January 1998): 28–51.

Huyssen, Andreas. "Mapping the Postmodern." In Linda Nicholson, ed., *Feminism/Postmodernism,* 234–79. New York: Routledge, 1990.

JanMohamed, Abdul R., and David Lloyd, eds. *The Nature and Context of Minority Discourse.* New York: Oxford University Press, 1990.

Jenkins, Richard. *Rethinking Ethnicity: Arguments and Explorations.* 2d ed. Los Angeles: Sage, 2008 (1997).

John, Mary E. *Discrepant Dislocations: Feminism, Theory, and Postcolonial Histories.* Berkeley: University of California Press, 1996.

Kaplan, Caren. *Questions of Travel: Postmodern Discourse of Displacement.* Durham: Duke University Press, 1996.

————. "Deterritorializations: The Rewriting of Home and Exile in Western Feminist Discourse." In Abdul R. JanMohamed and David Lloyd, eds., *The Nature and Context of Minority Discourse*, 357–68. New York: Oxford University Press, 1990.

Kaplan, Robert D. "The Coming Anarchy." *Atlantic Monthly* 273, no. 2 (1994): 44–77.

Katrak, Ketu H. "Colonialism, Imperialism, and Imagined Homes." In Emory Elliott, ed., *The Columbia History of the American Novel*, 649–77. New York: Columbia University Press, 1991.

Keller, Catherine, Michael Nausner, and Mayra Rivera, eds. *Postcolonial Theologies: Divinity and Empire.* St. Louis: Chalice, 2004.

Kim, Chol-jun. "Backwardness of Korean History." *Korea Journal* 6, no. 3 (March 1966): 16–20.

Kim, Helen. *The Role of Women in the Next Half Century.* Seoul: Ewha Woman's University Press, 1968.

Kim, Sejin. *The Politics of Military Revolution in Korea.* Chapel Hill: University of North Carolina Press, 1971.

Kim, Yung-Chung, ed. *Women of Korea: A History from Ancient Times to 1945.* Seoul: Ewha Womans University Press, 1976.

Kincheloe, Joe L., and Shirley R. Steinberg. *Changing Multiculturalism.* Berkshire, UK: Open University Press, 2011 (1997).

King, Anthony. *Culture, Globalization and the World-System: Contemporary Conditions for the Representation of Identity.* Minneapolis: University of Minnesota Press, 1997.

Kirshenblatt-Gimblett, Barbara. "Spaces of Dispersal." *Cultural Anthropology* (August 1994): 339–44.

Kristeva, Julia. *About Chinese Women*. Trans. Anita Barrows. New York: Marion Boyars, 1986 (1977).

Kwok, Pui Lan. *Introducing Asian Feminist Theology*. Sheffield, UK: Sheffield Academic Press, 2000.

Kymlicka, Will. *Contemporary Political Philosophy: An Introduction*. 2d ed. New York: Oxford University Press, 2002.

_____. *Politics in the Vernacular: Nationalism, Multiculturalism, Citizenship*. New York: Oxford University Press, 2001.

_____. *Multicultural Citizenship: A Liberal Theory of Minority Rights*. New York: Oxford University Press, 1998.

_____, ed. *The Rights of Minority Cultures*. New York: Oxford University Press, 1995.

_____, and Wayne Norman, eds. *Citizenship in Diverse Societies*. New York: Oxford University Press, 2000.

Laclau, Ernst. "Politics and the Limits of Modernity." In Andrew Ross, ed., *Universal Abandon? The Politics of Postmodernism*, 63–82. Minneapolis: University of Minnesota Press, 1989.

Lazare, Bernard. *Job's Dungheap: Essays on Jewish Nationalism and Social Revolution*. Trans. Harry L. Binsse. New York: Schocken, 1948.

Lebacqz, Karen. *Justice in an Unjust World: Foundations for a Christian Approach to Justice*. Minneapolis: Augsburg, 1987.

Lee, Jung Young. *Marginality: The Key to Multicultural Theology*. Minneapolis: Fortress Press, 1995.

Lee, Kuan-Yew. "In Defense of Asian Values: Singapore's Lee Kuan Yew." *Time*. March 16, 1998.

Lee, Woo Chung. *Hankuk Kidogkoe Yesung Baknundi Baljachi* [*A Hundred Years of History of Korean Christian Women*.] Seoul: Minjung, 1985.

Legge, James, trans. *The Four Books: Confucian Analects, the Great Learning, the Doctrine of the Mean, and the Works of Mencius*. New York: Paragon, 1966 (1923).

Lefebvre, Henri. "Toward a Leftist Cultural Politics." In Cary Nelson and Lawrence Grossberg, ed., *Marxism and the Interpretation of Culture*, 75–88. Urbana: University of Illinois Press, 1988.

Lerner, Gerda. *The Creation of Patriarchy*. New York: Oxford University Press, 1986.

Lévinas, Emmanuel. *The Lévinas Reader*. Ed. Sean Hand. Oxford: Blackwell, 1989.

————. *Totality and Infinity: An Essay on Exteriority*. Trans. Alphonso Lingis. Pittsburgh: Duquesne University Press, 1969 (1961).

Li, Chenyang. "The Confucian Concept of Jen and the Feminist Ethics of Care: A Comparative Study." *Hypatia* 9, no. 1 (Winter 1994): 70–89.

Li Chi: Book of Rites. Trans. James Legge. Ed. C. C. Chai and W. Chai. New York: University Books, 1967.

Liu, Melinda. "Confucian Comeback: China Remains Divided Over Reviving its Ancient Sage." *Newsweek*. September 10, 2012.

Lloyd, Moya. *Beyond Identity Politics: Feminism, Power and Politics*. London: Sage, 2005.

Lorde, Audre. *Sister Outsider: Essays and Speeches*. Freedom, CA: Crossing Press, 1984.

Lugones, Maria. "Playfulness, 'World'-Traveling, and Loving Perception." In Gloria Anzaldua, ed., *Making Face, Making Soul/Haciendo Caras: Creative and Critical Perspectives by Feminists of Color*, 390–402. San Francisco: Aunt Lute, 1990.

Lyotard, Jean-Francois. *The Postmodern Condition: A Report on Knowledge*. Trans. Geoff Bennington and Brian Messumi. Minneapolis: University of Minnesota Press, 1984.

Mabubani, Kishore. *Can Asians Think? Understanding The Divide between East and West*. South Royalton, VT: Steerforth, 2002.

Mace, David Robert, and Vera Mace. *Marriage: East and West*. Garden City, NY: Doubleday, 1959.

Mahmood, Saba. "Religion, Feminism, and Empire: The New Ambassadors of Islamophobia." In Linda Martin Alcoff and John D. Caputo, eds., *Feminism, Sexuality, and the Return of Religion*, 77–102. Bloomington: Indiana University Press, 2011.

Mannheim, Karl. *Ideology and Utopia: An Introduction to the Sociology of Knowledge*. New York: Harvest/HBJ Books, 1985 (1936).

Marks, Elaine, and Isabelle de Courtivon, eds. *New French Feminisms: An Anthology*. Amherst: University of Massachusetts Press, 1980.

Marty, Martin, and R. Scott Appleby, eds. *Religion, Ethnicity, and Self-Identity: Nations in Turmoil*. Salzburg Seminar. Hanover, NH: University Press of New England, 1997.

Massey, Doreen. *Space, Place, and Gender*. Minneapolis: University of Minneapolis Press, 1994.

McHale, Brian. *Postmodernist Fiction*. New York: Methuen, 1987.

McLaren, Peter. "White Terror and Oppositional Agency: Towards a Critical Multiculturalism. In David Theo Goldberg, ed., *Multiculturalism: A Critical Reader*, 45–74. Oxford: Blackwell, 1994.

Melville, Stephen W. *Philosophy Beside Itself: On Deconstruction and Modernism*. Theory and History of Literature. Minnesota: University of Minnesota Press, 1986.

Memmi, Albert. *The Colonizer and the Colonized*. Boston: Beacon, 1967.

Mencius. In *A Source Book in Chinese Philosophy*, 49–83. Trans. and compiled by Wing-Tsit Chan. Princeton: Princeton University Press, 1963.

Mencius. In *The Four Books: Confucian Analects, the Great Learning, the Doctrine of the Mean, and the Works of Mencius*. Trans. James Legge. New York: Paragon, 1966 (1923). **Page Nos.?**

Mignolo, Walter. *Local Histories/Global Designs: Coloniality, Subaltern Knowledge and Border Thinking*. Princeton: Princeton University Press, 2000.

_____. "The Many Faces of Cosmo-polis: Border Thinking and Critical Cosmopolitanism." *Public Culture* 11, no. 3 (Fall 2000): 721–48.

Mohanty, Chandra Talpade. *Feminism Without Borders: Decolonizing Theory, Practicing Solidarity.* Durham: Duke University Press, 2003.

_____. "Women Workers and Capitalist Scripts: Ideologies of Dominion, Common Interests, and the Politics of Solidarity." In M. Jacqui Alexander and Chandra Talpade Mohanty, eds., *Feminist Genealogies, Colonial Legacies, Democratic Futures*, 3–29. New York: Routledge, 1997.

_____. "Cartographies of Struggle: Third World Women and the Politics of Feminism." In Chandra Talpade Mohanty, Ann Russo, and Lourdes Torres, eds., *Third World Women and the Politics of Feminism*, 1–49. Bloomington: Indianapolis University Press, 1991.

_____. "Under Western Eyes: Feminist Scholarship and Colonial Discourses." In Chandra Talpade Mohanty, Ann Russo, and Lourdes Torres, eds., *Third World Women and the Politics of Feminism*, 51–80. Bloomington: Indiana University Press, 1991.

_____, Ann Russo, and Lourdes Torres, eds. *Third World Women and the Politics of Feminism.* Bloomington: Indiana University Press, 1991.

Moore, Stephen D., and Mayra Rivera, eds. *Planetary Loves: Spivak, Postcoloniality, and Theology.* New York: Fordham University Press, 2011.

Moraga, Cherrie, and Gloria Anzaldua, eds. *This Bridge Called My Back: Writings by Radical Women of Color.* New York: Kitchen Table/Women of Color, 1983.

Mosse, George. *Nationalism and Sexuality: Respectability and Abnormal Sexuality in Modern Europe.* New York: Howard Fertig, 1985.

Mouffe, Chantal. "Feminism, Citizenship, and Radical Democratic Politics." In Judith Butler and Joan W. Scott, eds., *Feminists Theorize the Political*, 369–84. New York: Routledge, 1992.

Moya, Paula M. *Learning from Experience: Minority Identities, Multicultural Struggles.* Berkeley: University of California Press, 2001.

_____. "Postmodernism, 'Realism,' and the Politics of Identity: Cherrie Moraga and Chicana Feminism." In M. Jacqui Alexander and Chandra Talpade Mohanty, eds., *Feminist Genealogies, Colonial Legacies, Democratic Futures*, 125–50. New York: Routledge, 1997.

Nader, Laura. "Orientalism, Occidentalism and the Control of Women." *Cultural Dynamics*. 2, no. 3 (July 1989): 323–55.

Nancy, Jean-Luc. *Being Singular Plural*. Stanford: Stanford University Press, 2000.

Nandy, Ashis. *The Intimate Enemy: Loss and Recovery of Self Under Colonialism*. Delhi: Oxford University Press, 1988.

Narayan, Uma. "Essence of Culture and a Sense of History: A Feminist Critique of Cultural Essentialism." In Uma Narayan and Sandra Harding, eds., *Decentering the Center: Philosophy for a Multicultural, Postcolonial, and Feminist World*, 80–100. Bloomington: Indiana University Press, 2000.

_____. *Dislocating Cultures: Identities, Traditions, and Third World Feminism*. New York: Routledge, 1997.

_____, and Sandra Harding, eds. *Decentering the Center: Philosophy for a Multicultural, Postcolonial, and Feminist World*. Bloomington: Indiana University Press, 2000.

Nederveen Pieterse, Jan. "Globalization as Hybridization." In Mike Featherstone, Scott Lash, and Roland Robertson, eds., *Global Modernities*, 45–68. London: Sage, 1995.

Nicholson, Linda. *Feminism/Postmodernism*. New York: Routledge, 1990.

_____, and Steven Seidman, eds. *Social Postmodernism: Beyond Identity Politics*. Cambridge: Cambridge University Press, 1995.

Nietzsche, Friedrich. *Twilight of the Idols*. In Walter Kaufmann, ed. and trans., *The Portable Nietzsche*, 463–564. New York: Viking, 1954.

Nussbaum, Martha. *Frontiers of Justice: Disability, Nationality, Specific Membership*. The Tanner Lectures on Human Values. Cambridge: The Belknap Press of Harvard University Press, 2007.

_____. *Women and Human Development: The Capabilities Approach.* Cambridge: Cambridge University Press, 2000.

_____. *Poetic Justice: The Literary Imagination and Public Life.* Boston: Beacon, 1995.

Omolade, Barbara. "Black Women and Feminism." In Hester Eisenstein and Alice Jardine, eds., *The Future of Difference*, 247–57. New Brunswick: Rutgers University Press, 1985.

Ong, Aihwa. *Flexible Citizenship: The Cultural Logics of Transnationality.* Durham: Duke University Press, 1999.

_____. "On the Edge of Empires: Flexible Citizenship among Chinese in Diaspora." *Positions* 1, no. 3 (Winter 1993): 745–78.

Onishi, Norimitsu. "Korean Men Use Brokers to Find Brides in Vietnam." *New York Times*. February 22, 2007.

Owen, Stephen. "Stepping Forward and Back: Issues and Possibilities for 'World' Poetry." *Modern Philology* 100, no. 4 (May 2003): 532–48.

_____. "The Anxiety of Global Influence: What is World Poetry?" *The New Republic* 203, no. 21 (November 19, 1990): 28–32.

Parekh, Bhikhu. *Rethinking Multiculturalism: Cultural Diversity and Political Theory.* Cambridge: Harvard University Press, 2002.

Patton, John, and Brian H. Childs, *Christian Marriage and Family: Caring for Our Generations.* Nashville: Abingdon, 1988.

Perdue, Leo G. *Reconstructing Old Testament Theology: After the Collapse of History.* Minneapolis: Fortress Press, 2005.

Peters, Ted. *God—The World's Future: Systematic Theology for a Postmodern Era.* Minneapolis: Fortress Press, 1992.

Peterson, Mark. "Women without Sons: A Measure of Social Change in Yi Dynasty Korea." In Laurel Kendall and Mark Peterson, eds., *Korean Women: View from the Inner Room*, 33–44. New Haven, CT: East Rock, 1983.

Phillipson, Robert. *Linguistic Imperialism.* New York: Oxford University Press, 1992.

Pogge, Thomas W. *World Poverty and Human Rights: Cosmopolitan Responsibilities and Reforms.* Cambridge, UK: Polity, 2002.

_____, ed. *Global Justice.* Oxford: Blackwell, 2001.

Powell, Timothy B., ed. *Beyond the Binary: Reconstructing Cultural Identity in a Multicultural Context.* New Brunswick, NJ: Rutgers University Press, 1997.

Radhakrishnan, R. *Theory in an Uneven World.* Malden, MA: Blackwell, 2003.

_____. *Diasporic Mediations: Between Home and Location.* Minneapolis: University of Minnesota Press, 1996.

_____. "Is the Ethnic 'Authentic' in the Diaspora?" In Karin Aguilar-San Juan, ed., *The State of Asian America: Activism and Resistance in the 1990s,* 219–34. Boston: South End, 1994.

Razack, Sherene. *Looking White People in the Eye: Gender, Race, and Culture in Courtrooms and Classrooms.* Toronto: University of Toronto Press, 1998.

Research Center for Peace and Unification. *The Identity of the Korean People: A History of Legitimacy on the Korean Peninsula.* Seoul: Research Center for Peace and Unification, 1983.

Ricoeur, Paul. *Lectures on Ideology and Utopia.* Ed. George H. Taylor. New York: Columbia University Press, 1986.

Rich, Adrienne. *Blood, Bread and Poetry: Selected Prose, 1979–1985.* New York: Norton, 1986.

Richard, Nelly. "Postmodernism and Periphery." In Thomas Docherty, ed., *Postmodernism: A Reader,* 463–70. New York: Columbia University Press, 1993.

Robertson, Roland. "Glocalization: Time–Space and Homogeneity–Heterogeniety." In Mike Featherstone, Scott Lash, and Roland Robertson, eds. *Global Modernities,* 25–44. London: Sage, 1995.

Roman, Leslie G. "White Is a Color!: White Defensiveness, Postmodernism, and Anti-racist Pedagogy." In Cameron McCarthy and Warren Crichlow, eds., *Race, Identity, and Representation in Education*, 71–88. New York: Routledge, 1993.

Rosello, Mireille. *Postcolonial Hospitality: The Immigrant as Guest*. Stanford: Stanford University Press, 2001.

Rosemont, Henry. "Why Take Rights Seriously? A Confucian Critique." In Leroy Rouner, ed., *Human Rights and the World's Religions*, 167–82. Notre Dame: University of Notre Dame Press, 1988.

Rosenau, Pauline Marie. *Post-Modernism and the Social Sciences: Insights, Inroads, and Intrusions*. Princeton: Princeton University Press, 1992.

Ross, Andrew, ed. *Universal Abandon? The Politics of Postmodernism*. Minneapolis: University of Minnesota Press, 1989.

Rorty, Richard. *Consequences of Pragmatism*. Minneapolis: University of Minnesota, 1982.

Rouner, Leroy, ed. *Human Rights and the World's Religions*. Notre Dame: University of Notre Dame Press, 1988.

Rowbotham, Sheila. *Women, Resistance, and Revolution: A History of Women and Revolution in the Modern World*. New York: Vintage, 1971.

Ruether, Rosemary Radford. *Women and Redemption: A Theological History*. Minneapolis: Fortress Press, 1998.

Russell, Letty. "Minjung Theology in Women's Perspective." In Jung Young Lee, ed., *An Emerging Theology in World Perspective: Commentary on Korean Minjung Theology*, 75–98. Mystic, CT: Twenty-Third Publication, 1988.

Rutherford, Jonathan, ed. *Identity: Community, Culture, Difference*. London: Lawrence & Wishart, 1990.

Safran, William. "Diasporas in Modern Societies: Myths of Homeland and Return." *Diaspora* 1, no. 1 (Spring 1991): 83–99.

Sakai, Naoki. *Translation and Subjectivity: On "Japan" and Cultural Nationalism*. Minneapolis: University of Minnesota, 1997.

_____. "Modernity and Its Critique: The Problem of Universalism and Particularism." *The South Atlantic Quarterly* 87, no. 3 (1988): 475–504.

Said, Edward W. *Reflections on Exile and Other Essays.* Cambridge: Harvard University Press, 2000.

_____. *Representations of the Intellectual.* The 1993 Reith Lectures. New York: Vintage, 1996 (1994).

_____. *Culture and Imperialism.* New York: Vintage, 1993.

_____. "Reflections on Exile." In Russell Ferguson, et al., eds., *Out There: Marginalization and Contemporary Cultures*, 357–66. Cambridge: MIT Press, 1990.

_____. *After the Last Sky: Palestinian Lives.* Photographs by Jean Mohr. New York: Pantheon, 1986.

_____. *Beginnings: Intention and Method.* New York: Columbia University Press, 1985.

_____. *Orientalism.* New York: Vintage, 1978.

Salih, Sara. *Judith Butler.* New York: Routledge, 2002.

Scheffler, Samuel. *Boundaries and Allegiances: Problems of Justice and Responsibility in Liberal Thought.* New York: Oxford University Press, 2001.

Scherpe, Klaus. "Dramatization and De-dramatization of 'The End': The Apocalyptic Consciousness of Modernity and Post-modernity." *Cultural Critique* (Modernity and Modernism, Postmodernity and Postmodernism issue) 5 (Winter 1986–87): 95–129.

Schreiter, Robert J. *The New Catholicity: Theology between the Global and the Local.* Maryknoll, NY: Orbis, 2004.

Schüssler Fiorenza, Elisabeth. *Jesus—Miriam's Child, Sophia's Prophet: Critical Issues in Feminist Christology.* New York: Continuum, 1995.

_____. "Introduction: Transforming the Legacy of the Woman's Bible." In Elisabeth Schüssler Fiorenza, ed., *Searching the Scriptures, Vol. 1: A Feminist Introduction*, 1–24. New York: Crossroad, 1995.

_____. *Discipleship of Equals: A Critical Feminist Ekklesia-logy of Liberation.* New York: Crossroad, 1994.

_____. *In Memory of Her: A Feminist Theological Reconstruction of Christian Origins.* New York: Crossroad, 1983.

Sen, Amartya. *Identity and Violence: The Illusion of Destiny.* New York: Norton, 2006.

Shackleton, Mark, ed. *Diasporic Literature and Theory—Where Now?* Newcastle upon Tyne, UK: Cambridge Scholars Publishing, 2008.

Shain, Yossi. *Kinship and Diasporas in International Affairs.* Ann Arbor: University of Michigan Press, 2007.

Sharma, Arvind, ed. *Women in World Religions.* New York: State University of New York Press, 1987.

Sheffer, Gabriel, ed. *Modern Diasporas in International Politics.* New York: Harcourt, 1986.

_____, ed. *Diaspora Politics: At Home Abroad.* New York: Cambridge University Press, 2003.

Sherwood, Yvonne, ed. *Derrida's Bible (Reading a Page of Scripture with a Little Help from Derrida).* New York: Palgrave Macmillan, 2004.

Shohat, Ella. "Post–Third-Worldist Culture: Gender, Nation, and the Cinema. In M. Jacqui Alexander and Chandra Talpade Mohanty, eds., *Feminist Genealogies, Colonial Legacies, Democratic Futures,* 183–211. New York: Routledge, 1997.

Sollors, Werner, ed. *The Invention of Ethnicity.* New York: Oxford University Press, 1989.

Song, Choan Seng . *Jesus, the Crucified People.* New York: Crossroad, 1990.

_____. *Theology from the Womb of Asia.* Maryknoll, NY: Orbis, 1986.

_____. *Third-Eye Theology.* Maryknoll, NY: Orbis, 1979.

Spelman, Elizabeth V. *Inessential Woman: Problems of Exclusion in Feminist Thought.* Boston: Beacon, 1988.

Spivak, Gayatri Chakravorty. *A Critique of Postcolonial Reason: Toward a History of the Vanishing Present.* Cambridge, MA: Harvard University Press, 1999.

_____. *The Spivak Reader.* Ed. Donna Landry and Gerald Maclean. New York: Routledge, 1996.

_____. *Imaginary Maps: Three Stories by Mahasweta Devi.* New York: Routledge, 1995.

_____. *Outside in the Teaching Machine.* New York: Routledge, 1993.

_____. "French Feminism Revisited: Ethics and Politics." In Judith Butler and Joan W. Scott, eds., *Feminists Theorize the Political,* 54–85. New York: Routledge, 1992.

_____. "Neocolonialism and the Secret Agent of Knowledge: An Interview with Robert J. C. Young." *Oxford Literary Review* (Neocolonialism issue) 13, no. 1 (July 1991): 220–51.

_____. *The Postcolonial Critic: Interviews, Strategies, Dialogues.* Ed. Sarah Harasym. New York: Routledge, 1990.

_____. "Who Claims Alterity?" In Barbara Kruger and Phil Mariani, eds., *Remaking History: Discussions in Contemporary Culture,* 269–92. Seattle: Bay Press, 1989.

_____. *In Other Worlds: Essays in Cultural Politics.* New York: Routledge, 1988.

_____. "Can the Subaltern Speak?" In Cary Nelson and Lawrence Grossberg, ed., *Marxism and the Interpretation of Culture,* 271–313. Urbana: University of Illinois Press, 1988.

Stanton, Elizabeth Cady. "Introduction." In Elizabeth Cady Stanton and the Revising Committee, eds., *The Woman's Bible.* New York: European Pub. Co., 1898. **Page Nos.?**

Sugars, Cynthia, ed. *Unhomely States: Theorizing English-Canadian Postcolonialism.* Ontario: Broadview, 2004.

Swidler, Leonard. "Human Rights: A Historical Overview." In Hans Küng and Jürgen Moltmann, eds., *The Ethics of World Religions and Human Rights. Concilium* (1990/2). London: SCM Press, 1990.

Tanesini, Alessandra. *An Introduction to Feminist Epistemologies.* Oxford: Blackwell, 1999.

Taylor, Mark C. *Erring: A Postmodern A/theology.* Chicago: University of Chicago Press, 1984.

Theweleit, Klaus. *Male Fantasies.* Minneapolis: University of Minnesota Press, 1987.

Thiel, John E. *Nonfoundationalism.* Guides to Theological Inquiry. Minneapolis: Fortress Press, 1994.

Thompson, Laurence. *Chinese Religion: An Introduction.* Belmont, CA: Wadsworth, 1989 (1979).

Tölölyan, Khachig. "The Nation-State and Its Others: In Lieu of a Preface." *Diaspora* 1, no. 1 (Spring 1991): 3–7.

Trinh T. Minh-ha. *Woman, Native, Other: Writing Postcoloniality and Feminism.* Bloomington: Indiana University Press, 1989.

UNICRI (United Nations Interregional Crime and Justice Research Institute). Thirteenth Coordination Meeting of The United Nations Crime Prevention and Criminal Justice Programme Network. Courmayeur, Mont Blanc, Italy, 23-24 September 1998. Prepared by UNICRI.

Vanhoozer, Kevin J., ed, *The Cambridge Companion to Postmodern Theology.* Cambridge: Cambridge University Press, 2003.

Vattimo, Gianni. *After Christianity.* Trans. Luca D'Isanto. New York: Columbia University Press, 2002.

Waldron, Jeremy. "Minority Cultures and the Cosmopolitan Alternatives." In Will Kymlicka, ed., *The Rights of Minority Cultures.* New York: Oxford University Press, 1995.

Walker, Alice. *The Color Purple.* London: Women's Press, 1983 (1982).

Wallace, Michele. "Multiculturalism and Oppositionality." In Henry Giroux and Peter McLaren, eds., *Between Borders: Pedagogy and the Politics of Cultural Studies*, 180–91. New York: Routledge, 1994.

Waters, Malcolm. *Globalization*. New York: Routledge, 1995.

Weber, Elisabeth, ed. *Living Together: Jacques Derrida's Communities of Violence and Peace*. New York: Fordham University Press, 2013.

Welch, Sharon. *After Empire: The Art and Ethos of Enduring Peace*. Minneapolis: Fortress Press, 2004.

————. *Communities of Resistance and Solidarity: A Feminist Theology of Liberation*. Maryknoll, NY: Orbis, 1985.

West, Cornel. "The New Cultural Politics of Difference." In Russell Ferguson, Martha Gever, Trinh T. Minh-ha, and Cornel West, eds., *Out There: Marginalization and Contemporary Culture*, 19–38. New York: New Museum of Contemporary Art/Cambridge: MIT Press, 1990.

Wise, J. Macgregor. "Home: Territory and Identity." *Cultural Studies* 14, no. 2 (2000): 295–310.

Woessner, Martin. *Heidegger in America*. Cambridge: Cambridge University Press, 2010.

Wolff, Janet. "On the Road Again: Metaphors of Travel in Cultural Criticism." *Cultural Studies* 7, no. 2 (1993): 224–39.

Wong, Loong . "Colour-Blind and Exclusive: The Internet and Asian Women." 2003. http//:www.mngt.waikato.ac.nz/ejrot/cmsconference/2003/proceedings/exploringthemeaning/Wong.pdf.

Wong, Angela Wai Ching. "Women Doing Theology with the Asian Ecumenical Movement." In Ninan Koshy, ed., *A History of the Ecumenical Movement in Asia*, vol. 2: 85–114. Hong Kong: CCA, 2004.

Wren, Brian. *What Language Shall I Borrow? God-Talk in Worship: A Male Response to Feminist Theology*. New York: Crossroad, 1991.

Yoshino, Kosaku. *Cultural Nationalism in Contemporary Japan: A Sociological Inquiry*. New York: Routledge, 1992.

Yegenoglu, Meyda. *Colonial Fantasies: Towards a Feminist Reading of Orientalism.* Cambridge: Cambridge University Press, 1998.

Young, Robert J. C. *Postcolonialism: An Historical Introduction.* Oxford: Blackwell, 2001.

Yun, Sung Bum. *Ethics East and West: Western Secular, Christian, and Confucian Traditions in Comparative Perspective.* Trans. Michael C. Kalton. Seoul: Christian Literature Society, 1977 (1973).

————. *Sungeui Sinhak* [*Theology of Sung*]. Seoul: Sungkwangsa, 1973.

Yuval-davis, Nira, Kalpana Kannabiran, and Ulrike M. Vieten, eds. *The Situated Politics of Belonging.* London: Sage, 2006.

Zakaria, Fareed. "The Rise of Illiberal Democracy." *Foreign Affairs* 76, no. 6 (1997): 22–43.

————. "Culture is Destiny: A Conversation with Lee Kuan Yew." *Foreign Affairs* 73, no. 2 (March–April 1994): 109–127.

Zizek, Slavoj, Eric L. Santner, and Kenneth Reinhard. *The Neighbor: Three Inquiries in Political Theology.* Chicago: University of Chicago Press, 2005.

Index